流畅美语会话系列

Fluent American English for College Life

校园流畅美语

邱立志 编著
张道真

北京大学出版社
PEKING UNIVERSITY PRESS

图书在版编目(CIP)数据

校园流畅美语 / 邱立志编著. —北京：北京大学出版社，2008.12
（流畅美语会话系列）
ISBN 978-7-301-14567-8

Ⅰ.校… Ⅱ.邱… Ⅲ.英语–口语–美国 Ⅳ.H319.9

中国版本图书馆 CIP 数据核字(2008)第 176236 号

书　　　　名：	校园流畅美语
著作责任者：	邱立志　编著
责 任 编 辑：	徐万丽
标 准 书 号：	ISBN 978-7-301-14567-8/H·2143
出 版 发 行：	北京大学出版社
地　　　　址：	北京市海淀区成府路 205 号　100871
网　　　　址：	http://www.pup.cn
电　　　　话：	邮购部 62752015　发行部 62750672　编辑部 62765014
	出版部 62754962
电 子 邮 箱：	xuwanli50@yahoo.com.cn
印　刷　者：	北京汇林印务有限公司
经　销　者：	新华书店
	650 毫米×980 毫米　16 开本　18.5 印张　299 千字
	2008 年 12 月第 1 版　2010 年 5 月第 2 次印刷
定　　　价：	36.00 元（配有光盘）

未经许可，不得以任何方式复制或抄袭本书之部分或全部内容。
版权所有，侵权必究　举报电话：010-62752024
　　　　　　　　　　 电子邮箱：fd@pup.pku.edu.cn

Preface（前言）

　　说起来真是惭愧，教英语二十余年却教出了很多不会说英语的"哑巴"学生，他们会读会写，就是听不懂，说不出。有人将此归咎于学生的不勤奋和考试制度的弊病，对此，我觉得这只怪我们做老师的懒惰，惰在没有把英语这门外语当作一种交际技能和工具教给学生，而过分强调了考试和考试的成绩。语言是一种交际工具，学习一门外语就是要学会用这种语言去跟别人开展交际活动，对学生来说就是一种技能了。阅读和写作是书面的交际技能，而听说则是口头的交际技能。

　　检讨以往的过失，不能仍然停留在原来的状态，那是不思进取的表现。所以，笔者觉得要做一些事情，不为别的，就是为了使得有觉悟的英语学习者真正把英语当作一项全面的技能去培养，听、说、读、写四项技能同步发展。鉴于目前仍有相当多的读者在英语听说方面存在障碍，本套书编写重在口头交际技能的培养和训练。当然，市场上关于英语口语训练方面的书籍种类繁多，但是水平也良莠不齐，存在着这样或那样的问题，最明显的一点是落后于时代步伐，很多口语书使用的材料过于陈旧，说法也已经过时。而英语是有生命力的，随着时代的前进，英语也在发展、变化，口语表达习惯更是与时俱进、不断变化的。还有就是许多书中并没有能够反映英语口语的客观实际，一些编写者对英语日常交流用语并不是很了解，所谓的"典型句型"并不是人们经常使用的，而很多常用的表达方式却没有反映出来。因此，学习者只学到了皮毛，在肤浅的框架式英语结构中原地踏步，不能贴切或正确地运用到交流中去。

　　读者的选择往往是多方面的，不同的读者群有不同的偏好和需要，本系列力图覆盖以下几个方面。

　　出国之旅：出国的梦想是令人激动的，之所以激动是因为走出国门可以开阔眼界、感受异域风情；但是手续的繁杂、文化的差异，尤其是语言的障碍让很多人或者望而却步，或者倍感艰难，从而使许多人的出国梦想不得不搁浅。所以，这一专题细致入微地呈现了签证、登机等场景所需的习惯表达方式，让你从容踏上出国之旅。

　　日常交往：异域生活是新鲜的，同时也是琐碎的。我们每天都要面对：衣食住行、购物买菜、朋友聚会、生日宴会、乔迁之喜、结婚晚宴，以至生病住院等各个生活场景,这些都是在海外生活的每个人必须亲历的。而作为一个新的参与者,要想生活惬意,能够无障碍地交流,避免文化冲突,你就必须做一个有准备的人。

校园生活:海外求学是很多有志青年追求的人生目标。海外校园生活是丰富多彩的,许多情况与国内迥然不同,如果你不了解,感到茫然是不可避免的,从申请入学、注册、选课、咨询教授、学分等级、奖学金到校内打工等具体问题是无法从教科书中得到答案的。

旅游参观:在今天,到国外旅游已是人们尤其是越来越多时尚年轻人假期的主题活动。入住酒店、景点参观、客房服务、餐厅服务、通讯服务等既是旅游六要素"行、住、食、购、娱、游"的具体表现,又是旅游中不可或缺的环节,此专题让你在旅游中克服语言的不便,充分享受游玩的乐趣。

求职工作:不管是在境外公司,或是在中国外资企业的蓝领、白领甚至金领,还是到外资公司跃跃欲试的求职者,你都必须跟"老外"打交道。在车间、办公室、会议等各个场景你想躲都躲不掉,不能够灵活地沟通交流,将会给工作带来极大的障碍。

本系列可读性强,语言地道,内容权威,因为书中70%的语言材料来自于笔者本人在美国生活、学习的语言记录,并加以整理和提炼,生动而不失规范;30%的语言材料来自于已经出版的书籍、文献和网络等媒体,并根据本系列书的需要而采取了改编、吸收和融合等手段,以采众家之所长;张道真教授多年以来对笔者关怀备至,对本系列书稿进行了校订,修改了不少错讹和疏漏之处,并把自己在美国生活十多年的感受和经验融合其中。

口头交际技能的培养,不能只是学会英语句子,学习者还必须了解英语国家的政治经济制度、文化习俗、教育体系、消费习惯、历史传统等多个方面的内容,才能把已经学到的句子应用到真实的交际环境中去。正是基于如上的考虑,本系列各书的主题框架设计如下:

话题导言(Topic Introduction)和背景知识(Background)是会话主题所在的文化氛围。一句话说出来是否得体,是要以其所在的文化背景来判断的。我们把这称作"交际的得体性(Communication Appropriateness)"。一句话说出来不得体,还不如不说,因为不得体的话轻则会让听者不知所云,或者会得罪人,或者会丧失生意机会,从而达不到交际的目的甚至起到相反的作用;重则可能影响国家之间的关系,造成不可挽回的损失或恶果。所以,得体性意识的培养是口头交际训练中不能缺少的一个环节。

Preface

　　情景对话(Situational Dialogs)和典型句型(Typical Sentences)是语言的具体运用。任何一个句子只有存在于一定的语言环境(contexts)中才有确定的实际的交际意义。把话题置于情景和大的文化背景之下,就是想尽可能地展现语言的实际应用状态,让学习者在一定的实际状态下学习真实的交际技能。

　　难点注释(Notes)对情景对话和典型句型中的词语用法、特殊的语法现象、特别的含义以及理解困难的语句进行注解。

　　大道理谁都明白,归结到一点:掌握一种外语的口头交际技能,得体地有效地开展交际活动,最好的方式就是开口说出来!找到一切可能的机会与说英语的人保持交流!这样才能给书上死的句子赋予生命力!

邱立志
2008年5月5日

Contents (目录)

1. Applying to College ·········· 1
   申请入学
2. Accepted to College ·········· 6
   批准入学申请
3. Applying for a Student Visa ·········· 12
   学生签证
4. Arriving at College ·········· 18
   到达学校
5. At International Students Office ·········· 25
   在国际学生办公室
6. About Language Program ·········· 32
   语言培训项目
7. At an Orientation ·········· 38
   就学指导会
8. Obtaining Student ID ·········· 45
   办理学生证
9. Paying Tuition for Registration ·········· 51
   交费注册
10. Selecting Courses ·········· 57
    选课
11. Buying Textbooks ·········· 64
    购买教材
12. Computer and Software ·········· 69
    电脑和软件
13. Campus Network Account ·········· 75
    校园网账号
14. Consulting Department Head ·········· 81
    咨询系主任
15. Meeting with Major Professor ·········· 87
    会见专业导师

16. About Credits 93
    关于学分
17. Discussion with Classmates 99
    与同学讨论问题
18. Questioning In and Out Class 105
    课堂内外提问
19. About Assignments 111
    关于作业
20. At a University Library 117
    大学图书馆
21. Online Library 123
    网络图书馆
22. Seminars and Presentations 130
    研讨课与演示会
23. Tests and Examinations 136
    关于考试
24. Academic Paper and Thesis Defense 142
    论文与答辩
25. Trying to Win Scholarship 148
    争取奖学金
26. Transferring to Another University 154
    转学
27. Changing Major 159
    转专业
28. Sports Activities 166
    体育活动
29. Festivals and Holidays 171
    节日假期
30. Recreational Activities 177
    娱乐活动
31. Chinese Spring Festival 182
    中国春节
32. International Friendship Association Activities 187
    国际学生联谊会活动

Contents

33. Being a Guest at Professor's Home 193
    到教授家做客

34. Being a Guest at Friends' Home 199
    到朋友家做客

35. Entertaining Guests 204
    招待客人

36. Dealing with Neighbors 210
    与邻居打交道

37. Renting a Bicycle 215
    租用自行车

38. University Cafeteria 221
    学校食堂

39. University Residence Hall 226
    学校宿舍

40. Off-Campus Housing 232
    校外租房

41. Utilities Sharing 238
    费用分摊

42. Finding an On-Campus Job 244
    校内找工作

43. Working On-Campus 250
    校内打工

44. TA and RA 256
    助教和助研职位

45. On-Campus Recruitment Fair 260
    校内招聘会

46. Practicum in Summer 266
    暑期实习

47. Students Health Service 272
    学生健康服务

48. Family to U. S. 278
    申请家属赴美

Acknowledgements (致谢) 283

Applying to College
申请入学

Topic Introduction
话题导言

出国留学是很多人梦寐以求的事情,而申请入学是关键的第一步,一定得把握好。除了书信、电子邮件、传真等通讯手段以外,也可以打一打越洋电话,可以比较真切地了解到对方大学的招生意向。已经身处外国的中国人申请入学也可以亲自到国际学生办公室(International Students Office)和所要申请的系里去与系主任(称作Department Head, Chairperson of the Department 或 Department Dean)或学术委员会成员谈一谈。

Situational Dialogs
情景对话

韩力刚(Ligang)要申请美国大学的计算机专业,国际学生顾问Mary接听了他的电话。

Dialog 1

Mary: Hello, admissions office.
您好,这里是招生办公室。

Ligang: This is Han Ligang from Peking University.
这里是北京大学,我叫韩力刚。

Mary: What can I do for you then?
那,我能给您帮什么忙?

Ligang: I am interested in your M. S. program in computer science. I am applying for admission① to your university as an exchange student. I am inquiring about the possibility of having a place at your university.
我对贵校的计算机科学理学硕士学位项目感兴趣。我要申请到贵校作交换学生。我要问一下在贵校就学的条件。

Mary: All right. Please tell me your address.
好的,请您告诉我您的地址。

Ligang: My address is ... Could you possibly send me an application form and a catalogue?
我的地址是……您能够寄给我一份招生简章和申请表格吗?

Mary: Certainly. Thank you for calling.
当然可以,谢谢您打来电话。

Dialog 2

Mary: Hello, this is admissions office.
您好,招生办公室。

Ligang: Good morning, this is Han Ligang. Thank you for your information materials.
早晨好,我是韩力刚。谢谢您寄给我的资料。

Mary: That's all right.
别客气。

Ligang: I am sending a copy of my notarized transcript and a list of my publication with a description of my research interest.
现寄上我的公证过的成绩单和发表过的作品目录清单,以及一份关于我的研究兴趣的描述。

Mary: OK.
好的。

Ligang: Please let me know in advance② if no place is available.
如果贵校没有空缺,请事先告知。

Mary: Yes, we will as soon as we finish evaluating your application.
好的,一完成对您的申请的评估,我们就会通知的。

Applying to College

Typical Sentences 典型句型

1) I graduated from Peking University.
   我毕业于北京大学。
2) I am interested in your Master of Science program in computer science.
   我对贵校的计算机科学理学硕士项目感兴趣。
3) I am applying for a Master's Degree program in biological chemistry.
   我要申请生物化学的硕士学位项目。
4) I am inquiring about the possibility of having a place at your university.
   我要问一下在贵校就学的条件。
5) Could you possibly send me an application form and a catalogue?
   你能够寄给我一份招生简章和申请表格吗?
6) What is the tuition for international students?
   留学生的学费是多少?
7) What is the English requirement?
   要求英语水平有多高?
8) I have asked ETS③ to send you my TOEFL score.
   我已经要求ETS把TOEFL考分寄给你。
9) I am enclosing a copy of my certified transcript and a list of my publications.
   我顺便寄上我的证明过的成绩单和发表过的作品目录清单。
10) I am sending you a description of my research interest.
    现寄上一份我的研究兴趣的描述。
11) I have enclosed my résumé and two sealed references.
    已经附上我的简历和两封密封的推荐信。
12) Please let me know in advance if no place is available.
    如果贵校没有空缺,请事先告知。

13) Could you please let me know early if I could waive my application fee?
你能尽早让我知道,我是否可以免交申请费吗?

14) I look forward to hearing from you.
望复。

背景知识

美国大学的招生:美国大学的招生体制和步骤与其他国家有很多不同。正常的招生程序是:

(1) 递交申请书(Application for Admission)给大学的招生办公室 (the Admissions Office) 或研究生招生办公室 (the Graduate Admissions Office),包括成绩单 (Academic Transcripts)、推荐信 (Letters of References,也叫 Letters of Recommendation)、资金证明 (如 Bank Statement)、申请费等材料;

(2) 招生官员收到材料后,如果材料完整,就开始审查入学资格;

(3) 符合学校总体入学要求的申请材料将转到相关系里,由系学术委员会进行再次审查,合格者的材料将退回到招生办公室,由招生办公室会同国际学生办公室发给申请者入学通知书和签证表即 I-20。

TOEFL (Test of English as a Foreign Language, 托福):这是由美国普林斯顿教育考试服务处 (Educational Testing Service,简称 ETS)主办的一种英语标准考试。其目的是测试申请去英语国家读本科或研究生课程的母语为非英语学生的英语熟练程度。TOEFL 成绩有效期为两年。两年以后,如果再需要 TOEFL 成绩,则必须重新参加考试。

MELAB (Michigan English Language Assessment Battery, 密执安考试):这是由美国密执安大学英语语言学院 (English Language Institute, University of Michigan)举办的一种英语标准考试,为全美国和其他一些国家的大专院校所承认和接受,旨在考核非英语国家留学生或进修生的英语水平。密执安考试和托福考试在美国和加拿大等国具有同等的效力。MELAB 成绩计算是通过将原始分变成换算标准分后取得的,考生所得的总分是各项考试换算分的平均分数。

注 释

① admission 的意思是"允许进入,许可入场(入学,入会);入场(入会)费",如:
Admission by ticket only. (凭票入场。)
亦可指"承认,坦白",如:
admission of blame (承认罪过)
② in advance 意思是"预先",如:
Commissions received in advance. (预收佣金。)
③ ETS,这是美国普林斯顿教育考试服务处 (Educational Testing Service)的简称。

Accepted to College
批准入学申请

Topic Introduction 话题导言

作为一个外国的留学申请者,就要按照学校的要求提供材料,经过审查,符合条件的就会发给入学通知书和签证表等材料。

无论你是否在美国,都应当与国际学生办公室(International Students Office)和系主任(Department Head)多交流,以加深印象,让他们在录取的过程中全面地了解你,特别是美国的大学教授普遍抱怨中国学生的托福考试成绩很高,GRE或GMAT成绩也很高,但听不懂也不会说流利的英语。英语听说能力好的申请者更是要多口头和他们联系。

Situational Dialogs 情景对话

韩力刚(Ligang)的申请得到了批准,交换学生杨佳欣(Jiaxin)想了解更多的信息,而已经在美国的李惠敏(Huimin)的读博申请遭到了拒绝。

Dialog 1

Ligang: Good morning, this is Han Ligang speaking.
早晨好,我是韩力刚。

Accepted to College

Mary: Good morning, I'd like to tell you something about your application.
早晨好,我想告诉您有关您申请的一些情况。

Ligang: This is what I need now.
这正是我现在所需要的。

Mary: I am now officially informing you of your admission. Our college has accepted you as a graduate student.
我现在正式通知你关于你申请的有关情况。学院已经决定接受你到这里攻读硕士学位。

Ligang: I'm glad to hear that. Thank you very much.
我很高兴听到这个消息。非常感谢。

Mary: Would you let me know the exact dates you plan to be in Los Angeles.
请告诉我你打算到达洛杉矶的确切日期。

Ligang: I am to get there in the middle of next month. And I will write you an email confirming the date.
我定于下个月到达,我会发电子邮件给你确认这个日期。

Mary: All right. On arrival, please contact my secretary, who will arrange everything.
好的。到达时,请与我的秘书联系,她将给你安排所有的事情。

Ligang: Thank you very much.
非常感谢。

Dialog 2

Jiaxin: Good morning, this is Yang Jiaxin.
早晨好,我是杨佳欣。

Steve: Good morning, what can I do for you?
早晨好,我能帮你干什么吗?

Jiaxin: I have received your admission letter last week. But I'd like to know something about my financial support.
我上周已经收到你们的批准通知,但是我想了解一些经济资助方面的问题。

Steve: Your support will be coming from the Ford Foundations. The graduate school will support partially.

你的资助将由福特基金会提供。研究生院将提供部分资助。

Jiaxin: That's fine. Thank you.
那很好,谢谢。

Steve: Could you tell me what expenses the Chinese side will provide?
能告诉我中国方面将提供哪些费用吗?

Jiaxin: The total living expenses will be provided by our government.
我国政府将给我提供生活费用。

Steve: Please contact us at the address in the admission letter if you have more questions about financial matters.
有关资助,如果还有问题请通过批准通知中的地址同我们联系。

Jiaxin: All right. Thank you.
好的,谢谢。

Dialog 3

Huimin: Good morning, sir. I'd like to know the status about my application.
先生,早上好,我想了解我的申请处理的情况。

Steve: Because of budget cut these years, we are not allowed to accept many Ph. D. program students. So I am very sorry that your application has been declined.
由于财政削减,我们不能招收很多博士研究生,所以,我感到非常抱歉,您的申请被拒绝了。

Huimin: It's pity. But I am really interested in this field. Is there anything else I can do in order to be a student in your department?
真可惜,但是我真的对这个领域很感兴趣。为了成为您这个系的学生,我还可以做点什么?

Steve: You may reapply for admission as a master program[①] student if you like.
如果您愿意,您可以重新申请先攻读硕士学位。

Huimin: Does that mean I can modify my application?
那是否意味着我可以修改我的申请?

Steve: Yes, correct. I'll ask the secretary to find your application materials and you may modify it. If you have any questions, I can help you.

対的,我会让秘书把您的申请找出来,您可以拿去修改。如果有问题,我可以帮您的忙。

Huimin: Yes, I understand. You are so kind. Thank you very much.
好的,我明白了。您这么好,太谢谢您了。

Steve: You bet.②
不用谢。

Typical Sentences
典型句型

1) I'd like to know the status about my application.
   我想了解我的申请处理的情况。
2) Could you tell me what happened to my application?
   您能否告诉我的申请的情况?
3) Must I submit additional documents?
   我要递交补充材料吗?
4) Does that mean I can modify my application?
   那是否意味着我可以修改我的申请?
5) I have received all information about my application.
   关于我的申请,我已经得到信息了。
6) I am ready to apply for the student visa.
   我已经准备去签证了。
7) I would be happy to consider your application.
   我将乐意考虑你的申请。
8) The application materials are enclosed here.
   现寄上申请所需材料。
9) I should appreciate your sending me a complete résumé.
   若能寄来一份完整的简历,我将十分感激。
10) Your support will be coming from the Ford Foundations.
    你的资助将由福特基金会提供。
11) The graduate school will support partially.
    研究生院将提供部分资助。

Background
背景知识

TSE(Test of Spoken English, 英语口语考试)：这是ETS为非英语国家的学生设置的英语口语水平考试。该项考试主要是用来考察考生的语音、语法水平以及使用英语的熟练程度。对象为申请去美国或加拿大院校担任助教职务或从事学术工作的人员。TSE成绩满分为300分。其有效期为一年半。

IELTS(International English Language Testing System, 国际英语测试系统,即雅思)：是为到英国各大学学习或进修的学生而设计的英语水平考试。它是英国文化协会和剑桥大学考试委员会(The British Council and the University of Cambridge Local Examinations Syndicate)于20世纪70年代末设计的,用于测试海外留学英国考生的英语能力。IELTS评分按9分制。最高分为9分,最低分为0分。

GRE(Graduate Record Examination, 研究生资格考试)：这是ETS提供的研究生入学资格考试。目前,GRE正成为美国各高等院校公认的研究生入学的一种权威性考试。凡欲进入研究生院深造,攻读硕士、博士学位的大学毕业生多数都必须通过该项考试。GRE分为能力考试(General Test或Aptitude Test)和专业科目考试(Subject Test或Advanced Test)。能力考试分3部分记分,即语言能力、定量能力和分析能力均单独记分,每部分满分为800分,其专业考试最高分数为990分。GRE成绩有效期为5年。

GMAT(Graduate Management Admission Test, 工商管理硕士入学考试)：这是GMAC (Graduate Management Admission Council)为美国工商管理硕士专业研究生举办的入学考试。世界上很多国家的管理学院（如College of Business Administration、College of Public Administration、College of Finance and Accounting）规定,凡是申请研究生奖学金的考生,无论是否来自英语国家,均要求参加GMAT考试。GMAT成绩满分为800分。GMAT的成绩有效期为5年。

注　释

① 很多美国大学的研究生入学申请不区分硕士和博士，但有的学校却分得很清楚。如果你是本科毕业生而直接申请读博士学位，是可行的；如果因为经费等原因，学校会建议你改申请读硕士学位。

② 这里是美国西北地区的方言，在爱达荷州及华盛顿州使用很普遍，意思是"不用谢"，和"You are welcome."一样。单词"bet"的原意是"打个赌"，所以，"I bet."或"I'll bet."是"我要打个赌。"的意思，表示"有信心"，如"I bet you are right."的意思是"我坚信你没有错。""You bet."的基本意思是"你跟我打个赌也可以。"和"sure, of course, certainly"意思相同。

Applying for a Student Visa
学生签证

Topic Introduction
话题导言

收到了大学的录取通知书和签证表，只是万里长征走完了第一步，更加艰苦的路程还在后面，签证是紧接着的关键一步，因为这么一小张"不干胶贴纸"就可以决定你是否能真正走出国门求学。国家不同，签证的方式也不同，英国只要求部分申请人面谈，澳大利亚基本上不面谈，美国则要求所有第一次申请签证者都必须面谈，加拿大、新西兰也各有自己的规定。根据经验，申请美国签证是最为困难的，拒签率比较高。

一般地，大学在发给你入学通知的同时也会给你几点提示，告诉你如何成功获取签证，概括起来无非是要你说明经济来源、所学专业对你个人发展的作用、国内有紧密联系（如配偶、房地产等）、毕业之后回国的必然性等等。

Situational Dialogs
情景对话

韩力刚(Ligang)和李惠敏(Huimin)的签证面谈很顺利，而杨洋(Yang Yang)却因为缺少证明文件而暂时遭到了拒绝。

Applying for a Student Visa

学生签证

Dialog 1

Ligang: Good morning, madam. My name is Han Ligang form Peking University. I'm here for the interview related to my visa application.
女士,早晨好。我是北京大学的韩力刚,我来想和您谈谈有关我的签证申请的事情。

Officer: Nice to see you. What are you going to do in the United States?
很高兴见到您。您到美国有何贵干?

Ligang: I am going to study for a master's degree.
我去攻读硕士学位。

Officer: You have been granted a full scholarship. And will you stay in the United States permanently?
您获得了全额奖学金。您会在美国永久逗留下去吗?

Ligang: No, sir. I'm sure to come back to China as soon as[①] I get my degree.
不会,先生。一旦获得学位,我肯定会回到中国的。

Officer: All right, you'll be able to get the visa.
好的,您会得到签证的。

Ligang: Thank you very much.
非常感谢您。

Dialog 2

Officer: Hello, Miss Li Huimin?
您好,李惠敏小姐?

Huimin: Hello, yes, I am Li Huimin.
您好,我是李惠敏。

Officer: So, the University of Chicago will provide you with a stipend of US$1200 dollars a month?
芝加哥大学每月给您提供1200美元的津贴,对吗?

Huimin: Yes, that's right.
是,对的。

Officer: How about the tuition and fees?
学费和杂费怎么办?

Huimin:	I have got a full tuition waiver, but this doesn't appear on the I-20. They sent me a letter verifying this after I got the I-20. 我得到了全免学费的奖学金，但是这一点没有能显示在 I-20 表上，我收到 I-20 表之后，他们又给了我一封信确认这一点。
Officer:	Can you show me the letter? 能给我看看那封信吗?
Huimin:	Yes, sure. 当然可以。
Officer:	Your application has been approved. Please come here at 3:00 tomorrow afternoon for your visa. 您的申请获得了批准，请明天下午 3:00 来取您的签证。
Huimin:	Thank you very much. 非常感谢。

Dialog 3

Officer:	Good morning, Mr. Yang Yang. 杨洋先生，早晨好!
Yang Yang:	Good morning, Madam. 女士，早晨好。
Officer:	Could you tell me your purpose of going to the United States? 您能否告诉我您去美国的目的?
Yang Yang:	I am going there for further study in order to get a master's degree. 我去那里是为了继续学习，以获得硕士学位。
Officer:	But your I-20 shows that you will study English. 但是，您的 I-20 表上说明您要去学习英语课程。
Yang Yang:	Yes, first I plan to go to the United States to study an intensive English program and then transfer to a master's degree program.② 是的，我打算先到美国去读一个强化英语课程，然后转到硕士学位课程。
Officer:	But your financial documents just cover your expenses during your English study. 但是您的资金文件只够你学英语期间的费用。

Yang Yang:	My uncle will provide me with the funds.	
	我叔叔将为我提供资金。	
Officer:	But you can't show us any statement from your uncle. I am sorry that your application cannot be approved.	
	但是,您没有能出示您叔叔的证明文件,很抱歉,您的申请不能获得批准。	
Yang Yang:	Thank you all the same.③	
	仍然要谢谢您。	

典型句型

1) I am going there for further study in order to get a master's degree.
   我去那里是继续学习,以获得硕士学位。
2) I plan to go to the United States to study an intensive English program.
   我打算到美国去读一个强化英语课程。
3) I have been granted a full scholarship.
   我已获得全额奖学金。
4) This is my financial certification.
   这是我的资金证明。
5) I will come back to China as soon as I finish the study there.
   我一完成学业就返回中国。
6) Because my wife and daughter are here, and my college will keep my teaching position for me.
   因为我的妻子和女儿还在这里,而且我们学院将保留我的教学职位。
7) How long will it take to process my application?
   要多长时间受理我的申请?
8) Your application is processed in turn.
   你的申请按照顺序被受理。
9) We need your marriage certificate and bank statement.
   我们需要你的结婚证明和银行证明。

10) It will be processed within 14 workdays
我们将在14个工作日内予以受理。

11) Are you bringing any dependant with you?
你是否随带家属？

12) Please show me your family photo.
请出示你的家庭合影。

13) Your visa application is granted.
你的签证申请被批准了。

背景知识

  学生签证的种类：不同类别的学生可以申请不同种类的学生签证。F-1：读本科或研究生或语言学生签证。F-2：学生的家庭成员签证。J-1：美国新闻署承认的交流人员赴美国学习、工作或培训者签证。J-2：J-1签证持有者的直系家庭成员签证。M-1：学习实用技术如飞行的学生签证。M-2：M-1签证持有者的家庭成员签证。

  学生签证的有效期：签证的有效期受I-94卡片标明日期的限制。进入美国国境时，要填写一张被称作"I-94"的白色卡片。移民局官员在卡片上加盖一个日期，如果在美逗留的时间超过这个日期，必须提前申请，否则会遇到很多麻烦，而且还可能影响到今后的入境。学生凭F-1进入美国，移民官会在I-94卡上盖一个章并标明逗留期限为"D / S"（D / S = duration of study），意思就是说只要你在美国是全日制学习，就可呆下去，但其实，这一点还受I-20表有效期的制约。所以，一旦你毕业了而还要呆下去，就要继续全日制学习，就要申请换发新的I-20表，或者申请移民。为防止非法居留造成失去学生身份(Out of Status)，要随时和国际学生顾问(International Student Adviser)保持联系。由于万不得已的原因造成了这种局面，要在国际学生顾问的帮助下向移民局申请恢复学生身份 (Reinstatement of F-1 Student Status)。

注 释

① as soon as 意思是"一……就",引导时间状语从句,时间状语从句还可以由以下连词引导,如:as, since, till / until, no sooner than, once, each time, the moment 等。

② 签证面谈时,自己所陈述的目的一定要和 I-20 表上的目的一致,即使你读英语只是暂时的,也要说是读英语;签证官问到英语学习完成后再做什么,可以回答"回国"或者"继续学习",文件一定要准备齐全。美国人更相信"口说无凭,有书为证"。

③ 短语 all the same 的意思和 anyway 的意思一样,表示"仍然,还是"。

Arriving at College
到达学校

Topic Introduction
话题导言

第一次到国外去留学,许多学生都怀着激动的心情登上国际航班,然后,经过长途旅行忐忑不安地到达目的地,心中一直在想:这学校是个什么样子?接我的人来了吗?我说的英语有人听得懂吗?……其实,事情总会过去,问题总会解决,飞机终究是要到达异国他乡的,不管接机的人到了没有,总要到学校去的。

从踏上国际航班的那一刻起,你就处在前往学校的过程了,一路上与人打交道的目的就是如何顺利达到学校。入境、过海关、转国内航班、领取行李、见到接机的人、到达学校、熟悉学校环境等等。遇到问题,要向熟悉的人们询问,常用的语句无非就是:Excuse me, where can I find Alaska Airlines gate? (请问阿拉斯加航空公司的登机口在哪里?) Excuse me, are you from the University of Idaho?(请问您是从爱达荷大学来的吗?) Excuse me, where can I get my baggage?(请问我在哪里可以拿到行李?)等等。

Situational Dialogs
情景对话

李惠敏(Huimin)和刘杭(Liu Hang)很顺利地到达了美国的大学。

Arriving at College

Dialog 1

Huimin: Hello, my name is Li Huimin. Are you from the University of Chicago?
您好,我叫李惠敏。您是芝加哥大学的吗?

Henry: Yes, I'm Henry. I'm meeting you here.
是的,我是亨利。我来接您的。

Huimin: It's nice to meet you. Thank you for picking me up at the airport.
见到您真高兴,谢谢您到机场来接我。

Henry: It's my pleasure. Can I help you with your luggage?
别客气,我可以帮您拿行李吗?

Huimin: Yes, please. I'm sorry to trouble you.
请吧,不好意思打搅您了。

Henry: It doesn't matter. The car is over there, please follow me.
没关系,车在那边,请跟我来。

Huimin: Yes, I will.
好的。

Dialog 2

Larry: Here we are going into the campus.
现在我们进了校园了。

Liu Hang: Oh, it's a beautiful place.
哦,是个漂亮的地方。

Larry: On your right is the university gymnasium, called Kibbie Dome. On your left is the area of residence halls.[①]
您的右边是大学的体育馆,叫做凯比多梦;左边是学生宿舍区。

Liu Hang: They are all wonderful places.
这些都是很好的地方。

Larry: Look, in the front is the university sports and recreation center.
瞧,前面是大学的运动与娱乐中心。

Liu Hang: So we can exercise ourselves over there.
这样我们可以到那儿锻炼身体了。

Larry:	The University is not very big and on the left is the teaching area. Look, the University Library and the College of Education, and the International Students Office is located in that three-storied building.

Larry: The University is not very big and on the left is the teaching area. Look, the University Library and the College of Education, and the International Students Office is located in that three-storied building.
我们大学并不大，左边是教学区域。瞧，大学图书馆和教育学院，并且国际学生办公室就在那栋三层的楼房里面。

Liu Hang: All the buildings are very beautiful. Are they red-bricked?
所有这些建筑物都非常漂亮，都是红砖砌的吗？

Larry: No, they are built of wood,② but the wall surface is covered with red bricks.
不，都是木头做的，但墙的表面贴了一层红砖。

Liu Hang: Really? Oh, I see.
真的吗？哦，我知道了。

Dialog 3

Larry: You told me you found a place to live in. Where is it?
您告诉过我您找到了住的地方，在哪里？

Liu Hang: It's on the Fourth Street. My roommate has given the keys to your secretary. He has gone to Seattle and won't be back until next Monday.
在第四街上，我的室友把钥匙给您的秘书了，他去了西雅图，到下个星期一才会回来。

Larry: My secretary? She never told me that. Just a second, please. I'm checking her.③
我的秘书？她从未告诉我这件事情。请稍等，我这就问问她。

Liu Hang: Sure.
好的。
……

Larry: The secretary said she had put the keys and a note from him into my mailbox.
秘书说她把钥匙和您室友的便条放在我的信箱里了。

Liu Hang: I think we can find the keys.
我想我们能找到的。

Larry:	Oh, they're here. Let me send you there. 噢，在这里呢。我送你去。
Liu Hang:	Thank you so much. 非常感谢。
Larry:	You bet. 不用谢。

Typical Sentences 典型句型

1) Excuse me, where can I find Alaska Airlines gate?
   请问阿拉斯加航空公司的登机口在哪里？

2) Excuse me, are you from the University of Idaho?
   请问您是从爱达荷大学来的吗？

3) Excuse me, where can I get my luggage?
   请问我在哪里可以拿到行李？

4) Hello, my name is Zhou Zhaoyang. Are you coming to pick me up?
   您好，我叫周朝阳。您是来接我的吗？

5) It's my pleasure. Can I help you with your luggage?
   别客气，我可以帮您拿行李吗？

6) They are all wonderful places. So we can exercise ourselves over there.
   这些都是很好的地方，我们可以到那儿锻炼身体了。

7) All the buildings are very beautiful. Are they red-bricked?
   所有这些建筑物都非常漂亮，都是红砖砌的吗？

8) They are made of wood, but the wall surface is covered with red bricks.
   都是木头做的，但墙的表面贴了一层红砖。

Background
背景知识

出国前必须解决的两个问题：现在新一代留学生大多是独生子女,父母对孩子留学海外在经济上是很舍得投资的,但他们出去之前都不了解所到之地的交通情况,以为发达国家的公共交通也很发达。不少人事先没有联系接机的有关事宜,等出了机场才感到了真正的无助,没有公共汽车,也见不到国内那成排等客的出租车,更找不到一个中国人可以帮一把,结果一打听才知道离学校还有七八十英里,鼻子一酸就吧嗒吧嗒地流出了眼泪。笔者在美国期间就多次听到中国学生"哭诉"他们到达异国他乡的痛苦经历。

所以,出国之前一定要联系好接机的事宜,包括告诉对方航班号、到达的机场名称、到达的具体日期和时间。中国人觉得又不认识别人,如何联系?其实完全不用担心那么多。新到一个国外大学上学,可以向如下一些单位或个人联系接机:国际学生办公室(International Students Office)、大学宿舍管理办公室(University Residence Office)、国际留学生联合会 (International Students Association)、中国学生学者联谊会(Chinese Students and Scholars Association)、房东(landlord / landlady)等。办法很简单,给每个机构或个人发一个电子邮件(email),咨询他们能否接机,待他们回信后选择一个来落实接你就可以了。到时候,就会有人手举招牌在机场等你了。

就算是接机的问题解决了,快到学校的时候接机的人会问你 Where should I leave you?(我应该把您送到哪里?)或者 Where will you live?(您要住在哪里?)如果你说不出地方,他就会把你送到学校附近的旅馆去。所以,住房问题是又一个要事先解决的问题。大学提供的宿舍往往要提前排队,且对于中国学生来说,也确实贵了一些。提前联系到住处非常重要,住几天旅馆的花费也确实难以承受。联系住房可以上学校的网,查阅房屋出租信息,从中可以找到你需要的住房,也可以与中国学生学者联谊会联系,他们一般会帮你的忙,或者帮你租到房子,或者让你到别的留学生那里暂住几日,是能解决一些问题的。

提醒一点的是，一定要提前几天到达学校，一来可以倒一倒时差，二来可以熟悉一下情况，特别是要多向老留学生请教。

美国高等教育主要类型：美国高等教育的类别比较丰富，有提供应用艺术、应用科学和职业培训的两年的社区学院（community college），也有进行各种职业技术培训的三年制专业技术学院，更多的则是提供综合性教育的四年制普通大学。

（1）两年制学院：通常称为社区学院（community college），很大程度相当于我国的大专，这些学院大部分是公立的，或得到当地社区支持，或由州政府协助兴办，学费比较低。未能进入四年制正规大学读书的人有机会受到高等教育等级的专业训练或职业培养。

（2）四年制学院：四年制学院（college）常被称作文科学院和文理学院。文科学院的课程包括人文科学、社会科学和行为科学。文理学院除上述文科课程之外，再加上自然科学课程。现在，大多数四年制学院增设了工商管理、护理和师资培训等课程，以满足学生和社会两方面的需求。一般来说，这类学院规模较小，每班学生人数也不多，学生与教授接触的机会较多，两者的关系也比较接近。

（3）四年制大学：大学（university）的规模和组织比学院既大得多，也复杂得多。大学分设数个学院，其课程范围和深度与那些独立的四年制学院不分上下，有的甚至大大超过。不过，大学的教学设备先进，图书资料丰富完整。但是，由于大学，尤其是名牌大学，强调科研成果和专著出版，所以教授们在教学方面花的精力和时间要少一些，学生与教授的关系也更疏远一些。

（4）专业学院：公立的专业学院（professional schools）大多附属于大学，私立的单独立户者居多。一般而言，专业学院包括医学院、法学院、牙科学院和兽医学院等专业性特强的学科。进入这些学院的学生，必须首先取得学士学位，然后才能到专业学院学习3到4年。这类学院的学费很昂贵，招生的名额也不多，进入专业学院读书仅属一小部分人的"特权"。

注 释

① 表示地点的介词短语开头的句子往往倒装,如:
On the hill stands a temple.(山上有座庙。)
有时候也可以用 there 来引导,如:
There stands a temple on the hill.(山上有座庙。)

② 用某种材料做成什么东西,可以用 be made of / be built of / be made from / be built from 来表达。材料没有发生明显变化,用 be made of / be built of,如:
This building is built of bricks.(这栋房子是砖砌成的。)
材料发生明显变化,用 be made from / be built from,如:
The paper is made from wood.(这种纸是木头制造的。)

③ check someone 是口头用语,意思是"找某人核实一下",可能是打电话,也可能是直接问一下,或别的什么方式,如:
I'll check you later.(我晚一点儿打电话问问你。)

At International Students Office
在国际学生办公室

Topic Introduction
话题导言

　　几乎所有的大学都设有管理外国留学生的专门机构,虽然名称可能略有差异,有的叫做国际学生办公室(International Students Office, ISO),有的叫做国际项目办公室(International Programs Office, IPO),有的叫做海外学生办公室(Overseas Students Office, OSO),有的叫做外国学生办公室(Foreign Students Office, FSO)等等,但都担负着同样的使命。这个机构的主要任务就是审查外国留学生的入学资格、管理外国留学生在校学习时的学生身份问题、为外国留学生提供必要的服务等。

　　作为一名留学生,有问题到ISO(或IPO或OSO或FSO)去请求帮助是理所当然的。新到美国大学,非常有必要到这个机构去走一趟,了解一下有关问题或开学时对外国留学生的活动安排,如留学生关心的"我凭这个签证能在这个国家呆多久"、"我的短期访问签证能否转为学生签证"、"假期回国后是否还需要新的签证"、"到第三国后再返回时是否需要新的签证"、"我的签证过期后如何获得合法身份"等等,都是留学生需要关心的问题。

Situational Dialogs
情景对话

初来乍到,刘杭(Liu Hang)经常去管理外国留学生的机构走走,这样不仅可以了解一些有关问题,也可以清楚一些对于外国留学生的活动安排。而李惠敏(Huimin)的身份却遇到了问题。

Dialog 1

Officer: May I help you?
可以帮您吗?

Liu Hang: I'm a new student from China. I'm wondering if there're some activities for us new international students.
我是来自中国的新学生,我想知道有没有为我们新来的国际学生举行的一些活动。

Officer: We're going to have an orientation for all new international students next Monday, a visit to nearby community next Tuesday and a seminar about student visas.
下个星期一有一个为所有新来的国际学生举办的就学指导会,星期二有一个到附近社区的参观活动和一个关于学生签证的咨询会。

Liu Hang: It is good for us to know something concerned.
这对我们了解一些有关的东西有用。

Officer: I hope so.① And, the International Students Union will host a potluck party tomorrow evening.
希望如此。还有,国际学生联合会明天晚上要举行一个百乐餐聚会。

Liu Hang: That'll be very interesting, I think.
我想那会很有意思。

At International Students Office

在国际学生办公室

Dialog 2

Officer: Hello, Liu Hang. May I help you?
刘杭,您好,有什么事吗?

Liu Hang: I'm surprised you remember my name. Could you tell me something about the student visa?
我很吃惊,您能记住我的名字。能告诉我一些关于学生签证的问题吗?

Officer: What would you like to know?
您想知道什么?

Liu Hang: How long can I stay here for full-time study?
在这里全日制学习,我可以呆多久?

Officer: As long as② you like until you finish your degree, but you must keep the status of a full-time student.
可以一直呆到您完成学位,但您必须保持全日制学生的身份。

Liu Hang: When I graduate from here and want to be a doctor, can I stay here any longer?
我从这里毕业并想读博士生时,我可以呆在这里更长一些吗?

Officer: Yes, you can. But you must obtain a new I-20 for your doctor program.
可以,但您必须获得读博士生的新 I-20 表。

Liu Hang: If I want to transfer to another university, what formalities must I go through?③
如果我想转学到另一所大学,我要办理哪些手续?

Officer: You must get a new I-20 from that university, and all the transcripts from this university.
您必须从那个大学获得新的 I-20 表,并从我们学校取得成绩单。
……

Dialog 3

Huimin: I'm told there's something wrong with my status.④
有人告诉我,我的身份有些问题。

Officer: What's the real problem?
究竟是什么问题?

Huimin: I finished my study here March 18, and my grace period ended May 18. But I just got my new I-20 last week; the date on it is July 21.

我3月18日完成了学习,我的宽限期在5月18日结束。但是我上个星期才得到新的I-20表,上面的日期是7月21日。

Officer: Oh, by gosh. That's a very serious problem! How did that happen?

噢,天哪。那是个严重的问题!怎么发生的呢?

Huimin: I don't know either. I submitted my application for Ph.D. Degree at graduate school February 15, but they declined the application, and I didn't receive any notice until May 27. I had to reapply for admission to a master's degree program, and they approved it. So I received a new I-20 last week.

我也不清楚。我2月15日向研究生院提交了读博士学位的申请书,他们拒绝了我,但直到5月27日我才收到通知。我不得不重新提交了读硕士学位的申请书,得到批准。这样我上个星期才收到新的I-20表。

Officer: Why did it happen? Why? I'm going to look into this matter.⑤ If it's true to what you told me, the ISO will help you to reinstate your status.

这事情怎么会发生呢?怎么会呢?我要查查这件事。如果您说的属实,国际学生办公室将帮助您恢复您的身份。

Huimin: I'm sorry to trouble you a lot.

对不起,打搅你这么多。

Officer: It's not your fault. Please write a statement of the whole process and give it to me next Monday.

不是您的错。请写一个整个过程的说明,下个星期一交给我。

Huimin: Yes, I will.

好,我会的。

Typical Sentences 典型句型

At International Students Office 5 在国际学生办公室

1) I'm a new student from China.
   我是来自中国的新学生。
2) Could you issue me a new I-20?
   您能给我签发一个新的I-20表吗?
3) Could you please issue an I-20 for my wife and daughter?
   您能为我的妻子和女儿签发一个I-20表吗?
4) I'm wondering if there're some activities for us new international students.
   我想知道有没有为我们新来的国际学生举行的一些活动。
5) We're going to have an orientation for all new international students next Monday.
   下个星期一有一个为所有新来的国际学生举办的就学指导会。
6) It is good for us to know something concerned.
   这对我们了解一些有关的东西有用。
7) Could you tell me something about the student visa?
   能告诉我一些关于学生签证的问题吗?
8) How long can I stay here for full-time study?
   在这里全日制学习,我可以呆多久?
9) As long as you like until you finish your degree, but you must keep the status of a full-time student.
   可以一直呆到您完成学位,但您必须保持全日制学生的身份。
10) I'm told there's something wrong with my status.
    有人告诉我,我的身份有些问题。
11) What's the real problem?
    究竟是什么问题?
12) Is there any special scholarship for us international students?
    有没有专门给国际学生的奖学金?

Background
背景知识

美国的学生签证：美国各驻外使、领馆颁发给外国留学生的签证种类有三种即 F-1(本科生、研究生、语言学生)、J-1(交换学生、访问学者)、M-1(学习实用技术的学生)。中国学生绝大部分是持 F-1 签证的，少数是 J-1 签证。对于学生签证，普通的中国学生和家长有许多模糊的认识，笔者根据自己的了解说明如下：

(1) 有效期。签证上面有一项是 Expiration Date(过期日)被很多人认为是到美国后只能呆到这一天为止，要想继续呆下去就得申请延期。其实，Expiration Date 的含义是，你在这一天之前到达美国就可以了，至于你在美国可以呆多久是入境时移民局官员决定的，学生到达美国时移民工作人员一般会在护照和入境卡(I-94)上加注"D/S"字样，表示"只要在全日制学习就可以呆下去(Duration of Study)"，同时，你的逗留期限还受 I-20 表上专业学习年限的限制。

(2) 临时回国。学习期间如果临时回国，当再次前往美国时，如果你上次签证的 Expiration Date 还没有到，就可以直接再次赴美。如果已经过了那个日期，就需要重新获得签证才能赴美，据说这种情况也有被拒签的个案。

(3) 去了第三国后再次赴美。"9·11"后的一般规定是，在签证的 Expiration Date 之前再次从第三国进入美国的，不需要重新签证，如果过了这个日期，你必须回国籍所在国或永久居住国重新获得签证，才能再次进入美国。而在"9·11"之前，只需要到邻国加拿大或墨西哥重新签证就可以了。

(4) 超期居留。美国移民局规定，外国学生学习完成后最多可以在美国多呆 60 天(被称作宽限期 Grace Period)，如果遇到两个项目的 I-20 表上的时间相隔超过 60 天，也被认为是超期居留或者失去了学生身份，需要在 ISO 的帮助下向移民局申请恢复学生身份。当然，专业实习 12 至 29 个月是不在此限的。

(5) 连续学习。如果本科毕业了，还要继续在美国读研究生，只需要在合法的期限内获得新的 I-20 表就可以了。其余的事情由

At International Students Office

ISO向移民局申报,不需要学生本人出面。毕业之后需要在美国工作可以申请工作签证或申请为期12至29个月的毕业实习许可证。

(6) 签证转换。以前曾有不少人持探亲或访问签证(B-1/2)滞美不归,为取得合法身份而到学校去当学生的情况,后来经过申请都得以转换为学生签证。"9·11"后这种申请就非常困难了,所以真想去学习就直接在国内申请学生签证。

注 释

① I hope so.是"我希望如此。"的意思,类似的说法有 I think so./I expect so. / I guess so.等。否定式各不相同,如:I hope not. / I don't think so. / I expect not. / I guess not.等。

② as long as 是"只要"的意思,相当于一个连词,如:
I will stay here as long as you are here. (你在这里呆多久,我就在这里呆多久。)

③ go through formalities 是"办理手续"的意思,如:
In the past if you wanted to go abroad, you had to go through many formalities. (过去如果你想出国,你必须办理很多手续。)

④ There is something wrong with ... 意思是"某人或某物有问题",如:
There is something wrong with the TV set. (电视机有些问题。)
也可以说 Something is wrong with ...,如:
Something must be wrong with her throat. (她的喉咙一定有些问题。)

⑤ look into 是"调查"的意思,如:
We must look into the whole matter. (我们必须对整个事情进行调查。)

About Language Program
语言培训项目

Topic Introduction
话题导言

在国内申请出国留学的朋友首先会想到的是英语要过关,具体来说就是托福(TOEFL 即 Test of English as a Foreign language)要多少分、雅思(IELTS 即 International English Language Testing System)要多少分。但是,其实没有英语成绩也是可以出国留学的,也就说,不参加托福或雅思考试照样可以进入美国等国的大学。

你会问,有窍门吗?没有。问题是申请出国留学的人们没有认真研究美国等国大学的入学规则。大多数大学对于外国人入学就读虽然有语言水平的要求,希望申请者的托福或雅思达到多少分,但这只是其中的一个标准,如果达到与其并列的其他标准中的一个也是被认可的,也具有和托福或雅思同等的效力。所以,英语水平达不到外国大学本科或研究生入学要求的朋友想到外国留学,可以首先考虑去读该大学设立的英语强化课程。

情景对话

杨洋(Yang Yang)遇到了大多数中国留学生同样存在的问题,英语不过关,他需要参加一段时间的英语强化课程。而刘杭(Liu Hang)的导师却建议她去学阅读与写作课。

About Language Program

语言培训项目

Dialog 1

Kate:	ALCP office, may I help you? 美国语言与文化项目办公室,能帮您忙吗?
Yang Yang:	I'd like to know something about your language program. 我想了解一下你们语言项目的情况。
Kate:	Our program is to improve your English level so that you can study undergraduate or graduate courses at our university.① 我们项目的目的是提高您的英语水平,让您好学习我们大学的本科或研究生课程。
Yang Yang:	What level should I pass if I'd like to enroll at graduate school? 我要是入读研究生院,我应该通过哪一个等级?
Kate:	Most of graduate programs require Level 6, but a few of them require only Level 5. 大多数研究生项目要求六级,但有一些只要求五级。
Yang Yang:	How about the tuition for each session? 每期的学费是多少?
Kate:	Around 1800 US dollars plus insurance. 大约1800美元,再加上保险费。
Yang Yang:	When is the next session going to begin? 下一期什么时候开始?
Kate:	January 14. 1月14日。
Yang Yang:	How can I get further information and how can I apply for admission? 我如何得到更加详细的信息? 我怎么申请入学?
Kate:	Please check our program's website. The Internet address is www.uidaho.edu/ipo/alcp. If you have any other questions, please call us again. Thank you for calling. Good luck. 请查阅我们项目的网站,互联网地址是 www.uidaho.edu/ipo/alcp,如果还有问题,请再给我们打电话。谢谢您打电话来,祝您好运。
Yang Yang:	Thank you. Good-bye. 谢谢,再见。

Dialog 2

Yang Yang: Excuse me, Kate, may I have a question?
凯特，打搅一下，可以问一个问题吗？

Kate: Yes?
什么事？

Yang Yang: I think my English is qualified for[2] graduate course study. I'm wondering if you could waive my ALCP.
我觉得我的英语学习研究生课程是合格的，我想您能否免掉我的美国语言与文化项目的课程。

Kate: You have to take the placement test this afternoon. If your English is really excellent, you could directly register graduate courses.
您必须参加今天下午举行的分班考试，如果您的英语确实很优秀，您就可以直接注册研究生课程。

Yang Yang: That's good enough.
那真是很好。

Kate: We arrange students to different ALCP levels according to their achievement in the placement test, but I suggest that you should do[3] our Level 6 Reading and Writing, for it's very useful for your graduate course study.
我们按照学生入学考试的成绩把学生分到不同的级别，但我还是建议您学我们的第六级阅读与写作，对您的研究生课程学习非常有用。

Yang Yang: That sounds very attractive.
那听起来非常有吸引力。

Dialog 3

Liu Hang: My major professor asks me to do some courses in ALCP.
我的专业导师要我在美国语言与文化项目学一些课程。

Steve: That's good. What kind of courses would you like to have?
那不错，您要学些什么课程？

Liu Hang: My professor suggests that I should take some reading and writing.
我的教授建议我学些阅读与写作。

About Language Program 6

语言培训项目

Steve: Is it good for us to put you into Level 6 Reading and Writing class? That's useful for you to master some skills and techniques in your graduate courses.
我们把您安排到第六级阅读与写作班,好吗?这对于您掌握研究生课程的一些技巧很有好处。

Liu Hang: I hope so. How much should I pay then?
希望如此,我应该付多少学费?

Steve: Level 6 Reading and Writing is half the whole level, so please pay half, that is, 900 dollars.
第六级阅读与写作课是整个级别课程的一半,所以请您支付一半,就是900美元。

Liu Hang: I see. Thank you very much.
我明白了,非常感谢。

Steve: You bet. If you have any questions, please check me again.
不谢。如果还有问题,请再来找我。

Typical Sentences 典型句型

1) I'd like to know something about your language program.
我想了解一下你们语言项目的情况。

2) How about the tuition for each session?
每期的学费是多少?

3) When is the next session going to begin?
下一期什么时候开始?

4) How long is a session?
一期是多长时间?

5) What level should I pass if I'd like to enroll at graduate school?
我要是入读研究生院,我应该通过哪一个等级?

6) What in case I can't pass Level 6?
万一我没有能通过六级怎么办?

7) May I use ALCP Level Certificate to substitute TOEFL?
我可以用ALCP水平证书代替托福?

8) How can I get further information and how can I apply for admission?

我如何得到更加详细的信息？我怎么申请入学？

9) I'm wondering if you could waive my ALCP.

我想您能否免掉我的美国语言与文化项目的课程。

10) Could you tell me my placement test score?

您能告诉我我的入学考试成绩是多少分吗？

11) My major professor asks me to do some courses in ALCP.

我的专业导师要我在美国语言与文化项目学一些课程。

12) My professor suggests that I should take some reading and writing.

我的教授建议我学些阅读与写作。

背景知识

英语强化培训：几乎各个大学都设立了英语强化培训机构，目的是为母语不是英语的外国留学生提高英语水平。这个项目在各个大学的名称各异，有的叫做强化英语项目 (Intensive English Program)、有的叫做美国语言与文化项目(American Language and Culture Program)、有的叫做强化英语中心(Intensive English Center)等等。

下面以美国爱达荷大学(the University of Idaho)为例，介绍这方面的内容。爱达荷大学在国际学生办公室(International Students Office)下设立了一个"美国语言与文化项目(American Language and Culture Program，简称ALCP)"专门负责国际学生的英语水平评估和教学。

(1) 参加对象：英语水平不够爱达荷大学本科和研究生入学要求的国际学生；虽然参加了托福或其他考试且成绩合格，但入学后导师认为不能正常学习的在校学生；国际交流的学生或教师；希望提高自己英语水平的其他人员。

(2) ALCP 等级：ALCP 共设有六个等级，开设听力、会话、语法、阅读、写作和课堂笔记技巧等课程。从一级到六级(Level 1, 2, 3, 4, 5, 6)分别换算成不同的托福成绩,通过了5级就可以读本科,通过了6级就可以读研究生。实际上,通过5级比托福考试的525分要容易一些,一般一期(8周)的学习可以提高一级。

(3) ALCP效用:完成并通过了5级或者6级的考试,将获得一个成绩证书,凭此证书就可以直接转读爱达荷大学的本科或研究生的任何一个专业。同时,爱达荷州的其他四所大学(Idaho State University, Boise State University, North Idaho College, Lewis-Clark College)也承认这个成绩,也就是说,你可以用这个证书代替托福成绩申请这四所大学。

(4) ALCP的期次:每年开五期:1月中旬至3月上旬;3月下旬至5月中旬;6月下旬至8月中旬;8月下旬至10月中旬;10月下旬至12月中旬。具体开学日期依照校历的变化略有变动。

(5) 报名信息:填写完整的报名表并签字;银行资金证明,每报一期要求至少提供3580美元的银行资金证明(以本人的名义或父母或其他赞助人的名义)。

(6) 签证:提供了完整、真实的信息之后,学校会逐一审查。对于符合要求的申请者,爱达荷大学将签发入学通知书、I-20表、签证说明书以及学校简介等资料。申请者就可以凭借这些资料、护照、资金证明等到美国领事馆申请学生签证(F-1)了。

注释

① so that 在这里引导的是目的状语从句,含有"以便"的意思,如:
She gets up early so that she can catch up the first train. (她起床早,以便赶上第一班火车。)

② be qualified for 的意思是"在某方面合格",如:
Am I qualified for joining in the contest? (我符合参加这个比赛的资格吗?)

③ 这里几次出现了 do 的一种用法,即用在口语中代替别的动词,如:study a course 说成 do a course (学习一门课程。)

At an Orientation
就学指导会

Topic Introduction
话题导言

我国的大学开学的头几天往往有一个叫做入学教育的活动，目的是让新生树立正确的行为规范、理想信念等。美国大学开学的时候也有一个类似活动叫做 orientation（就学指导会）。orientation 的本义是"确定方向、定位"，这样一个活动就是要你给自己在新环境中定一个位。其中有专门为外国留学生举办的 orientation，主要的内容包括大学介绍、学生签证的有关法律规定、选课的策略、学生医疗保险、学分与成绩问题、转学与转专业问题、校内工作机会介绍、聚餐等。这中间的活动很多都是以 seminar（讨论会）的形式进行的，主持人都是某个方面的专家，学生可以随意提问，学校相关部门（如 Graduate School, International Students Office, Registrar, Students Health Center 等）的负责人会到场解答有关问题。

新到的中国留学生很有必要参加这样一个活动，一来可以了解应该关心的问题，有些内容关系到留学生的切身利益；二来也是英语听力的第一次"风暴式培训"，没有翻译和思考的余地，你才能真正体会到"英语是什么"。纯正地道的语言对大脑是一个强烈的语言刺激。遇到问题要大胆提问，一定要丢弃中国学生害羞和爱面子的弱点，这就是开始。

At an Orientation

Situational Dialogs
情景对话

杨洋(Yang Yang)和刘杭(Liu Hang)去参加了一个就学指导会，这对他们所关心的问题很有帮助。

Dialog 1

Yang Yang: I hear there is an orientation. When will it begin?
我听说有一个就学指导会，什么时候开始？

Christiana: It begins Monday morning, eight-thirty.
星期一上午 8 点 30 分开始。

Yang Yang: Is there a special one for us international students?
有专门为国际学生举办的就学指导会吗？

Christiana: Yes, there is. The International Students Office holds it in the Students Activities Center. It'll begin at eight-thirty Monday morning.
有的，国际学生办公室在学生活动中心举办，也是星期一上午 8 点 30 分。

Yang Yang: Are you going there?
你去吗？

Christiana: Sure. You'd better sign up① for it at the Information Desk of ISO.
当然，你最好到国际学生办公室登记参加。

Yang Yang: Oh, I will. So see you Monday morning, eight-thirty.
噢，我会的。那么星期一上午 8 点 30 分见你了。

Christiana: Yes, please be punctual.② See you later.
好的，请准时，再见。

Dialog 2

Liu Hang: Excuse me, may I ask a question?
打扰一下，我可以问一个问题吗？

Host: Sure, please go ahead.
当然,问吧。

Liu Hang: Is the University Students Health Insurance mandatory?
大学学生健康保险是必须买的吗?

Host: Yes. Otherwise you mustn't register any courses.
是的,否则你就不能注册课程。

Liu Hang: But what if I have bought another kind of insurance with the same coverage?
但要是我已经买了别的保险且保障范围相同,怎么办?

Host: If so, you may apply for a waiver of the University Students Health Insurance. Please fill in the form titled Application for Health Insurance Waiver and turn it in to the International Students Office or the Students Health Center.
如果这样,你可以申请免除购买大学学生健康保险。请填写题为《健康保险免除申请表》的表格,然后交给国际学生办公室或学生健康中心。

Liu Hang: I see. Thank you. Can I have another question?
我明白了,谢谢。我可以还问一个问题吗?

Host: Sure, you can.
当然,你能问。

Liu Hang: Can I use distance courses to substitute in-class ones?
我可以用远程教育课程代替课堂课程吗?

Host: Yes, but your distance course credits cannot be more than a quarter of all the credits required for your degree.
可以,但你的远程教育课程学分不能超过你获得学位所需学分的四分之一。

Liu Hang: I need 36 credits for my master degree. As you said just now, I may take at most 9 credits by distance learning.[3]
我获得硕士学位需要 36 个学分,按照你所说的,我最多可以修 9 个远程教育学分。

Host: Correct.
正确。

At an Orientation 7

Dialog 3

Liu Hang: Excuse me, what if I meet with some trouble in my course work?
打搅一下,如果我学习功课遇到困难,怎么办?

Host: We have set up several centers to help you, such as writing center, disabled students aids center, statistical help center, and so on.
我们设立了几个中心帮助你,如写作中心、残疾学生协助中、统计帮助中心,等等。

Liu Hang: Are they free of charge or do I have to pay?
是免费的,还是我必须付钱?

Host: Completely free for first ten hours, and then you have to④ pay, but it's cheap.
前10个小时完全免费,然后你就要付钱了,但很便宜。

Liu Hang: That sounds wonderful.
听起来真是妙极了。

Typical Sentences 典型句型

1) I hear there is an orientation. When will it begin?
我听说有一个就学指导会,什么时候开始?

2) Is there a special one for us international students?
有专门为国际学生举办的就学指导会吗?

3) You'd better sign up for it at the Information Desk of ISO.
你最好到国际学生办公室登记参加。

4) Is the University Students Health Insurance mandatory?
大学学生健康保险是必须买的吗?

5) But what if I have bought another kind of insurance with the same coverage?
但要是我已经买了别的保险且保障范围相同,怎么办?

6) I'd like to know if you have jobs open to us new students.
我想知道你是否有工作给我们新生干。

7) If so, you may apply for a waiver of the University Students Health Insurance.

如果这样,你可以申请免除购买大学学生健康保险。

8) Can I use distance courses to substitute in-class ones?

我可以用远程教育课程代替课堂课程吗?

9) As you said just now, I may take at most 9 credits by distance learning.

按照你所说的,我最多可以修9个远程教育学分。

10) Excuse me, what if I meet with some trouble in my course work?

打搅一下,如果我学习功课遇到困难,怎么办?

11) Are they free of charge or do I have to pay?

是免费的,还是我必须付钱?

12) Does the International Students Union host many activities?

国际学生联合会举办很多活动吗?

背景知识

美国大学学位:美国各大学颁发的学位有准学士、学士、硕士和博士等四种。

(1) 准学士学位(Associate Degree):两年制的社区学院毕业可获得该学位,如理科准学士(Associate in Science,简称 A.S.)、文科准学士 (Associate in Arts,简称 A.A.)、商学准学士 (Associate in Business,简称 A.B.)等等。

(2) 学士学位(Bachelor Degree):进入四年制大学本科学习的学生,完成各门功课并取得规定的学分可获得该学位,如文科学士(Bachelor of Arts,简称 B.A.)、会计学学士(Bachelor of Accounting,简称 B.Acct.)、理学士 (Bachelor of Science,简称 B.S.)、工学士(Bachelor of Engineering,简称 B.E.)等。学士学位被称为第一学位,属于初级学位,是读研究生的先决条件。

(3) 硕士学位(Master Degree):具有学士学位者入读硕士研究

生课程，在导师的指导下，确定一门专修学科的学习计划，修完规定的学分，通过论文答辩，可获得该学位。有些学校的某些应用型专业也可以通过综合性考试代替论文写作以获得硕士学位。常见的硕士学位有：文科硕士（Master of Arts，简称 M.A.）、理科硕士（Master of Science，简称 M.S.）、工商管理硕士（Master of Business Administration，简称 M.B.A.）、公共管理硕士（Master of Public Administration，简称 M.P.A.）等。在美国，可授予硕士学位的大学有700所左右。

（4）博士学位(Doctoral Degree)：是大学颁授的最高学位，有哲学博士(Philosophical Doctor，简称 Ph.D.)和专业博士(Professional Doctor)两种。哲学博士又称为"研究博士(Research Doctor)"。攻读博士学位可以在获得硕士学位后攻读，如果专业相同且又是在同一所学校，获得硕士学位后大约还需2到3年；也可以在获得学士学位后直接攻读，但必须修读硕士学位课程，大约需要5到6年。

如果在中国已经获得硕士学位，到美国去读博士学位，除非个别情况，一般只按具有学士学位的研究生对待，需要5到6年才能得到博士学位。获得博士学位必须通过博士论文答辩，博士学位都需标明科目，如工商管理博士(Doctor of Business Administration，简称 D.B.A.)、自然资源学博士（Doctor of Philosophy in Natural Resources，简称 Ph.D.N.R.)、教育学博士(Doctor of Philosophy in Education，简称 Ph.D.E.或 Doctor of Education，简称 D.ED.)等。

还有些博士学位比较特殊如法学博士(Juristic Doctor，简称 J.D.)、牙医学博士(Doctor of Medical Dentistry，简称 D.M.D.)、医学博士(Medicine Doctor，简称 M. D.)等，因为这些专业的学士和博士之间没有硕士学位，学士毕业直接攻读博士学位。所以在美国没有法学硕士、医学硕士之类的学位名称。在美国，可授予博士学位的大学有200所左右。

注 释

① **sign up** 的意思是"登记"，目的是为了参加某个活动，以使主办方掌

握人数，方法是签下你的名字。

② be punctual 是"准时"的意思。表示时间的很多说法很容易混淆，注意下列几个：

Keep time, please.（请跟上节奏。）

My watch keeps good time.（我的表走得很准。）

We must make good time.（我们必须抓紧时间。）

Please be punctual.（请准时。）

I'll be there on time.（我将准时到达。）

They sent him to hospital in time.（他们及时送他到医院。）

Please be prompt.（请准时。）

Don't be tardy.（不要迟到。）

Don't be late.（不要迟到。）

③ at most 的意思是"最多，至多"；另有几个也属于同类短语，at least（至少）、at first（首先）、at last（最后）。

④ 美国英语中更多地使用 have got to 代替 have to，例如：

I've got to hit the road.（我得开路了。）

She's got to pay.（她必须付钱。）

Obtaining Student ID
办理学生证

Topic Introduction
话题导言

  美国等西方国家的大学也向学生颁发IC卡形式的学生证。各个大学的学生证都有着自己的名称，如爱达荷大学(the University of Idaho)的学生证就被称为Vandal Card，西肯塔基大学(Western Kentucky University)的学生证被称为Big Red Card。至于这些名字的来历，有些已很难考究其来历了。

  新生办理学生证要出示入学通知书等文件，到学生服务中心或注册处的某个机构进行。学生证上有姓名(名+姓)、身份(Student)、照片(数码像)、学号(入学年月含在学号内)、条形码(Bar Code)、持证人签名以及使用规定。学生证在大学内部的用途可以说是无所不能，既可以用于借书、吃饭、购物、运动、使用教学设施，也可以凭证免费使用自行车、球场。在校外还可以享受部分公交车的免费服务或者折扣优惠。

Situational Dialogs
情景对话

  刘杭(Liu Hang)作为新生入学，首先要做的事情当然是办理学生证了。而杨洋(Yang Yang)则是要换学生证。

Dialog 1

Clerk: Hello, may I help you?
您好,能帮您吗?

Liu Hang: I'd like to have my student ID.
我要办理学生证。

Clerk: Could you show me your letter of admission?
把你的入学通知书给我看看吧。

Liu Hang: Here it is. I'm a new graduate student here.
给你这个。我是新来的研究生。

Clerk: Please take a seat① over there and we'll take a picture of you. ... Perfect. Just smile at the camera slightly.
请到那边坐下,我们给你照张相。好极了,对着照相机稍微笑笑就可以了。

Liu Hang: Is it okay?
行了吗?

Clerk: Please wait a second. We'll have a second one, and then you can choose the better.
请稍等,我们再来一张,你可以从中选一张。

Liu Hang: OK. Thank you.
好的,谢谢。

Clerk: You bet.
别客气。

Dialog 2

Yang Yang: I'd like to change my student ID.
我想换学生证。

Clerk: Oh, why?
噢,为什么?

Yang Yang: I used to be a student of American Language and Culture Program, but now I have been admitted into Graduate School.
我原来是美国语言与文化项目的学生,但现在我被录取到研究生院了。

Obtaining Student ID 8
办理学生证

Clerk: Show me your letter of admission, and sit down there to take a picture.
请把入学通知书给我,坐在那里照张相。

Yang Yang: Here you are. I'd like to use the old picture. Could you find it in the computer?
给你。我想用那张旧照片,你能从电脑里帮我找出来吗？

Clerk: Sure. Just a second. ... Oh, look, is that you?
当然可以,稍等……哦,看,那是你吗？

Yang Yang: Yes, that's me. Does this look nicer than myself?
是我,是不是看上去比我本人要好看些？

Clerk: You look pretty[2] handsome. Do you like this old one?
你看起来很是英俊,喜欢这张旧照片吗？

Yang Yang: Yes, I do. Please use it.
我喜欢,就用这张吧。

Dialog 3

Liu Hang: Excuse me, could you tell me what the use of this bar[3] code is?
打扰一下,能否告诉我这个条形码的作用是什么？

Clerk: Sure. This bar code is designed for the computer bar code reader. When you scan it with the reader, the code will enter the computer automatically.
可以,这个条形码是专为电脑条形码阅读器设计的。用阅读器扫描时,这个号码就自动进入电脑了。

Liu Hang: Just like when we borrow books from a library?
就像我们在图书馆借书那样？

Clerk: Correct. And, when you're off campus and want to check something on the university library website, you have to enter your bar code.
正确,而且你不在学校而又想到图书馆网上查阅什么东西时,你就必须输入你的条形码。

Liu Hang: Oh, I see. Thank you very much.
噢,我明白了,非常感谢。

Typical Sentences
典型句型

1) I'd like to have my student ID.
   我要办理学生证。
2) I'd like to change my student ID.
   我想换学生证。
3) Could you show me your letter of admission?
   把你的入学通知书给我看看吧。
4) You may take the bus free of charge from here to Pullman by showing your student ID to the driver.
   出示学生证,你可以免费乘坐从这里到普尔曼的公共汽车。
5) Please take a seat over there and we'll take a picture of you.
   请到那边坐下,我们给你照张相。
6) I have been admitted into Graduate School.
   我被录取到研究生院。
7) I'd like to use the old picture. Could you find it in the computer?
   我想用那张旧照片,你能从电脑里帮我找出来吗?
8) Excuse me, could you tell me what the use of this bar code is?
   打扰一下,能否告诉我这个条形码的作用是什么?
9) This bar code is designed for the computer bar code reader.
   这个条形码是专为电脑条形码阅读器设计的。
10) What's the implication of the ID number?
    这个证的号码意味着什么?
11) It implies that you're a graduate student enrolled in the year 2002.
    这个号码意味着你是2002年入学的研究生。

背景知识

Obtaining Student ID — 办理学生证

美国大学教授： 英美大学，尤其是美国大学里的教授的称呼较多，绝不是一个 professor 就可以指代得了的。

(1) 正教授(full professor)：一般大学里，绝大多数的系都有一名正教授主持，规模较大的系可能由数名正教授主持，而由其中一名出任系主任。

(2) 副教授(associate professor)：其职位低于正教授，要协助正教授的工作。由担任过三年以上助理教授职位的教师提拔上来。

(3) 助理教授(assistant professor)：其职位低于副教授，也是要协助正教授的工作。一般获得博士学位者到大学任教时被聘为助理教授。

(4) 高级教授(senior professor)：在一些特定的时候才设立这个职位，担任此职位者多是资历深或成就卓越的人。

(5) 讲座教授(professor ordinaries 或 chair-professor)：这是各种教授中具有最高荣誉的教授。"讲座"的设立是因为一位教授在某一方面做出了重要贡献，大学便以他的名字设立一个基金会和研究所，并命名该学科的讲座。即便是在他退休或逝世后，讲座也永远保留其名称。除了是极高的荣誉之外，讲座教授还可以参加大学行政和管理工作，可以自由地处理自己所担任的科目。

(6) 名誉教授(emeritus professor)：教授在退休或光荣退职后，一般会获赠一个荣衔 (emeritus)，称为 "emeritus professor 或 professor emeritus"，即名誉教授。

(7) 客座教授(visiting professor)：是由大学领导特别聘任的教一学年或半学年的人士，甚至包括特邀到大学短期讲课的 guest professor。

(8) 交换教授(exchange professor)：是和其他大学交换，到大学担任一个时期课程的教授。

讲师种种： 一般称讲师为 lecturer，有些美国大学则称为 instructor，两者都是比教授地位低一级的大学教师。

在英国的大学里，因为一般的系中只有一位教授(大系可以有

多个),讲师的职位与权力相当于讲座教授,所以讲师也有高级讲师(senior lecturer)和普通讲师(lecturer)之分,而前者和美国大学的教授职位相等,后者则相当于副教授。讲师之下也有副讲师(associate lecturer)、助理讲师(assistant lecturer)和助教(teaching assistant)。讲师的地位虽然低于教授,但并不是说他们的学问不如教授。事实上,很多讲师都拥有博士学位。

美国大学里的讲师职位一般在学科力量比较薄弱的系里或者是讲授公共课的系(部)才存在。担任讲师职位的教师往往因为没有博士学位而永远也得不到"教授"的称号。

注 释

① take a seat 的意思是"就座",类似的短语很多,如 take a picture (照相)、take a note (记录)、take a walk (散步)、take a bath (洗澡)、take a swim (游泳)、take a look (看一看),等等。

② pretty 这里作副词用,意思是"相当",如:
She is a pretty beautiful lady. (她是个相当漂亮的女士。)

③ bar 指"条状物,柱状物",如:bar chart (柱形图)。另外列一些图形种类的表达方法:pie chart (饼图)、line chart / curve diagram (趋势曲线图)、table (表格图)、flow chart / sequence diagram (流程图或过程图)、processing / procedure diagram (程序图)。

Paying Tuition for Registration
交费注册

Topic Introduction
话题导言

注册是新生正式成为该大学学生的关键手续,广义上说,注册包括选课、交纳学杂费、购买健康保险,其中关键的一个步骤是交纳学费。正式开始上课的第一天往往是交纳学费的最后一天,如要迟交,就得交纳一定数额的滞纳金(late fee);而且这一天交费人很多,有时候要排队等候很长时间,所以能早交学费就早一点儿交,反正也躲不掉。

由于各人的情况不尽相同,有的有奖学金,有的没有奖学金。因此,有奖学金者需要先到校园网上进入到自己的账户确认所接受的奖学金,就可以知道自己还需要交纳多少钱。没有奖学金者,就要直接按照规定的数额交纳。学费交纳的方式也有许多种,可以在校园网上直接从你银行的存款账户划账给学校的学生财务账户(Bursar's Account),也可以到财务柜台去交纳现金或者支票,还可以用信用卡转账给财务账户。交了学费之后又获得奖学金的,学校奖学金管理部门(Scholarships and Financial Aids Office)会把所获得的金额开成现金或转账支票给学生。

Situational Dialogs
情景对话

注册最重要的一步肯定是缴纳学费了，刘杭(Liu Hang)今天需要去缴纳学费。

Dialog 1

Liu Hang: Hello, have you registered?
你好，你注册了吗？

Christian: Not yet. How about you?
还没有呢，你呢？

Liu Hang: No. I want to register tomorrow, but I'm afraid there'll be too many people.
没有，我想明天注册，但我怕人太多。

Christian: Yes, you have to line up① for at least one hour.
是啊，你得至少排队一个小时。

Liu Hang: One hour? But I feel they don't have so much room② for us to line up in the front of the Bursar's counters.
一个小时？但我觉得他们财务柜台前面没有那么大的地方让我们排队。

Christian: The Bursar's people will work in the conference hall on the second floor of the students' center building. It's big enough.
财务人员会到学生中心大楼二楼的会议厅办公，足够大。

Liu Hang: I didn't think of that point.③
我倒没有想到那一点。

Dialog 2

Clerk: Hi, how're you?
嗨，你好吗？

Liu Hang: Pretty good. How're you? How much should I pay?
很好，你好吗？我该付多少钱？

Paying Tuition for Registration 9

交费注册

Clerk: Your Student ID Card, please.
请出示学生证。

Liu Hang: Here you are.
给你。

Clerk: The total amount is 7237.80 dollars for this semester, but you have got a Non-resident Tuition Waiver④, that's 5800 dollars. 7237.80 less⑤ 5800 equals 1437.80, plus health insurance 240. So you should pay 1677.80 dollars.
这学期总共是7237.80美元，但你得到了州外费减免，是5800美元，7237.80减去5800，等于1437.80，再加上保险费240美元。这样你应该付1677.80美元。

Liu Hang: What if I don't want to buy the university insurance?
如果我不想买学校的保险，怎么办？

Clerk: You have to pay it first. If your waiver application for the university insurance is approved, we'll refund it to you.
你得先付了钱，如果你不买学校保险的豁免申请获得批准，我们将退钱给你。

Liu Hang: I see. Do you accept American Express credit card?
我明白了，可以用美国运通信用卡吗？

Clerk: Sorry, we don't. We accept Visa and MasterCard.
对不起，我们不接受。我们接受维萨和万事达卡。

Liu Hang: Can I write a check, then?
那么，我可开支票吗？

Clerk: Sure you can.
你当然可以。

Liu Hang: What should I put for "PAY TO"?
"支付给"这里该怎么填？

Clerk: Put "UI Bursar". That's right.
填上"UI Bursar"。对了。

Liu Hang: The amount is ONE THOUSAND SIX HUNDRED SEVENTY SEVEN DOLLARS and 80/100.⑥ Right?
数额是壹仟陆佰柒拾柒美元八十美分，对吗？

Clerk: Quite right. Thank you very much.
很对，谢谢你了。

Typical Sentences
典型句型

1) Have you registered?
   你注册了吗?

2) I want to register tomorrow, but I'm afraid there'll be too many people.
   我想明天注册,但我怕人太多。

3) The Bursar's people will work in the conference hall on the second floor of the students' center building.
   财务人员会到学生中心大楼二楼的会议厅办公。

4) How much do I need to pay?
   我要付多少钱?

5) What if I get some scholarships after I pay the tuition?
   如果我交了学费后又得到奖学金该怎么办呢?

6) What if I don't want to buy the university insurance?
   如果我不想买学校的保险该怎么办呢?

7) If your waiver application for the university insurance is approved, we'll refund it to you.
   如果你不买学校保险的豁免申请获得批准,我们将退钱给你。

8) I don't need to pay tuition, for I've got full tuition waiver.
   我不需要交学费,因为我得到了全免学费奖学金。

9) Do you accept American Express credit card?
   可以用美国运通信用卡吗?

10) Can I write a check, then?
    那么,我可开支票吗?

11) What should I put for "PAY TO"?
    "支付给"这里该怎么填?

Paying Tuition for Registration

Background 背景知识

美国大学的校历制度(Calendar System)：大体上可分为学期制、三学季制和三学期制等三种。

(1) 学期制(Semester System)：每学年的秋季学期(Fall Semester)为第一个学期，一般8月下旬或9月上旬开学，到12月下旬圣诞节之前结束；春季学期(Spring Semester)为第二学期，一般在1月中旬开始，到5月底或6月初结束。每个学期长度为15周。大多数学校在复活节期间放假一至两个星期。实行这种体制的学校大多在夏季(被称作Summer Session)也开设若干门功课，供有兴趣或有需要的学生修读，往往采取集中上课或实习的方式。

(2) 三学季制(Quarter System)：每学年分为3个学季(three quarters)，每个学季长度为11周。秋季从9月初到12月中旬，冬季从1月到3月，春季从3月到6月底。

(3) 三学期制(Trimester System)：每学年分为3个等长的学期，每个学期长度约为16周。秋季学期从8月到12月，冬季学期从1月到4月，夏季学期从5月到8月。

美国大学的选修制：目前，美国大学多采用必修课和选修课制度。前两年必修课分为自然科学、人文科学和社会科学三个领域，学生必须修读其中规定的课程，才能继续修读专业课程，目的是使学生得到全面的基础教育。后两年，学生要集中攻读一个专业领域，称为"主修"(specialized course 或 major)，以便在该领域有所作为和发展。除"主修"专业外，还有"副修"(sub-majoring 或 minor)课程。实际上，"副修"课程是第二专业课程的学习。

必修课(required courses)和选修课(elective courses)获得的总学分达到了规定的学位授予条件，就可以授予学位。有些学校的机制比较灵活，对于兴趣广泛，修读的课程跨越多个专业，让人说不出是哪个专业，而学分又达到学位授予数的学生，授予他们一个普通学习学位(Bachelor of General Studies)。对于中国人来说，这一点儿看起来也确实滑稽。

注 释

① **line up** 是"排队"的意思,如:
Please line up in front of the third counter. (请在三号柜台前排队。)
② **room** 这里做不可数名词,意思是"空间",如:
The boy made some room for me, and I put myself onto the ground.
(男孩给我让了一些地方,我一下子躺到了地板上。)
③ **point** 在这里做量词,指"点",如:different points of view。
④ **Non-resident Tuition Waiver** 也叫做 Out-of-state Tuition Waiver,是给外州学生和国际学生的一种奖学金。获得这种学费减免,就可以跟本州学生缴纳同等数额的学费了。
⑤ **less** 这里是介词,意思是"减去",和 **minus** 相同,如:
Ten less four is six. (十减四等于六。)
⑥ 填写支票时,除了要用阿拉伯数字外,还要用英语词语表达数额,且多数人写大写字母,就像中国人用大写数字一样。

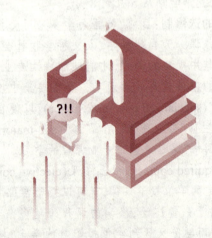

Selecting Courses
选课

Topic Introduction
话题导言

应该说,选课也是注册的重要部分。由于信息技术的发展,传统的选课方式使用得越来越少了。一般情况下,学生通过校园网就可以选课了,本科生一般可以选12到19个学分的课,研究生可以选9到15个学分的课,大学一、二年级学生还必须先修读必修课,经过批准才能选读高年级的课程。

首先学生要根据自己的专业和兴趣,选出一些课程,然后去和专业导师(major professor)或学业顾问(academic adviser)讨论,他会根据整个专业的知识面和专业技能要求,建议你选读哪些课程。讨论时要听从导师的意见,也可以和往届学长交流看法。

Situational Dialogs
情景对话

选课总是一件麻烦的事情,刘杭(Liu Hang)除了要先咨询导师的意见外,还碰上了很多其他的问题。

Dialog 1

Liu Hang: I'm coming to see you about selecting courses.
我来是为了选课的事情。

Professor: Yep. What're you thinking about then?
好的,你是怎么想的呢?

Liu Hang: I'm planning to do three elective courses besides① the three required ones.
我打算选三门必修课和三门选修课。

Professor: How many credits in all?
总共多少学分?

Liu Hang: Fifteen credits, with eight credits for the three required and seven for the three electives.
15个学分,三门必修课8个学分,三门选修课7个学分。

Professor: Generally, an American student takes twelve credits for the first semester. My opinion is that you'd better take ten.
一般地,美国学生第一个学期选12个学分,我的意见是你选10个学分。

Liu Hang: I'm just thinking I can graduate earlier if I take more.
我只是想,多选课可以早毕业。

Professor: Don't be too eager. You may take two required courses, RRT502 and RRT586, and two electives, RNG522 and BUS428.
别太急。你可以选两门必修课即RRT502和RRT586,以及两门选修课RNG522和BUS428。

Liu Hang: That's six credits for the required and five credits for the electives. I'm dropping the other two.
这样就是必修课为6个学分,选修课为5个学分。我要丢掉另外两门选修课。

Professor: If you think you are interested in the other two, you may audit them. You don't need to do anything except② show up in class and listen.
要是你认为你对另外两门感兴趣,你可以旁听。除了到课堂听课以外,什么也不用做。

Selecting Courses 10

Liu Hang: That's better for me. Thank you very much.
这对我更好,非常感谢。
Professor: You bet.
别客气。

Dialog 2

Liu Hang: Excuse me, professor. I'm considering dropping this course.
教授,打搅一下,我想丢掉这门课。
Professor: Well, do you think it is hard?
呃,你觉得难吗?
Liu Hang: I can't follow you in class. English is just my foreign language, and I'm new here. I'd like to take it when I'm used to listening to English.
我上课跟不上。英语是我的外语,我又刚来这里。我想等我习惯听英语了再上这门课。
Professor: That's no problem. You may take it next fall. We'll repeat it then.
没问题,你可以明年秋季听。那时我们要重开这门课。
Liu Hang: I feel sorry about that. I've discussed about it with my major professor[3] and the department head.
我对此感到抱歉,我已经和我的专业导师及系主任谈过这事。
Professor: Don't worry about that. Just concentrate yourself on the other courses.
别想那么多,只要集中精力到其他课上就行了。
Liu Hang: Thank you so much.
非常感谢。
Professor: Thank you for telling me.
谢谢你告诉我。

Dialog 3

Liu Hang: Excuse me, professor, I have a question.
请问,教授,我有一个问题。

59

Professor:	Yep. Go ahead. 好的,说吧。
Liu Hang:	I can't register Stat405, and I'm asked to take Stat278 first. But when I register Stat278, I'm asked to take Stat108. 我注册不了 Stat405,我被要求先修 Stat278,可当我注册 Stat278 时,我又被要求先修 Stat108。
Professor:	Oh, I see. Did you take some similar courses like Stat278 and Stat108 when you were an undergraduate? 哦,我明白了。你以前读本科的时候学过类似 Stat278 和 Stat108 的课程吗?
Liu Hang:	I think so. You may check my previous transcripts. 我想我学过,你可以查我以前的成绩单。
Professor:	Please fill in the form and I'll sign it. Take this form to the registrar. They will register Stat405 directly for you. 请填写这个表格,我给你签字。拿着这个表格去注册处。他们就会直接为你注册 Stat405 了。
Liu Hang:	Thank you very much. 非常感谢。
Professor:	Think nothing of it.④ 别客气。

典型句型

1) I'm coming to see you about selecting courses.
   我来是为了选课的事情。

2) How many courses have you taken?
   你选了几门课?

3) I'm planning to do three elective courses besides the three required ones.
   我打算选三门必修课和三门选修课。

4) How many credits in all?
   总共多少学分?

5) I need to take an English Conversation course to improve my spoken English.

我需要选英语会话课来提高我的英语口语。

6) Generally, an American student takes twelve credits for the first semester.

一般地，美国学生第一个学期选12个学分。

7) You may take two required courses and two electives.

你可以选两门必修课和两门选修课。

8) If you think you are interested in the other two, you may audit them.

要是你认为你对另外两门感兴趣，你可以旁听。

9) I suggest you take an easier course first.

我建议你先选一门容易一些的课。

10) I'm considering dropping this course.

我想丢掉这门课。

11) I guess that is too heavy a load for you.

我觉得这对你来说负担太重了。

12) That sounds like what I'm looking for.

这好像正是我要选的课。

背景知识

选修课程：到美国去上大学你要自主规划自己的专业，你得考虑自己该学什么，包括整个专业你都可以换掉。选课是一件头痛的事情，要考虑方方面面。

（1）编号：美国各大学对课程编号都有自己的一套体系，有的是三位数，有的是四位数。大多数学校的情况是：1字头的为大学一年级；2字头为大学二年级；3字头为大学三年级；4字头为大学四年级；5字头为研究生课程；6字头以上为研究课程。跨年级选课，特别是低年级选修高年级的课，需要得到专业导师(major professor)或学业顾问(academic adviser)的批准。

(2) 类别：本科课程一般分为基础必修课、专业必修课、专业选修课和自由选修课四个类型，其中必修课是必须修读的，不能不修；而专业选修课则是要求从规定的课程中选择一部分修读，达到学分要求就可以了；在此之外的选修课一般不作限制，可以根据爱好和兴趣自由选择，只要是本校开设的课程都可以。

　　(3) 先修：选课的时候会遇到一种情况，就是当你选择一门课时，电脑系统提示你不能选择这门课，而必须先选择另外一门编号低一些的课程，后者被称为先修课。比方说，当你选择 Stat405(统计学 405) 时被拒绝，要求你先选 Stat278(统计学 278)，后者就是前一门课的先修课。所以，整个学习期间一定要有整体规划，不能盲目。但是，如果你已经在其他大学学过类似 Stat278 的课，就可以要求免除先修课，而直接修读较高编号的课程。

　　(4) 特别程序：当你不能在校园网上自由选课的时候，就要启动特别程序，实际上是手工程序。一是要求有先修课，一是没有正式注册为本科或研究生而属于非学位学生(non-degree student)，再有就是语言中心的学生，还有就是访问学者或本校教师等，如果要注册自己感兴趣的课程，要填写选课申请表，并需要系主任(department head)或学业顾问的签字，才能到注册处(registrar)进行手工注册。

　　(5) 候补名单：有时候你碰到自己想选的课程，可是选这门课的人太多，电脑系统就告诉你，已经把你放到候补名单上(waiting list)了。美国大学规定一个班只能容纳多少人，先选课的人先进入这个班，后选的只能等着别人退出(drop off)这门课，再按照候补名单的顺序递补上去。看来，不管做什么都要做到别人前面，因为大家都要遵守先到先得(First come, first served)的游戏规则。

　　(6) 选课时间：选课其实并不是开学头几天的事情，从上个学期中就开始了，这种选课只能算是预注册，要等到交了学费，才算是正式注册。录取的新生往往会收到注册表和选课说明，现在多数学校只告诉你如何上网选课的方法，所以录取通知书给你的学生代码(student ID number)和登陆注册网页的密码(PIN)就很重要了。选好课以后，从开学起的两个星期以内，都可以自由调整，或增加，或减少，国际学生必须保持全日制学生所要求的学分数的底限，如本科生必须至少选 12 个学分，研究生至少 9 个学分。过了这个期限虽然也可以减少课，但会麻烦得多。

Selecting Courses 10

注 释

① besides 的意思是"除了……以外,还有",如:
We went to the zoo besides Tom. (除了汤姆,我们也去了动物园。)
这个例子中,"我们"和"汤姆"都去了动物园。

② except 的意思是"不包括……在内",很容易与 besides 混淆,如:
We went to the zoo except Tom. (除了汤姆没有去动物园,我们都去了。)
这个例子中,"我们"去了动物园,而"汤姆"没有去动物园。

③ discuss about something with someone 意思是"与某人讨论某事",如:
They discussed about his promotion with several professors yesterday.
(他们昨天和几位教授讨论了他的晋升问题。)

④ Think nothing of it. 是对表示感谢的另一种答语,本义是"不要想这件事",引申为"别客气,不用谢"。

Buying Textbooks
购买教材

Topic Introduction
话题导言

我们在中国读大学,大多数情况下教材是学校统一购买之后发放给学生的,教材的费用作为一项收费已经和学费一同收走了,我们不担心用什么教材上课的问题。美国大学的做法与我们不同,教材要学生自己购买,是否买教材完全取决于学生本人。

美国大学都有自己的书店,名字就叫做"某某大学书店",如"爱达荷大学书店"(University of Idaho Bookstore)就是专门经营教材和学习用品的店。书店里教材的摆放按照专业和学科的编号与字母顺序。所以,要买什么教材首先要知道课程编号和教师是谁,因此得按照选好的课程从校园网上把课程表打印下来,带上课程表上大学书店购买教材,才能买到教师指定的教学用书。一般地,学生都在听了第一次课后才买教材,原因是这时才决定是否选修这门课。

Situational Dialogs
情景对话

选好课之后,刘杭(Liu Hang)要做的就是选购教材了。当她决定不修某门课后,又去退回先前购买的教材。

Buying Textbooks 11

购买教材

Dialog 1

Justin: Have you got the books for RNG 428, Liu Hang?
刘杭，您买了 RNG 428 的教材了吗？

Liu Hang: Not yet. Are there required books for this course?
还没有，有这门课的指定用书吗？

Justin: No. The professor just recommended some, I guess.
没有，我想，教授只是推荐了几本。

Liu Hang: What is the difference between the new books and used ones?
新书和旧书的区别在哪里？

Justin: Ah ... the new books were printed this year but the used ones were not, and they have been used once or more. Most important of all, the price is quite different.
啊，新书是今年印刷的，旧书不是，而且旧书被人用过一次或多次。最重要的，价格很是不同。

Liu Hang: But are all the texts the same?
但是，内容一样吗？

Justin: Yes, they are the same edition.
一样，是同一个版本。

Liu Hang: If so, I prefer① used books.
如果这样的话，我宁愿要旧书。

Dialog 2

Liu Hang: I'm a freshman of the University. Can you help me find my books?
我是本大学的新生，您能帮我找到我要的书吗？

Bookseller: Certainly. Have you got your school schedule? The books are arranged by course number and instructor.
当然可以，您有课程表吗？所有的书都是按照课程编号和任课教师排列顺序的。

Liu Hang: Oh, I see. I've got it in my schoolbag. ... Here it is.
哦，我明白了，我把课程表放在书包里。找到了，给您。

Bookseller: Wait a minute. I'm looking for them.
等一下，我这就去找。

……

Bookseller:	We have found all the books on your schedule except one. Would you like to order it? 除一本之外，我们找到了您课程表上所有的书。要不要订购这本？
Liu Hang:	When will you have this book in stock? 你们什么时候会有这本书？
Bookseller:	In a week. 一周之后。
Liu Hang:	Please reserve a copy and call me when it arrives. 请帮我留一本。书到了之后，请给我打电话。
Bookseller:	Certainly, we will call you as soon as it arrives. 当然，书一到就打电话给您。
Liu Hang:	Thank you. 谢谢。

Dialog 3

Liu Hang:	Excuse me, sir, can I return these books? 打搅一下，先生，我能退了这几本书吗？
Bookseller:	When did you buy them? 您什么时候买的？
Liu Hang:	Last Friday. 上个星期五。
Bookseller:	I think you can. All the books you bought within them past two weeks can be returned if you think you don't need for class. 我想可以，您买的所有的书只要不超过两个星期，如果您觉得上课用不上的话，都可以退。
Liu Hang:	I paid for them by credit card. How can I get my money back? 我用信用卡付的账，我如何得到我的钱？
Bookseller:	We'll give your credit back to your account. Please sign here. 我们将把您使用的信用额度退回到您的账户，请签字。
Liu Hang:	It is finished. Thank you. 好了，谢谢您了。

Buying Textbooks

Typical Sentences
典型句型

1) I need to buy some books for class.
   我需要买一些课程用书。
2) Where can I find the textbooks for RRT 511?
   我在哪里可以买到 RRT511 的课本？
3) I am wondering if I could buy all the books required by the professor.
   我想知道我能否买到教授指定的所有的书籍？
4) This book is a little expensive.
   这本书有些贵。
5) Can I get a student discount?
   我能得到学生优惠吗？
6) I prefer new books to used ones.
   我宁愿买新书,而不买旧书。
7) What is the difference between the new books and used ones?
   新书和旧书的区别在哪里？
8) I prefer used books because they are much cheaper.
   我喜欢旧书,因为旧书便宜。
9) Do you still have used textbooks for this course?
   您是否还有这门课的旧书卖？
10) This book has torn pages.
    这本书有破损印页。
11) Can I pay these books by the student ID card[②] or cash?
    我是要用学生证付钱,还是付现金？
12) I want to return these three books.
    我要退回这三本书。
13) I don't need the teacher's book; I just need this one for students.
    我不需要教师用书,我只要这本学生用书。

背景知识

大学教材：各大学都设立了书店专门经营教材和文具，我们可以从这几个方面了解美国大学的教材：

(1) 教材都是由教这门课的教师指定(required)或推荐(recommended)的，一般来说，指定教材都是课堂教学的依据，应该购买，而推荐用书可以不买。

(2) 大学教材不像我们中国出版的图书都有定价，价格由书店决定，因为你要上课就要买书，所以教材价格奇贵。这样，许多学生都愿意购买便宜的旧书(used books)，买书也要趁早，不然旧书就卖完了。一个学期的用书消费一般在300美元上下。

(3) 美国学生大多在新书用了之后，都退回给学校的书店，根据损坏和新旧的程度，一般书店回购旧教材的价格是原价格的50%—60%，但保留课本的价值对于中国学生来说远远不是卖掉旧课本得到的那几块钱所能比的。

注释

① 单词 prefer 的意思是"宁愿，喜欢"，如：
I prefer this style. (我喜欢这个样式。)
很多时候可以表示比较：
I prefer this shirt to that one. (比起那件衬衫，我更喜欢这件。)
I prefer staying home to watching the game. (我宁愿呆在家里也不愿看比赛。)

② 很多大学的学生证由于采用了新技术，具有和银行卡一样的功能，你把钱存进去就可以在校内消费。学校为了鼓励这种做法，往往对持学生证的消费给予折扣。

Computer and Software
电脑和软件

Topic Introduction
话题导言

现在上大学,只有教科书、纸和笔,已经不能完成学习任务了,这也是时代发展的必然。电脑和电脑软件成为课堂上课和课后完成作业的必备工具。大部分的课程依赖于学校提供的电脑设备以及装载于电脑系统内的共享软件,是可以完成学习任务的。但是,某些专业性很强的课程,仅仅依靠学校的电脑网络已经做不到了。关键在于学校电脑系统没有装载所需要的应用软件,你也没有在校园网络上装载软件的权限。

购买电脑和电脑软件对部分学生而言是开课前的任务之一。各人有各人的考虑,但一定要等到任课老师公布对于作业的要求,如果在学校的电脑系统上能把作业完成,也就没有必要购买电脑和软件了。电脑可以临时租用或借用,但上课和作业所需要的特殊软件不要借,特别不要向美国同学借,因为他们保护知识产权的意识很强。

Situational Dialogs
情景对话

没有电脑,学习和生活都不太方便,刘杭(Liu Hang)决定去买台电脑和一些电脑软件。

Dialog 1

John: Hello, this is John.
你好,我是约翰。

Liu Hang: Hello, I saw a poster of selling a computer on the bulletin board①. Is that yours?
你好,我看见布告牌上贴了一个卖电脑的广告。是你的吗?

John: Yes, it's mine. It's a very excellent one and very cheap.
是我的。这电脑非常不错,也非常便宜。

Liu Hang: I need a computer for my course work. I'm wondering when I can have a look at the computer.
我需要电脑学习功课,我想什么时候看看电脑。

John: Let me check my schedule. ... How about tomorrow afternoon, three thirty?
我来查一下时间安排表,……明天下午3点30分如何?

Liu Hang: OK, my friend and I will be at your place tomorrow afternoon, three thirty. Please tell me your address.
好的,我和我的朋友明天下午3点30分到你家去,请告诉我你的地址。

John: No. 4, 207 Jackson Street. Got it?
杰克逊大街207号之四。记住了吗?

Liu Hang: No. 4, 207 Jackson Street. OK, I got it.
杰克逊大街207号之四。好的,我记下来了。

Dialog 2

John: Hello, I'm John. Please come in.
你好,我是约翰。请进。

Liu Hang: We're coming to look at the computer.
我们来看看那个电脑。

John: It's here in my bedroom. Wait a second. I'm moving it out.
在我的卧室里,稍等,我就把它搬出来。
……

John: Let me turn it on. Look, it runs perfectly almost without any noise.
我来开机。瞧,运转很好,几乎没有噪音。

Computer and Software 12

电脑和软件

Liu Hang: Are the configurations completely the same with what you said on your poster?
这规格和你的广告上说的完全一样吗？

John: Completely the same. 2.8 G CPU; 1024 MB; etc.
完全一样，2.8 G CPU；1024 MB 等等。

Liu Hang: Would you please let me check something inside?
让我检查一下里面的东西，好吗？

John: Yes, please.
好的，请吧。

Dialog 3

Shopper: Good morning, Madam. How can I help you?
小姐，早晨好。我怎么帮你？

Liu Hang: I'm a new student here, and I need a computer for my course work. Could you tell me something about your computers?
我是这里的新学生，我需要电脑学习功课。能介绍一下你的电脑吗？

Shopper: Sure. We have name-brand computers such as Compaq, Dell, IBM and Toshiba. We also build computers on request.
当然可以。我们有名牌电脑，如康柏、戴尔、IBM 和东芝。我们也按照要求组装电脑。

Liu Hang: That's great. I'd like to have your price list first and shop around②.
好极了，我想先看看你的报价单，到别处也看看。

Shopper: Here you are. Welcome back.
给你，欢迎回来。

Dialog 4

Liu Hang: Do you have a kind of software called ΣPlot 6.0?
你有一种叫做西格玛图表 6.0 的软件吗？

Shopper: Yes, we do. We have two editions, one for students and one for professionals. Which one would you like to have?
有，我们有两个版本，一个是学生版，一个是专业版。你要哪一个版本？

Liu Hang:	The student edition, I guess.
	我想是学生版。
Shopper:	99 dollars.
	99美元。
Liu Hang:	OK, I take it.
	好的,我买了。

Typical Sentences
典型句型

1) I saw a poster of selling a computer on the bulletin board. Is that yours?

   我看见布告牌上贴了一个卖电脑的广告。是你的吗?

2) I need a computer for my course work. I'm wondering when I can have a look at the computer.

   我需要电脑学习功课,我想什么时候看看电脑。

3) We're coming to look at the computer.

   我们来看看那个电脑。

4) Are the configurations completely the same with what you said on your poster?

   这规格和你的广告上说的完全一样吗?

5) Would you please let me check something inside?

   让我检查一下里面的东西,好吗?

6) Could you tell me something about your computers?

   能介绍一下你的电脑吗?

7) We have name-brand computers such as Compaq, Dell, IBM and Toshiba.

   我们有名牌电脑,如康柏、戴尔、IBM和东芝。

8) We also build computers on request.

   我们也按照要求组装电脑。

9) I'd like to have your price list first and shop around.

   我想先看看你的报价单,到别处也看看。

Computer and Software

10) Do you have a kind of software called ΣPlot 6.0?
   你有一种叫做西格玛图表 6.0 的软件吗？
11) We have two editions; one is student edition and the other is professional edition.
   我们有两个版本，一个是学生版，一个是专业版。

背景知识

购买电脑的途径：对于学习而言，并不需要很高档次的电脑，再说，高档次电脑也比较贵，对于节衣缩食的中国学生来说无疑增加了经济上的困难。

(1) 从其他同学那里购买二手电脑。学校里很多公共布告栏都有各种各样的广告，开学的时候有很多毕业的同学需要离开学校，就要把多余的东西卖掉，包括用过一年半载的电脑。如果自己不是很在行，一定要找懂行的同学帮忙检查，看硬件和软件是否适应学习的需要。中国学生出于习惯，容易轻视软件问题。美国的软件很贵，也没有盗版的买，更不能借来装。如果买到与你同专业的同学的电脑，那要省很多钱，因为电脑里应该装有你以后学习需要的软件。

(2) 从品牌机厂商拍卖网站购买。美国很多大公司、机构、大学等并不购买电脑供员工使用，而是从品牌机生产厂商那里租用一大批电脑分发给员工，使用一到两年后再还回厂商。厂商就把这种电脑进行彻底的检修，称之为 refurbished computers（更新电脑），然后在本公司的网站上拍卖。这种品牌机质量比较有保证，价格要靠运气，因为有时候买的人少，价格就会降下来，买的人多，价格就被抬了起来。可以定一个底价后再上网，不要盲目跟高，更不能斗气。

(3) 到附近的电脑商店去买一台组装机。与中国一样，你也可以到电脑商店去选购各种配件，然后组装，只要保证学习的功能就可以了。组装电脑叫做 build computers，找一个懂行的同学一起到电脑商店去咨询一下价格、软件和维修等问题。

(4) 购买品牌机。如果经济条件比较好，可以考虑购买一台品

牌机，可以从网上购买，也可以到专门的电器商店购买。最好是选择一个比较好的时机，如感恩节的第二天或圣诞节后就是大减价的时候。

软件问题：一般的软件在学校的电脑系统上都有，但某些课程的软件则需要自己购买。同样一个软件往往有多个版本，如果某一门课需要特殊的软件才能完成学习任务，主讲教授往往会向大学书店提出集中采购某种软件的要求，价格会比市场价便宜很多。这种软件只有凭该教授的书面证明才能买到，因为书店是按照学生数量准备的。

注　释

① **bulletin board** 是指"公共布告栏，公共广告牌"，在大学里的图书馆、教学楼、实验室的入口都辟有这样的地方，供校内师生张贴通知、广告等信息。

② **shop around** 是买东西时候的用语。当遇到比较贵、对商品不满意、没有下决心购买的时候，要和店主结束谈话就用这句话：
I think I'll shop around.（我想到别处再看看。）

Campus Network Account
校园网账号

Topic Introduction
话题导言

　　信息和网络技术的发展给美国的高等教育带来了翻天覆地的变化,远程授课、异地存取资料、网上图书馆、教案及作业电子化网络化已经成为现实。美国大学都有自己的校园网络,电脑实验室、教室、办公室、图书馆等各个角落的电脑都已经联结成一体,这一内部网络又通过学校的计算机与信息中心的主机房和互联网连成一气。

　　到美国大学留学的新生,首先要做的一项重要事情就是申请校园网账号。校园网账号是由诸如计算机与信息中心(Computer and Information Center)这样的机构管理和维护的,新生也需要向这个中心申请自己的账号。一般地只要出示入学通知书或学生证就可以办理了,给出的账号名称是根据姓名编排的,而密码则是难以记忆的随机密码,需要修改。

情景对话

刘杭(Liu Hang)和杨洋(Yang Yang)买了电脑之后,下一步就是申请校园网账号了。网络信息中心的工作人员 Andrew 和 Alice 接待了他们。

Dialog 1

Liu Hang: Hello, I'd like to apply for a computer lab account.
你好,我要申请电脑实验室账号。

Andrew: Yap. Your letter of admission or your student ID, please.
好的,请出示你的入学通知书或者学生证。

Liu Hang: Here it is the letter of admission. I haven't got my student ID.
这是入学通知书,我还没得到学生证。

Andrew: That's OK. Just a second. ...
那就行,稍等。……

Liu Hang: Ready?
好了?

Andrew: Yap. Please notice some of the instructions, such as the password. The network gave the password randomly, and it's hard to remember. You may modify it.
是的,请注意说明中的一些内容,如密码。网络任意给你一个密码,很难记住。你可以修改。

Liu Hang: Yes, it's so long. I'll change it.
好的,太长,我会改的。

Andrew: You can use any of the computers on campus in thirty minutes. If you have questions, please come to the help desk, or phone 57888.
30分钟之后你就可以使用校园里的任何一台电脑,如果有问题,请到咨询台来,或者打电话57888。

Liu Hang: I will. Thank you very much.
我会的,非常感谢。

Dialog 2

Alice: May I help you?
能帮你吗?

Yang Yang: Yes. I received an email from the Campus Network Center, telling me that my account will be closed within four weeks[①]. I'd like to know why.
是的,我收到校园网络中心的一封电子邮件,说我的账号四个星期之内要关掉。我想知道是怎么回事儿。

Campus Network Account 13

校园网账号

Alice:	Your name of account, please.
	请告诉我你的账号名称。
Yang Yang:	yang5566.
	是 yang5566。
Alice:	We close an account according to the regulations of campus network administration. You're an ALCP student and your sponsor② is Steve Springer. When you applied for your account, a letter from Steve Springer was sent to us.
	我们根据校园网络管理的规定关闭一个账号。你是美国语言与文化项目的学生,你的赞助者是史蒂夫·斯普林格。当你申请这个账号时,他的一封信就给了我们。
Yang Yang:	About my account?
	关于我的账号?
Alice:	That's right. The letter listed your account's opening and closing dates. That's the reason.
	正确,这封信列举了你的账号开始和关闭的日期。这就是原因。
Yang Yang:	Oh, I see. But my status has been changed. I used to be a language student at ALCP. Now I'm a graduate student.
	噢,我明白了。但是我的情况已经变了,过去我是美国语言与文化项目的学生,而现在我是研究生。
Alice:	Show me your new letter of admission, please.
	请你把新的入学通知书给我。
Yang Yang:	Here it is.
	这就是。
Alice:	We're sorry for that. Now take it easy③, and we'll change your account as one for a graduate.
	对此我们感到抱歉。现在请放心,我们将把你的账号改为研究生用的账号。
Yang Yang:	You mean my account won't be closed.
	你是说我的账号不会关闭了。
Alice:	Correct. Your account is OK.
	正确,你的账号没问题了。

Dialog 3

Liu Hang: I can't enter my account. Could you help me?
我进不去我的账号,您能帮我吗?

Andrew: Yes. Have you changed your password recently?
能,您最近改过密码了吗?

Liu Hang: No. I never changed it.
没有,从未改过。

Andrew: How many days have you used the previous one?
你的前一个密码用了多少天了?

Liu Hang: I'm not sure. I guess it's more than four months.
我不太肯定,我想超过四个月了。

Andrew: One password can only be used for 120 days. You have to change it. Possibly you forgot to change it.
一个密码只能用120天,你得把它改了。可能你忘记了。

Liu Hang: Perhaps.
也许。

Andrew: It's easy. I'll activate your account, and you'd better change the password.
很容易,我将激活你的账户,你最好把密码改了。

Liu Hang: Sure, I will. Thank you.
当然,我会的。谢谢。

典型句型

1) I'd like to apply for a computer lab account.
我要申请电脑实验室账号。

2) Can I go to the Internet through campus network?
通过校园网络,我可以进入互联网吗?

3) I received an email, telling me that my account will be closed within four weeks.
我收到一封电子邮件,说我的账号四个星期之内要关掉。

Campus Network Account

4) The letter listed your account's opening and closing dates.
这封信列举了你的账号开始和关闭的日期。

5) Now take it easy, and we'll change your account as one for a graduate.
现在请放心,我们将把你的账号改为研究生用的账号。

6) Have you changed your password recently?
您最近改过密码了吗?

7) How many days have you used the previous one?
你的前一个密码用了多少天了?

8) One password can only be used for 120 days.
一个密码只能用 120 天。

9) I'll activate your account, and you'd better change the password.
我将激活你的账户,你最好把密码改了。

Background 背景知识

　　校园电脑网络的作用:一旦申请了账号,学校的任何一台公用联网电脑都可以自由免费使用。电脑、网络设备的价格目前来说还是比较昂贵的,各个大学都不惜血本地添置这些设施,以供教师和学生使用。其功能主要是:

　　(1) 辅助教学:校园电脑网络的基本作用就是辅助教学,教师可以通过网络向学生发布教学信息、指定教学材料、布置作业、解答疑问等,学生则可以利用电脑完成作业、上交作业、提出教学意见、向老师提问。

　　(2) 研究工具:以前做研究往往要写很多信、跑很多地方、找很多人、花很长时间才能得到一些资料,现在利用网上图书馆或互联网信息就可以查阅到大量的有用资料。而且,校园网电脑上还有多种工具软件帮助解决具体研究过程中的问题,如图形设计、计算等繁琐的工作都可以让电脑去做。

(3) 对外交流:校园网账号不仅可以让你进入电脑系统以帮助你学习、研究,还可以通过电子邮件、语音网络通话和聊天工具等与外界进行紧密的联系。

　　(4) 娱乐休闲:也许在电脑实验室你可以注意到有一部分人在听音乐、看电影等,这都是学习累了以后的一种休闲方式。你可以戴上耳机听自己喜欢的歌曲、看网络电影或和别人聊天。

注 释

① **telling me that my account will be closed within four weeks** 是个现在分词短语,用来说明前述电子邮件的内容。

② **sponsor** 的本义是"(金钱的,物资的)赞助者",这里指的是校园网络账号使用的要求人,一般在大学里学生的账号都是由系主任或专业导师或项目负责人向计算机与信息中心提出要求,得以开户,只不过学生并不知道这一层。

③ **take it easy** 的意思是"别紧张,放轻松些"。

Consulting Department Head
咨询系主任

Topic Introduction
话题导言

　　一般地,一个系有一个系主任,另外有一名秘书和一名行政助理协助系主任的日常工作。系主任是一个系负责教学和行政事务的头目。对学生而言,他掌握着新生录取、奖学金分配、助教职位的聘用、专业导师的安排等事务的主导权力。说是主导权力,是因为他要推动这些事务的展开、过问进展情况和在意见分歧时起决定作用。

　　同时,系主任往往是一个系学术水平最高的教授,也有自己的教学和研究工作,行政管理工作只占总工作量的百分四十。所以,别指望能随时见到系主任,有问题咨询要首先和秘书或行政助理预约时间才能到办公室面谈。适宜和系主任交谈的应该是些事务性的问题,如要求调整申请类别(如博士改硕士)、导师小组的组成、寻求证明信、奖学金和助教职位的申请,以及需要和学校其他部门打交道的事务。细枝末节的小问题则应该由秘书或行政助理解决,而课程问题则是专业导师或学业顾问的管辖范围。

Situational Dialogs
情景对话

刘杭(Liu Hang)总是有很多问题需要咨询系主任 Steve Smith,例如她的研究生指导教授小组组成,是否能得到助教奖学金,或是开证明信。

Dialog 1

Liu Hang: Hello, Steve①, could you spare② me several minutes?
史蒂夫,您好,我能耽搁您几分钟吗?

Steve: Sure. What do you need?
可以,你要什么?

Liu Hang: When must I organize my graduate group of professors?
我什么时候必须组织好我的研究生指导教授小组?

Steve: Before the end of your first year of study.
在你学习满一年之前。

Liu Hang: I'm not sure who are qualified for my group.
我不太肯定谁合适到我的小组。

Steve: Your major professor is an essential member of the group. At least one of the other two must be from outside the department. There're no other restrictions.
你的专业导师是不可缺少的成员,其余的两个成员中至少有一个必须是外系的,没有别的限制了。

Liu Hang: I see. I'll discuss about it with my major professor.
我明白了,我将和我的专业导师讨论这个问题。

Steve: You should talk to him earlier about what you're thinking.
你应该早一些告诉他你是怎么想的。

Dialog 2

Liu Hang: Excuse me, Dr. Smith. I'd like to know if I could get a Teaching Assistantship.
史密斯博士,打搅一下,我想知道我能否得到助教奖学金。

Consulting Department Head 14

Dr. Smith:	We are discussing this matter in two weeks③.
	我们将在两个星期后讨论这个问题。
Liu Hang:	Do I have to submit an application?
	我得交申请吗?
Dr. Smith:	No, you don't have to. I'll make a document of all graduates' requests about TA or RA, and then let it go around the faculty④.
	不必,我会把各位研究生的助教和助研要求做成一个文件,然后在全系教师中传阅。
Liu Hang:	Thank you very much.
	非常感谢。

Dialog 3

Liu Hang:	Excuse me, Dr. Smith, could you write a letter for me?⑤
	史密斯博士,打搅一下,给我写封信,好吗?
Dr. Smith:	For what?
	为什么?
Liu Hang:	I need my husband and daughter to come here to stay with me. I think it better for you to write a letter to state that I'm a full-time graduate student.
	我需要我丈夫和女儿来这里。如果你写一封信说明我是这里的全日制研究生,会好一些。
Dr. Smith:	To whom?
	给谁?
Liu Hang:	To the United States Consulate General in Guangzhou.
	给美国驻广州总领事馆。
Dr. Smith:	That's no problem. But, please write a draft and send it to me by email.
	那没问题。但是,请你写一个草稿并用电子邮件发给我。
Liu Hang:	OK. I'll do it this afternoon. Could you let me get the letter next Monday?
	好的,我今天下午就做。我星期一能得到这封信吗?
Dr. Smith:	I'll put it in your mailbox. You may check next Monday.
	我会放到你的信箱里,下周一你看一下。
Liu Hang:	Thank you very much.
	非常感谢。

Typical Sentences
典型句型

1) Hello, Dr. Smith, could you spare me several minutes?
史密斯博士,您好,我能耽搁您几分钟吗?

2) When must I organize my graduate group of professors?
我什么时候必须组织好我的研究生指导教授小组?

3) Your major professor is an essential member of the group.
你的专业导师是不可缺少的成员。

4) You should talk to him earlier about what you're thinking.
你应该早一些告诉他你是怎么想的。

5) I'd like to change my application, from Ph.D. to Master.
我想改变我的申请,从博士变为硕士。

6) I'd like to know if I could get a Teaching Assistantship.
我想知道我能否得到助教奖学金。

7) I'd like to take courses instead of doing research.
我想上课,而不想做研究。

8) We are discussing this matter in two weeks.
我们将在两个星期后讨论这个问题。

9) Do I have to submit an application?
我得交申请吗?

10) Can I get my master degree by taking courses only?
我只是上课能得到硕士学位吗?

11) Could you write a letter for me?
给我写封信,好吗?

12) I need my wife and daughter to come here to stay with me. I think it better for you to write a letter to state that I'm a full-time graduate student.
我需要我妻子和女儿来这里。如果你写一封信说明我是这里的全日制研究生,会好一些。

Background 背景知识

美国大学的基本结构：美国的大学规模一般比较大，小型大学也有学生超过5000人，学生人数在数万人的不在少数。这么大的学校有什么样的运行机制呢？

(1) 校长(president)：州立大学的校长是由州政府面向全国乃至全世界招聘并经过董事会任命的，私立大学的校长则是由董事会选聘的，都是某学科知名的专家或社会名流。校长的权力比较有限，要接受董事会(Board of Trustees)、教师代表大会(Congress of Faculty)和学生代表大会(Congress of Students)的监督。而且私立大学校长还必须是募捐能手，能为学校找来"钱"。校长的工资收入不算高，但享受了很好的勤务服务，官邸、出行、日常生活都得到了很好的安排。校长之下往往有若干名副校长，分别负责学生事务、教学工作、行政工作等，校长之下还设有教务长(provost)一职，负责协调各相关学院的教学和研究工作。

(2) 行政机构(executive organs)：美国大学的行政机构比较简单，主要有招生办公室(Admissions Office 和 Graduate Admissions Office)、国际学生办公室(International Students Office)、注册办公室 (Registrar 或 Registration Office)、奖学金和财务办公室(Scholarships and Financial Office)、计算机和网络管理中心(Computer and Campus Network Center)、人力资源服务处(Human Resource Service)、研究生院(Graduate School 或 College of Graduate Studies)等。

(3) 学院(college)：学院是大学的教育实体单位，专业的开设、研究生的培养等都是以学院为单位组织实施的。学院设有比较简单的行政机构，处理学院的日常事务。与校长一样，院长(dean)也是面向全美选任的，往往是有名气的教授并要特别能募捐到"钱"，且院长一般不从事教学工作，而是专门的管理官员，也通常有两到三名副院长(vice dean)协助工作。研究生院虽然也称之为college或school，但并不担当教学工作，只是各学院研究生教育工作的协调机构。学院的名称多种多样，有college, school, faculty, institute 等，有的在college之下还有school这样的设置。

（4）系(department)：系具体落实学院的教学任务，是一个完全的教学单位，一般以学科为单位组成一个系，也有几个相近的学科合起来组成一个系的，多数叫做 department，也有少数叫做 division 的。大系有数十名教师，小系只有七、八名教师或更少。一个系设一名系主任，没有副系主任，另有行政助理和秘书处理日常工作。全体教师叫做 faculty，行政人员被称作 staff。系里的决策往往是比较民主的，遇到一项事情要决定，就由系主任制作一个文件，由行政助理让每个教师提出意见。然后以大多数人的意见为主决策，遇到双方意见势均力敌的时候，系主任就是很关键的因素，决定权就在系主任手里了。

（5）研究所(institute)：研究所是大学主要从事科学研究的学术单位，一般也招收研究生，并往往是某个学院的一个部分，如商学院(College of Business)下可能设有消费科学研究所(Institute of Consumers' Science)。研究所的教授也可能受聘到别的系担任本科生的教学工作。

（6）研究中心(research center)：研究中心的组织没有研究所紧密，往往是来自于多个系有共同研究兴趣的教授形成的一个研究机构，各位教授并不脱离原来系里的教学岗位。

注　释

① 这是一种比较随意的说法，关系比较熟悉的人之间说话往往没有那么讲究客气和用词，对教授和系主任也可以直呼其名，甚至是称呼他们的小名。

② spare 这里指"匀出，抽出(时间或钱)"，如：
Could you spare me a few litres of petrol? (你能匀给我几升汽油吗？)

③ in two weeks 的意思是"两个星期之后"，如：
He will be back to school in three hours. (他三个小时后返回学校。)

④ go around / round the faculty 指的是"在全体老师传递"。

⑤ 系主任经常被外国留学生提出这样的要求，目的是证明一个学生是美国大学的全日制学生，以便回国后能重新得到签证或使家属得到赴美签证。但是，这种信函的作用越来越弱了。

Meeting with Major Professor
会见专业导师

Topic Introduction
话题导言

美国大学的研究生教育和国内大学的形式是基本相同的，特别是依靠研究方式攻读学位的研究生。到美国大学的研究生院攻读博士或硕士学位的时候，系主任就会根据你的兴趣、爱好、教育背景、工作经历等给你指定一位专业导师，被称之为 major professor 或 academic advisor 等。研究生与导师的关系往往比较紧密，更多的时候，研究生是导师研究和教学的助手和合作伙伴，和导师见面是很平常的事情。

入读美国大学的本科专业，和只修读课程不做学位论文的研究生一样，没有指定的专业导师，但系里会有一个教授在学业上（如选课）对你提出建议，也称之为 academic advisor，且多半由系主任担任这一角色。作为学生，你可以从不和他近距离接触，甚至他并不认识你，你也不认识他。

Situational Dialogs
情景对话

刘杭（Liu Hang）同导师见面之后，还需要同导师确定研究项目的题目。

Dialog 1

Liu Hang: Good morning, the department head asked me to meet you this morning.
早晨好，系主任要我今天早上来见您。

Bill: Yap. I'm William Black. I was assigned to be your major professor. You may call me Bill.
好的，我是威廉·布莱克，我被指定为你的专业导师。你可以叫我比尔。

Liu Hang: Yes, Steve has told me you would be my major professor.
是的，史蒂夫告诉我您是我的专业导师。

Bill: I'd like to know your education background and working experience.
我想了解你的教育背景和工作经历。

Liu Hang: I've got a bachelor's degree in Accounting and a master's degree in Chinese History. I've been an accountant for more than ten years.
我有会计学的学士学位，以及中国历史的硕士学位。我当了十年以上的会计。

Bill: Perfect. So, you have a very good background to do your second master's degree.
好极了，这样你就有很好的基础来这里做你的第二个硕士学位。

Liu Hang: I hope I can be an excellent student.
我希望我能成为一名优秀的学生。

Bill: Sure, you can.
当然你能。

Dialog 2

Liu Hang: I'm coming to see you because I'd like to discuss the research proposal① with you.
我来见您是因为我想和您讨论我的研究方案。

Bill: Yap. What's your topic?
好的，什么题目？

Liu Hang: It's about visitors' impacts to a national scenic resort in China.
是关于旅游者对中国的一个国家级名胜区的影响的。

Meeting with Major Professor 15

Bill: Do you have something written for that?
你有书面的东西吗？

Liu Hang: Yes, I do. Here you are.
有的，给您。

Bill: Let me see. ...
我看看，……

Liu Hang: I need your suggestions, Bill. I've never done such a proposal.
我需要你的意见，比尔。我从来没有做过这样一个方案。

Bill: Yap. Could you narrow down the range of the topic? I mean you could deal with a more concrete field.
好的，能把你的题目的范围缩小吗？我是说你可以论述一个更加具体的方面。

Liu Hang: I'm thinking about that point.
我正在考虑这一点。

Bill: Let's list some possible things concerned with your topic, and then we can discuss later.
我们先列出一些与你的题目有关的东西出来，下次再讨论。

Liu Hang: Thank you very much. How about next Wednesday morning, ten o'clock?
非常感谢，下个星期三上午10点钟，如何？

Bill: Let's also set a time② we meet every week. The same time as today?
我们就确定一个每周见面的时间吧。今天这个时间怎么样？

Liu Hang: I'm available, and that's every Wednesday morning, ten o'clock.
我可以，就是每个星期三上午10点钟。

Bill: Perfect. Let's make it.
好极了，就这样吧。

Dialog 3

Bill: I have listed several aspects of your topic. How about yours?
我已经列了你题目的几个方面，你的呢？

Liu Hang: I've done it. Here it is.
我也列了，给你。

Bill: Let's make them together. Now, we have ten different points and every point can be a topic that you can do. Choose one among them that interests you most.
我们放到一起吧，现在我们总共有10个不同的点，每一点都可以成为你要做的题目。从中选一个你最感兴趣。

Liu Hang: I think No. 7 is suitable for me.
我想第7个适合我做。

Bill: That's good. I'll list several books and articles for you to read, and you may go to the library to check them out③. If you can't find them, please come here to get them.
好的，我将为你开列几本书和一些文章阅读，到图书馆去借出来，如果找不到，请到这里来拿。

Liu Chang: All right. Thank you very much, professor.
好的，教授，非常感谢您。

Typical Sentences
典型句型

1) Steve has told me you would be my major professor.
史蒂夫告诉我您是我的专业导师。

2) I'd like to know your education background and working experience.
我想了解你的教育背景和工作经历。

3) I'm coming to see you because I'd like to discuss the research proposal with you.
我来见您是因为我想和您讨论我的研究方案。

4) It's about visitors' impacts to a national scenic resort in China.
是关于旅游者对中国的一个国家级名胜区的影响的。

5) I need your suggestions, Bill. I've never done such a proposal.
我需要你的意见，比尔。我从来没有做过这样一个方案。

6) Could you narrow down the range of the topic? I mean you could deal with a more concrete field.
能把你的题目的范围缩小吗？我是说你可以论述一个更加具体的方面。

Meeting with Major Professor 15

7) Let's also set a time we meet every week. The same time as today?
   我们就确定一个每周见面的时间吧。今天这个时间怎么样?

8) I have listed several aspects of your topic. How about yours?
   我已经列了你题目的几个方面,你的呢?

9) Choose one among them that interests you most.
   从中选一个你最感兴趣。

导师制:国内大学研究生培养的导师制和美国大学的有很大程度上的类似,但具体做法还是不同。实际上,国内各大学的制度也不是一样的。这里介绍的也只是笔者熟悉的一种制度。

导师往往是由系主任或系学术委员会主席根据学生的专业背景、工作经历、培养目标等指定的教授。该教授一定是你将要学的这个专业领域的专家甚或是顶尖人物,具有很高的学术地位。

除导师本人以外,还有由三人组成的导师小组,组成人员包括专业导师和另外两位教授。这两位教授当中,其中要求至少有一名是本系以外的教授,也可以是外校的。如果你的研究方向和教育有关,还必须有另外一名来自于教育学院的教授参加这个导师组,这样,导师组就有四人了。

除导师以外的其他导师组成员,由攻读学位的研究生选择教授组成,要和他本人商量,看他是否同意担任这个成员。也可以在征求导师意见的基础上再确定人选,注意不能选择导师不喜欢的、相互瞧不起的人进入导师组,最好选择导师的朋友。导师组设立的主要目的是开阔研究视野,确定研究方案和实施细则,指导学位论文的写作,评定论文的成绩。导师组一般要求在学生入学满一年之内确定,人员选定之后报告给系主任或系学术委员会主席,再报告给研究生院备案。

美国大学教师和学生的词汇:

　　professor 教授　　　　　　university/college student 大学生

associate professor 副教授	freshman 大学一年级学生
visiting professor 访问教授	sophomore 大学二年级学生
guest professor 客座教授	junior 大学三年级学生
assistant professor 助理教授	senior 大学四年级学生
lecturer 讲师	undergraduates 本科生
instructor / instructress 讲师	underclassmen 前两年级大学生
assistant 或 tutor 助教	upperclassmen 后两年级大学生
full-time teacher 专职教师	graduate / postgraduate 研究生
part-time teacher 兼职教师	research student 研究生

注 释

① **research proposal** 指的是研究生入学后,要确定一个研究的方向和课题,以后的学位论文就要围绕这个题目去做。一般包括导言、对以前别人研究的综述、基本理论、要弄清楚的问题、新在什么地方、具体的研究办法等等。

② **set a time** 意思是"定一个时间",为了约会、会议、上课等确定一个具体的时间,如:
Have you set a time to discuss the question?(你们确定了讨论的时间了吗?)

③ **check out** 指的是"(将图书)借出来、(旅馆住宿)结账",如:
All the books I need have been checked out.(我所需要的书都被借走了。)

About Credits
关于学分

Topic Introduction
话题导言

美国大学的二年级学生(sophomore)很可能读了三年了,因为他们划分的依据是看你读了多少学分而不是读了多长时间。这就跟每学期选修课程的量有关系,1至32个学分是 freshman,33至64个学分是 sophomore,65至96个学分为 junior,96个学分以上为 senior。这和我们头脑中的概念完全不同。

学分的说法在英语中也不尽相同,有 credit、credit hour、semester credit 等。学分是一个问题,跟学分有关的成绩档次是另一个重要问题,两者合起来就是通常的 GPA。

Situational Dialogs
情景对话

刘杭(Liu Hang)和朋友 David 正在讨论和中国完全不同的学分记分方法。

Dialog 1

Liu Hang: How many credits should I get for my master degree?
要多少学分我可以获得硕士学位?

David:	At least 36. You can get at most 6 credits by research. 至少 36 学分，做研究最多可以获得 6 个学分。
Liu Hang:	Do I have to get 18 credits for the required courses? 我必须修读必修课来获得 18 个学分吗？
David:	Not necessarily. You may take other courses as well instead of some of them, but you have to ask for permission in advance[①]. 不一定，你也可以通过修读其他课程，但事先要获得批准。
Liu Hang:	That sounds reasonable. What's the requirement for GPA? 听来有道理。对 GPA 有什么要求？
David:	The minimum requirement for GPA is B, namely, 3.0. 最低是 B, 就是 3.0。
Liu Hang:	Oh, I see. 哦，我明白了。

Dialog 2

Liu Hang:	Are you going to graduate next spring? 你明年春季毕业吗？
David:	No, I cannot. I've just got 58 credits, and I need 70 credits more. There is a long way to go. 不，我毕业不了。我才得到 58 个学分，我还差 70 个学分。路还长着呢。
Liu Hang:	So you're still a sophomore. 所以，你是二年级。
David:	Not completely. I'm a student between a sophomore and a junior. I'm trying to finish my school here next fall. 不完全，我是一个介于二年级和三年级的学生。我努力在明年秋季完成学业。
Liu Hang:	So, you are to finish your bachelor's degree within three years! 这样，你三年之内就把学士学位完成了！
David:	Absolutely right. 绝对正确。
Liu Hang:	Smart guy, I envy you! 聪明的家伙，我羡慕你！

About Credits 16

关于学分

Dialog 3

Liu Hang: I hear there's a seminar held by Professor Cliff Johnson next semester.
我听说下学期克里夫·约翰逊教授要开设讨论课。

David: I know that.
我知道。

Liu Hang: But, there's something I can't understand.
但是,有些东西我搞不懂。

David: About what?
关于什么的?

Liu Hang: The bulletin writes: This seminar is designed for you to gain one, two or three credits. It's strange that a course may be awarded different credits.
告示说:这个讨论课你可以获得一个、两个或三个学分。奇怪,一门课怎么可以给不同的学分。

David: It's not strange at all. If you need one credit, just show up[②]. If you need two credits, show up and write a summary of previous research. If you need three credits, show up and turn in a research proposal[③].
一点儿也不奇怪。如果你想得到一个学分,只要参加就可以了;如果你要得到两个学分,出席加上写一个以前研究的综述;如果你要得到三个学分,出席加上写一个研究方案。

Liu Hang: I understand. I'm willing to just get one by only showing up in class.
我懂了,我愿意只到课堂去露露面而得到一个学分。

David: I prefer three.
我愿意得三个学分。

典型句型

1) How many credits should I get for my master degree?
要多少学分我可以获得硕士学位?

2) You can get at most 6 credits by research.

研究最多可以获得6个学分。

3) Do I have to get 18 credits for the required courses?

我必须修读必修课来获得18个学分吗?

4) What's the requirement for GPA?

对 GPA 有什么要求?

5) I've just got 58 credits, and I need 70 credits more.

我才得到58个学分,我还差70个学分。

6) I'm a student between a sophomore and a junior.

我是一个介于二年级和三年级的学生。

7) It's strange that a course may be awarded different credits.

奇怪,一门课怎么可以给不同的学分。

8) If you need one credit, just show up.

如果你想得到一个学分,只要参加就可以了。

9) If you need two credits, show up and write a summary of previous research.

如果你要得到两个学分,必须出席并写一个以前研究的综述。

10) If you need three credits, show up and turn in a research proposal.

如果你要得到3个学分,必须出席并写一个研究方案。

11) I'm willing to just get one by only showing up in class.

我愿意只到课堂去露露面就得到一个学分。

背景知识

大学学分(credits):美国大学实行完全的学分制,一门课可以获得几个学分是根据该门课在一个学期中每周上课几个课时来决定的,如某门课每周上课两课时,如考试合格就获得两个学分。全日制本、专科学生一个学期可以注册12到19个学分的课程,全日制研究生可以注册9到15个学分的课程。一般说来,取得准学士

About Credits 16

关于学分

学位需60到64个学分,学士学位需120到128学分,硕士学位需要30到38个学分,博士学位需要68到90个学分。只要按照规定修满学分就可以获得相应学位,而不限制修读年限,所以你可以三年读完本科,也可以七年读完本科。

除学分外,大多数学校还计算所谓"平均成绩"(Grade Point Average,即GPA)。一般规定,GPA至少在2.0即C级以上才能获得学位,而只有本科GPA达到3.0以上者才能读研究生。学生的学习成绩分为:A为优秀(计为4.0),B为良好(计为3.0),C为中等(计为2.0),D为及格(计为1.0),F为不及格(计为0,为无效成绩,必需补修或重修或用别的课程代替)。一般90分以上为A,80分以上为B,70分以上为C,60分以上为D,低于60分为F。所谓"平均成绩"是指学生各种成绩乘以其学分加起来的平均数。举例说明:功课01、02、03、04、05、06、07分别获得A、A、B、B、C、A、B的成绩,而各科的学分数分别为3、4、2、3、3、1、3,这样GPA就是:

GPA = (3A+4A+2B+3B+3C+1A+3B)÷(3+4+2+3+3+1+3)
    = (3×4+4×4+2×3+3×3+3×2+1×4+3×3)÷19
    = 62÷19
    ≈ 3.26

除了上述五个等级的计分之外,还有一些讲座或技巧训练课程只计为合格(P=Pass)或不合格(F=Fail),这样的课程不参加GPA的计算,但照样获得学分。

注 释

① in advance 的意思与 ahead of time / ahead of schedule 相同,"提前"的意思。如:
I want to finish the task in advance. (我想提前完成这个工作。)

② show up 的意思是"露面,出席,参加",如:
Did everyone you invited show up? (你邀请的每个人都到了吗?)

③ 学分得的越多,要做的事情也就越多,研究生课程经常有这种类型,难度由自己选择,学分由自己把握。比如这门课,出席就可以得到一

个学分;多写一个以前别人研究的综述,就可以得到两个学分;而要做一个研究方案可以得到三个学分。这第三种情况其实包含了前两种情况的所有内容,因为研究综述是研究方案的必要部分。把一件大的事情(这门课)分成三件来做(听课、研究综述、研究设计),做第一件得一学分,做前两件得到两个学分,三件都做得到三个学分。

Discussion with Classmates
与同学讨论问题

Topic Introduction
话题导言

同学之间讨论问题不仅是学习知识的需要,更是教师教学计划的安排内容之一。之所以这样说,是因为很多时候老师布置的作业就要求两人或多人合作完成,课堂发言一般要求先按组讨论后派代表发言,以及不懂的时候请教同学等。

作为一个中国留学生,英语又不是母语,讨论的时候一定要大胆发言;同时,分组选择的时候要注意到对亚洲人比较友好的同学那个组去,对于有"种族歧视"倾向的同学不要过多理睬,除非他或她有挑衅性的行为或言辞。

Situational Dialogs
情景对话

刘杭(Liu Hang)要跟同学分组讨论问题。小组成员间合作得都很默契。

Dialog 1

Liu Hang: Tony, can I join your group's discussion?
托尼,我可以加入你这组的讨论吗?

Tony: Yes. But we have a precondition.
好，但是我们有一个先决条件。

Liu Hang: What's that?
什么条件？

Tony: You do the presentation for our group.
你代表我们小组上台报告。

Liu Hang: No problem. I'm willing to do that.
没有问题，我愿意做。

Dialog 2

Tony: Let's get down to our discussion about the assignment. I'm to take notes of today's work①.
我们着手讨论作业问题吧，我来做今天的记录。

Liu Hang: Pardon me,② should we each report our parts respectively?
打搅一下，我们应当每个人分别报告自己的那部分吗？

Tony: Yes. Who'll be the first?
是的，谁先说？

Liu Hang: I will. Mine is about the questionnaire. I've designed eighteen questions in all. Some are multiple choices, some are descriptive, and the others are yes-no questions.
我先说吧。我的是关于问卷的，总共设计了18个问题，一些是多项选择，一些是描述性的，其余的是是否问题。

Tony: Do you have something printed to deliver to us?
你有印好的东西发给大家吗？

Liu Hang: Yes, I've prepared some handouts③ for you. Please come up with④ your opinions.
有，我印好了一些东西发给大家，请多提意见。

All: Thanks.
谢谢。

Discussion with Classmates 17
与同学讨论问题

Dialog 3

Tony: I have generalized what we discussed last time, and we have to make it a research report. Now I'm thinking we all should go over the whole thing.
我把我们上次讨论的东西进行了总结，而我们必须写成报告。现在我想我们把整个内容过一遍。

Liu Hang: I agree.
我同意。

Mary: After this discussion, should we make it finished?⑤
这次讨论之后，我们就完成了吗？

Tony: I hope so. But we need a person to polish it up and a person to make the presentation.
希望如此，但我们还需要一个人润色这个报告，一个人作讲解。

Liu Hang: I'm willing to make the presentation.
我愿意作讲解。

Tony: That's perfect. Who's to polish it up?
好极了，谁愿意润色报告？

Christine: I can do that.
我可以做。

Liu Hang: You are very excellent at⑥ writing reports, as everyone knows.
你写报告是非常优秀的，人人都知道。

Tony: If so, our group will get an A without any question whatsoever.⑦
如果这样，我们小组得到 A 是没有疑问的。

1) The professor asked us to have a group discussion.
教授要同学们分组讨论。

2) Tony, can I join your group's discussion?
托尼，我可以加入你这组的讨论吗？

3) You do the presentation for our group.
   你代表我们小组上台报告。
4) Let's get down to our discussion about the assignment.
   我们着手讨论作业问题吧。
5) Pardon me, should we each report our parts respectively?
   打搅一下,我们应当每个人分别报告自己的那部分吗?
6) I totally agree with you.
   我完全同意你的说法。
7) Try to express your own opinion.
   试着表达你自己的看法。
8) I've prepared some handouts for you. Please come up with your opinions.
   我印好了一些东西发给大家,请多提意见。
9) After this discussion, should we make it finished?
   这次讨论之后,我们就完成了?
10) You are very excellent at writing reports, as everyone knows.
    你写报告是非常优秀的,人人都知道。

背景知识

分组作业(group assignment): 对于研究生课程来说,老师布置的作业多半属于问题研究式的,需要查阅大量的资料才能完成,并在综合了这些资料的基础上提出观点。比较简单一些的,通常要求一个人独立完成;而比较复杂的,则要求两人或多人合作完成。

这种分组作业的完成也是分成几个部分后分别去做,然后组织一至两次的讨论,直到最后完成定稿。参与这种讨论前,一定要做好充分的准备,说出自己的观点和看法,特别是要有独特的见解,这样才能博得同学的好评,以后有这样的作业和讨论时就会被别人抢着要。不然,在以后的分组学习和讨论中可能就没有人要了。

作业完成之后,往往还要求在全班交流,每个小组挑选一个发言人,也可以主动提出担任小组发言人。这也是展示自己实力和信

Discussion with Classmates 17

心的时候。

研究方法课(courses for research methods)：这是为研究生开设的课程，主要内容是学会与本专业相关的各种研究方法、了解本学科领域的研究流派和研究动态。研究方法课一般是几门课程分为一个组，称为 Big Three 或 Big Four。这种课程往往是做课题设计的基础和理论，通常包括研究流派介绍和研究方法、文献综合、学科理论基础等主干课程，为相近专业学科研究生的必修课。

因而，以前本科如果是本专业的毕业生学起来会轻松很多，而其他专业毕业的本科生就会觉得很难。开设此类课程的专业往往也是研究性很强的专业，大部分研究生都准备读完博士学位。国内的同学申请的时候一定要看看整个研究生阶段的课程安排，不然到时候会叫苦不迭。

注　释

① be to do something 的意思是"确定要做什么事情"，如：
President Bush is to visit China next October.（布什总统定于明年10月访问中国。）

② pardon me 的意思在这里与 excuse me 相同，用于打断别人谈话、请求别人谅解等，如：
Pardon me, how can I get to the bookstore?（请问，我怎么去书店？）

③ handout 是老师上课发给学生的参考资料或布置的作业，小组讨论时也可以准备材料发放给同一个小组的人。

④ come up with 意思是"提出，拿出"，如：
She came up with many questions at yesterday's meeting.（她在昨天的会议上提出了很多问题。）

⑤ make + object + object complement 是一种常用的结构，其中的宾语补足语(object complement)可以是名词、动词不定式、现在分词、过去分词、副词或介词短语等。例如：
We made him our monitor.（我们选他当班长。）
They have made him what he wants to be.（他们使他如愿以偿。）

She made the boy do the exercise once again.（她让男孩重做练习。）
Don't make him waiting for me so long.（不要让他等我那么久。）
Ignorance makes him cheated.（无知使他受骗。）
You must make the quarrel over.（你必须让争吵停止。）
The people made him into power.（人民使他掌权。）

⑥ be excellent at 的意思是"在……方面优秀"，其结构与 be good at 一样，还有 be clever at 等。

⑦ without any question whatsoever 意思是"毫无疑问"，如：
I will stand by you without any question whatsoever.（我会毫无疑问地支持你。）

Questioning In and Out Class
课堂内外提问题

Topic Introduction
话题导言

大家都熟悉"提问"这个词,指的是课堂上教师为了检验学生是否掌握授课内容而向学生发问。这一种教学技巧在美国的大学、中小学课堂使用也很普遍,但更多的是学生向老师提问题,希望得到老师的即时解答。这在中国的课堂上比较少。

在美国大学上课时,学生通常可以随时打断教授的讲课,提出自己不明白的问题。有的问当时讲的内容,有的联系到以前的内容,有的要求老师重复一遍刚说过的话,有的要老师解释一下某个词或某句话,还有的请求老师把速度放慢一些,甚至还有的学生问某个词如何拼写,等等。总之,你什么都可以问,教授都不会反感。但学生所使用的语言一般都是比较客气的,如 Isn't that true ...?或者 Would you please explain ...?或 Couldn't you say ...?等。如果有问题需要讨论,可以下课以后再问,或约个时间专门讨论。课间休息时间不要耽搁教授太多的时间,因为他可能接着还要给别的班上课。

Situational Dialogs
情景对话

杨佳欣(Jiaxin)虽然选择了环保专业,但对企业管理也很感兴趣,所以她选了 Jack Campbell 教授的课。

Dialog 1

Jack: Good morning, everyone. Welcome to my class. My name is Jack Campbell. I'm expecting to cooperate with you in BUS511, that is, Partnerships and Development. Now I'm passing out the syllabus. Get one copy and see if you have any questions.

各位,早晨好。欢迎到我这个班。我叫杰克·坎贝尔。盼望大家和我合作 BUS511 课,就是《合伙企业及其发展》。现在我发放课程大纲,取一份,如果有问题请提出来。

Jiaxin: Besides the term paper, a mid-term, and a final, do we have pop quizzes[①]?

除了学期论文,期中考试和期末考试,有没有临时测验?

Jack: Yes. We have around five pop quizzes.

有,我们有 5 次。

Jiaxin: Is there a grade for class participation?

上课参加活动是否也打分数?

Jack: Yes, there is. I encourage you to attend class, for your grade depends on class activities as well.[②]

要的,我鼓励大家上课,因为你们分数也取决于课堂活动。

Jiaxin: There're too many assignments. How many are required to finish?[③]

太多作业了,多少次是必须完成的?

Jack: At least ten of them.

至少 10 次。

Dialog 2

Jiaxin: Excuse me, Professor Campbell. I'd like to talk with you about some questions.

打搅一下,坎贝尔教授,我想和您讨论几个问题。

Jack: No problem.

没问题。

Jiaxin: When is good for you?[④]

什么时候可以?

Jack: Come to see me during my office hours. Let me see.... Tomorrow morning, from ten to eleven.

办公时间到我的办公室来,我看看……明天上午 10 点到 11 点。

Questioning In and Out Class 18

课堂内外提问题

Jiaxin: But I have class then. How about tomorrow afternoon?
但我有课上，明天下午呢？

Jack: OK. From three thirty to four thirty.
好的，3点30分到4点30分。

Jiaxin: All right. See you then.
好的，到时候再见。

Typical Sentences 典型句型

1) I can't handle that professor's lectures.
我跟不上那个教授的课。

2) How do you spell that word?
如何拼写那个词？

3) Prof. Wells, I'm quite worried about today's lecture.
韦尔斯教授，我实在着急今天的课。

4) Could you explain these definitions again?
你能再解释一下这些定义吗？

5) Do you think I can still change my mind?
你认为我还能改选别的课吗？

6) Besides the term paper, a mid-term, and a final, do we have pop quizzes?
除了学期论文，期中考试和期末考试，有没有临时测验？

7) Is there a grade for class participation?
上课参加活动是否也打分数？

8) There're too many assignments. How many are required to finish?
太多作业了，多少次是必须完成的？

9) Prof. Campbell, I'd like to talk with you about some questions.
打搅一下，坎贝尔教授，我想和您讨论几个问题。

10) Don't be afraid to ask questions.

不要怕问问题。

11) I have a question.

我有疑问。

12) I can't get your point.

我不太了解你的重点。

13) Could you explain that again?

你可以再解释一下吗？

教学安排大纲(syllabus)：每个学期开学的第一次课一般都不讲授实质性的教学内容，教授要对整个课程安排做一个比较详细的说明，叫做 introduction；同时，教授要发放本学期的课程安排大纲，内容包括授课计划、详细的时间安排、测试次数、作业布置、成绩评定方法等，并附上教材名称和阅读的书目。下面以《行为理论》课为例(节录部分)：

PSC488: Introductory to Behaviorism

Syllabus

Instructor: Tommy Wells   Title: Assistant Professor; Ph.D.

Office: 209 ADB   Phone: 5-6789

Hours: 10:00–11:00 Mon & Thu or when open

Purpose Description: PSC488 is designed for upperclassmen and graduates to lay a solid foundation in conducting research of human behaviors. ...

Questioning In and Out Class

Date	Chapter	Assignment	Test	Note
01/16	Introduction	Ex 2: 1/5/7/9 (Due 01/18)		
01/18	Ch 1	Ex 2: 2/3/9 (Due 10/22)		
01/23	Ch 1	Ex 3: 7/18 (Due 01/30)		
01/25				No Class
01/30			Test1	211 MOR
02/01	Ch 2	Ex 1: 2/7/8 (Due 02/06)		
…	…	…	…	…

Grading Policy: Participation 10%

      Assignments 20% (At least 10 times)

      Tests 30% (At least 5 times)

      Final 50%

Grades: A—90% or above

    B—80%～89%

    C—70%～79%

    D—60%～69%

    F—59% or below

Texts: Slant, T. (2002), Introductory to Behaviorism, ABC Press: Seattle

Readings: check my website: www.xysw.edu/twells/course/PSC488

现在，很多教授都将课程大纲放在个人网页上，当你选课的时候就可以点击教师姓名进入教授的个人网页，查阅相关细节。有些词汇可能比较生疏，不过看多了就知道是什么意思了。

注　释

① pop quiz 是指平时上课临时进行的"课堂测验"。

② as well 和 also 是同义的，表示"也"的意思，如：I know him as well.（我也认识他。）

③ 大学教授布置的作业有时候并不要求每次都完成，而是要求完成其中的大部分，一般为80%，如布置10次作业，只要完成8次就可以得到作业的满分。

④ good 在这里的意思是"合适,适合"，如：
That color is good for me.（那种颜色适合我。）

About Assignments
关于作业

Topic Introduction
话题导言

学生完成作业是天经地义的事情。在国内的时候听人说美国的学校最讲究"突出个人"和培养"创新能力",想像着可能不用做很多的作业。可没曾想,一进入课堂首先感到的就是繁多作业的重压。美国大学老师布置作业就像中国的中学老师一样,每次上课之后都有要完成的作业,而且要求还很严。

首先是规范化,整个作业都有非常细的规定,包括标题样式、用几号字、多大的行距、打印在多大的纸上、姓名学号在什么地方,甚至是多少页纸,多一行少一行都不行,看起来近乎死板。其次是交作业的时间,规定到某日几点几分,晚一分钟就不要了,笔者就曾遇到这样的尴尬。再次就是绝对不能抄课本,强调一定要自己总结后再做答案,如果跟课本上的一模一样,肯定是零分。

一个学期所有要布置的作业都在第一次上课时发放的课程大纲(syllabus)上面,很少有临时增加或减少的情况。虽然很多中国学生由于英语听说的困难而在课堂上表现不够主动,但是在作业这方面往往表现很优秀,都能严格按照要求去做,所以最后的总成绩也不错。笔者曾问过一名学生为什么会这样,得到的回答是"中国学生的主要功夫花在课外"。

Situational Dialogs
情景对话

美国全新而且严格的作业形式,困扰着很多留学生。杨洋(Yang Yang)与同学 Mary 讨论了作业问题;刘杭(Liu Hang)请教了她的老师。

Dialog 1

Yang Yang: How's everything going with your class?①
你的功课都进行得怎么样?

Mary: Well, not too bad. But the math assignments often bother me, actually. They are really hard.
哦,不太坏。但其实,数学作业总是烦着我,真的很难。

Yang Yang: It happens that I find math so easy; maybe I can help you out②
碰巧我觉得数学很容易,也许我可以帮你的忙。

Mary: Nothing could be better than that.
那是再好不过了。

Yang Yang: At the same time you can help me with my English composition.③
同时,你也可以帮一下我的英语作文。

Mary: Certainly I will.
我当然愿意。

Dialog 2

Liu Hang: Excuse me, Professor. I don't know how to finish the assignment.
打搅一下,教授,我不知道如何完成这个作业。

Professor: Eh, where is your trouble?
哦,你的困难在哪里?

Liu Hang: I can't classify these figures.
我不会给这些数字分类。

About Assignments 19

关于作业

Professor: Okay, don't bother yourself too much. First make them into④ two main types, and then it'll be easier.
好的，别太为难自己，先把它们分成两大类，然后就容易些了。

Liu Hang: That sounds reasonable. I'll have a try.
听起来有道理，我试一下。

Dialog 3

Mary: What does this assignment mean?
这个作业是什么意思？

Yang Yang: The professor asked us to find at least 25 articles and 5 books, and these items have to be closely related to the topic we choose.
教授要我们找到至少 25 篇文章和 5 本书，而且这些东西必须和我们选的题目密切相关。

Mary: Just find the titles or the whole articles and books?
只找到题目，还是整篇的文章和整本的书？

Yang Yang: I guess the titles should be OK, for we've got to turn them in next Monday.
我想题目就可以了，因为我们下个星期一就得交。

Mary: Possibly you're right. Do you understand the format?
可能你对了，你懂得这个格式吗？

Yang Yang: I think so. APA format should be author's family name, initials of given names, date of publication in brackets, title of article or book, name of journal or press, and last publishing place.
我想我懂。APA 格式应该是作者的姓、名的缩写、出版日期放在括号内、文章或书的标题、杂志或出版社的名称，最后是出版地点。

Mary: It's so complicated. She should give us a model.
这么复杂，她应该给我们一个示例。

Yang Yang: It's not necessary. We can do it by the software called APA Library or something.
没有必要，我们可以用叫做"APA 图书馆"之类的软件来做。

Mary: Smart guy. You are correct.
真聪明，你说的对。

Typical Sentences
典型句型

1) How's everything going with your class?
   你的功课都进行得怎么样?

2) The only thing I don't understand is yesterday's assignment.
   我唯一不明白的是昨天的作业。

3) Math assignments often bother me, actually.
   其实,数学作业总是烦着我。

4) I think I know something about it.
   我想我略知一二。

5) At the same time you can help me with my English composition.
   同时,你也可以帮一下我的英语作文。

6) Professor, I don't know how to finish the assignment.
   教授,我不知道如何完成这个作业。

7) Could you check my composition for me?
   您能帮我检查一下作文吗?

8) I can't classify these figures.
   我不会给这些数字分类。

9) What does this assignment mean?
   这个作业是什么意思?

10) I wish I could find another method to work out the problem.
    我希望我能找到另外一个方法解答这个问题

11) Possibly you're right. Do you understand the format?
    可能你对了,你懂得这个格式吗?

12) It's unfair that she just scored a B to my essay.
    她给我的论文只评了一个B,不公平。

13) It's so complicated. She should give us a model.
    这么复杂,她应该给我们一个示例。

14) It's most important for you to submit your assignments on time.
    准时交作业极为重要。

About Assignments 19

Background 背景知识

作业类型：大学功课的作业量大，类型也很多样，主要包括：

(1) 问题解答(Questions)，主要是课本后面的问题，要求就题答题，不要求扩展，表现为计算、解答、比较等方式。

(2) 自由问题(Designation)，这也是课本中的一种问题，结合自己实际情况或他人的经验进行总结或设计，回答方式和长短也是比较自由的，但一定要应用学过的原理理论，做到自圆其说。

(3) 参考文献(References)，这是高年级或研究生的作业，往往是老师给题目或自选一个题目，要求查找能够参考的文献资料，这种作业往往被称为 library work。看起来简单，实际上有严格的规范，如文献内容的列举多推荐美国 APA 格式(APA 是美国心理学会 American Psychological Association 的简称)。

(4) 问题列举(Question List)，这也是研究生的一种作业，目的是为研究选题。老师通常要求列出感兴趣的问题，说明可能的研究范围，能够参考的书籍杂志，哪些机构能为研究提供资助，研究结果的学术或应用价值等。

(5) 小论文(Essays)，这是高年级或研究生课程的作业，往往是理论课或概论课老师为了让学生理解一些基本的理论问题而设计的，如 What Is Science? / What Is Theory? / The Definition of Tourism 等，长度要求在 4 页左右。特别重视的是概括能力，即能够从不同观点进行总结，引用别人的观点要求很严格，必须按照 APA 格式注明出处。

(6) 课程论文(Course Essays)，这是为了某门课而设立的作业，往往用以代替期末考试。题目必须与课本内容有密切关系，有独立的见解或观点才可能得到较高分数，如推导出一个新的个人所得税计算公式，或把某一概念的应用范围扩大到其他领域等。学期论文(Term Paper)也有些类似于课程论文。

(7) 研究方案(Research Proposal)，这是研究生为了完成学位论文而向专业导师或导师组提交的报告，在研究生教育中，这个方案起着十分重要的作用。同时，也是几门研究方法课的联合作业，

分别由数位老师从不同侧面打分。

(8) 综合论文(Integrated Paper)，在导师的指导下，选定一个比较小的题目，为学位论文的写作打基础。完成后，导师经过评价给出一个等级分数，可以算作通过研究得到的学分。

注　释

① "How's everything going with something?"意思是"什么事情进行得怎么样？"如：

How's everything going with your research? （你的研究进行得怎么样了？）

类似的表达还有：

How are things going with your company? （公司情况如何？）

How are you getting along with your work? （工作情况如何？）

② help out 指的是"帮助别人摆脱困境"，如：

My father helped me out with money when I lost my job. （我失业的时候，爸爸给我钱帮我渡过难关。）

③ help somebody with something 意思是"在某方面帮助某人"，如：

She often helps me with my spoken English. （她常常在英语口语方面帮助我。）

④ make into 意思是"把……转变成……"，如：

The local cinema has been made into a hall. （当地电影院已经改建成了礼堂。）

At a University Library
大学图书馆

Topic Introduction
话题导言

中国学生在国外留学很大程度上就是在教师指导下的自学,尽可能地利用图书馆这一现代化知识与信息中心,对于取得优异的学业成绩是至关重要的。出国留学深造的学生,一般都把大部分业余时间花在图书馆里。对大多数中国留学生来说,他们去图书馆,主要是为了查阅与自己专业有关的书籍。当你有问题时可以随时向图书馆工作人员提问,他们都十分乐意帮助你。

大学图书馆每天从上午 7:00 至午夜 12:00 开放,部分区域还是 24 小时开放。书库里备有桌椅,你可以在书库内的书架上任意查找所需要的书,然后取出来坐下阅读,读后放在桌子上就可以了。书库里还有供研究生租用的一间间自习室(study room),室内安静舒适,是从事学术研究、著书撰文的最佳场所。由于申请自习室的人很多,因此要提前很久预订。

Situational Dialogs
情景对话

图书馆无疑是个查找资料的好地方,就算遇到了问题,也可以向图书馆员提问。刘杭(Liu Hang)和杨洋(Yang Yang)经常使用图书馆,而且刘杭还想申请一间自习室便于平时的学习。

Dialog 1

Yang Yang: Excuse me, where should I put the books I just read?
请问，我应当把读过的书还在什么地方？

Mary: Don't worry about that. Just put them on the desk.
别管这一点，放在桌子上就行。

Yang Yang: You mean I don't need to put them back where I got them.
您是说我不必要把书放回原处。

Mary: Correct. Look, there is a sign, "Don't Reshelf① Books".
正确。瞧，那儿有个牌子，写的是"不要把书还回原架"。

Yang Yang: What does it mean?
什么意思？

Mary: That means that you should not put the books you just read back to the shelf.
意思是说，您不要把书放回原来的书架。

Yang Yang: But who will put them back?
但是，谁放回去呢？

Mary: This is the librarians' job. They will do it.
这是图书馆员的工作，他们会做的。

Dialog 2

Liu Hang: Excuse me, where can I find some academic journals published in China?
请问，我在哪里可以找得到中国出版的学术期刊？

Librarian: I'm sorry to say we just have very few such journals. Probably we have only three kinds. They are *Journal of Peking University, Journal of Tsinghua University*, and the other one I can't remember.②
非常遗憾地告诉您，我们只有很少几种，可能我们只有三种，《北京大学学报》、《清华大学学报》，还有一种我记不起来了。

Liu Hang: Do you have any Chinese newspapers?
您这里有中文报纸吗？

At a University Library

Librarian:	We have *People's Daily*, the *Chinese Times*, and the *World Journal*.
	我们有《人民日报》、《中国时报》以及《世界日报》。
Liu Hang:	That sounds not too bad.
	听来还不算太坏。
Librarian:	If you need more Chinese journals, we can connect to the Library of Congress in Washington DC.
	如果您需要更多的中文期刊，我们可以联系在华盛顿特区的国会图书馆。
Liu Hang:	Thank you for your offer. I'll get in touch with③ my friends in China. They may be of a great help.
	谢谢您主动提出帮我。我会与中国的朋友联系，也许他们能帮上大忙。

Dialog 3

Liu Hang:	Excuse me, can I apply for a study room?
	请问，我能申请一间自习室吗？
Librarian:	Are you a grad or under④?
	您是研究生还是本科生？
Liu Hang:	I'm a graduate.
	我是研究生。
Librarian:	So you can apply for one. But you can't have it now. I can just put you on the waiting list⑤.
	那么，您可以申请。但您现在得不到，我可以把您放到候补名单上。
Liu Hang:	What formalities?
	什么手续？
Librarian:	We need your major professor's reference or a letter from your department head, and your Student ID Card, and a deposit of $100. Please fill the form and sign here.
	我们需要您的专业导师的推荐信或系主任的信，您的学生证，以及押金100美元。请填写这个表并在这里签字。
Liu Hang:	Okay, I see. Thank you.
	好的，谢谢。

Typical Sentences 典型句型

1) I'd like to borrow some books on Shakespeare's plays.
   我想借关于莎士比亚戏剧的书。
2) Then in what way can I get such books?
   那么,我可以用什么方法得到这些书呢?
3) I'd like to take those two out and return these three.
   我想借那两本,还这3本。
4) I just got an overdue notice from the library.
   我刚接到图书馆的一张过期罚款单。
5) I've been looking for this book in the stacks but haven't found it yet.
   我一直在书架上找这本书,可是没找到。
6) Excuse me, where should I put the books I just read?
   请问,我应当把读过的书还在什么地方?
7) Where can I find some academic journals published in China?
   我在哪里可以找得到中国出版的学术期刊?
8) Do you have any Chinese newspapers?
   您这里有中文报纸吗?
9) Excuse me, can I apply for a study room?
   请问,我能申请一间自习室吗?

Background 背景知识

大学图书馆基本介绍:西方国家的图书馆与我国的图书馆一样都设有书库、阅览室、工具书室、复印室、电脑查询室和报告厅等最基本的设施,还提供音像资料(如录像带、录音带、影音光碟等)的借阅,并设有电脑室供需要的读者免费上网和发送 e-mail。具体介绍如下:

At a University Library

(1) 布局：进入图书馆就可以看到咨询台(Reference Desk)，也有的设有问讯处(Information Desk)，在这里你可以了解图书馆的整个布局。你可以取一张说明，上面具体说明了各学科的图书所在的位置。

(2) 目录：图书馆的现代化使读者不用再查目录卡，图书目录已经电脑化了，直接在电脑中输入你要的书名的关键词，电脑系统瞬间就能全部列举出来，你可以选择具体需要的那一本，再根据 Call Number 到相应的区域去找就很容易了。

(3) 借书：借书时凭学生证，在流通部柜台(Circulation Desk)将图书消磁就可以了；续借通过校园网进行网上续借即可。学校对于本科生、研究生、教师的借书规定是不同的。一般地，本科生只能借五本书，且只能持有四个星期，只能续借一次；研究生和教师不限借书数量，可以持有一个学期，可以续借一次。

(4) 还书：俗话说"有借有还，再借不难"，其实还书特简单，只要随时丢进图书馆的归还箱就可以了，不需要到流通部柜台。一旦持有某本书超过一个星期，而有人急需且预借(reserve)了该书，你就会被通知在一个星期之内归还。不管因什么原因而导致图书超期归还，都要被罚款。

(5) 急需：如果遇到你要的书被人借走未还，并在 Status 一栏获知是 Check Out 且有到期日期，你可直接在网上要求 Reserve 这本书。图书馆员就会立即催前面的读者在一周内还书，这样你很快就可以得到该书了。

(6) 网借：如果本校图书馆没有你要借的书，图书馆员还会通过馆际互借网络向其他图书馆"调兵谴将"(即 inter-library loan)。是否付费根据馆际协议执行。

(7) 规则：阅览室内保持安静，不大声喧哗，爱护图书，书库及阅览室内禁止吸烟，不许吃东西。若带点东西当作午餐固然很好，但必须到休息室或走廊去吃，还可取用饮用水，既方便又省事。

注　释

① 美语中有些词的使用非常灵活，这里的 reshelf 就是由"前缀 re + shelf"构成的，而 shelf 是名词（书架）作为动词（放置到书架上）使用了，所以 reshelf 的意思就是"重新放回到书架上"。
② 这句话属于宾语前置，正常的语序是 I can't remember the other one.
③ get in touch with 和 connect to 的意思都是"与某某人取得联系"。还有 be in touch with（与某某人有联系），keep in touch with（与某某人保持联系），lose in touch with（与某某人失去联系）等。
④ 这里 grad 和 under 是两个缩写词：grad = graduate（研究生），under = undergraduate（本科生），口语中交谈常用。
⑤ waiting list（候补名单）指的是虽然目前没有空位，但一旦有空位就按照一定的顺序递补上去的名单，如租学生宿舍、选课、申请工作职位等等。

Online Library
网络图书馆

Topic Introduction
话题导言

  人类已经进入所谓"信息社会",信息社会的技术标志就是"信息高速公路"。美国各大学图书馆的管理可以说已经网络化,不管你在世界的哪个角落,只要你能上互联网并拥有该大学的证件就可以查阅到该大学图书馆的一切信息:进入图书馆,输入证件条形码(bar code)就可以跟在校内一样使用图书馆的网上资料了。

  美国各大学图书馆为了方便本校教师和研究生的研究工作,订购了大量的学术期刊(academic journals/periodicals),这些期刊既有普通版本的也有网络版的,本校师生可以直接从网上浏览到最新的文献而不用付费,也可以保存在自己账号下的文件夹内或者直接打印出来。若需要本校没有订的期刊的文章,要想阅读或打印就要按标价付钱。

Situational Dialogs
情景对话

  要想尽快熟悉使用网络图书馆,除了不要错过"如何使用图书馆"的讲座之外,刘杭(Liu Hang)还需要掌握一些搜索技巧。

Dialog 1

Liu Hang: I noticed there will be a lecture about how to use the library.
我注意到有一个关于如何使用图书馆的讲座。

Erick: Yes, it's 7:00 tonight.
是的，今晚7点。

Liu Hang: Where shall we meet?
我们在哪里集合？

Erick: I remember it's around the reference desk or something.
我记得是在咨询台附近还是什么地方。

Liu Hang: Do you know what they will tell us?
您知道会讲些什么？

Erick: Probably mainly about the online library, or campus library network. Actually I don't know either.
大概主要是关于网络图书馆的，或者是校园图书馆网络。其实我也不知道。

Liu Hang: Whatever, we'll be there at 7:00 tonight. Sorry, I'm rushed.
管它如何，我们今晚7点钟到那儿吧。不好意思，我要有急事。

Erick: OK. See you later.
好的，再见。

Dialog 2

Liu Hang: Excuse me, can I ask a question?
打搅一下，我可以问个问题吗？

Librarian: Yes, go ahead, please.
可以，请问吧。

Liu Hang: Can I get into the library network when I go back to China during vacations or when I travel around the United States?
如果假期我回中国或者出去旅行，我能进入图书馆网络吗？

Librarian: Sure, you can. But you have to remember to take your Student ID Card with you, because you need to enter the bar code of the Student ID Card.
当然，您能进入。但是，记住带上学生证，因为您需要输入学生证上的条形码。

Online Library

网络图书馆

Liu Hang:	It's great. Thank you very much. 太好了,非常感谢。
Librarian:	You are welcome. 不用谢。

Dialog 3

Liu Hang:	Hello, Erick. Are you busy now? 您好,埃里克,忙吗?
Erick:	Not very busy. What's up?① 不是很忙,什么事情?
Liu Hang:	The professor asked us to find an article using any of qualitative methods. Have you found it? 教授要我们找一篇关于定性分析的文章,您找到了吗?
Erick:	Yes, I have. Do you have any trouble? 我找到了,您有什么困难?
Liu Hang:	I found one but the author charges 18.99 dollars. I don't know why I couldn't find one for free. 我找到一篇,但作者要我付 18.99 美元。我不知道我为什么不能找到一篇免费的。
Erick:	Okay, let me show you. Just enter "Library Website", then "Find Articles", then "General Studies", type "qualitative" under "Key Words" and last "Search". Look, there comes a list of articles that include the word "qualitative". You can look through several of them and you will find which is the best. 好的,我来告诉您。只要进入"图书馆网站",然后到"找文章",然后到"一般研究",在"关键词"处输入"qualitative",最后"查询"。瞧,含有单词"qualitative"的文章都列了出来。您可以浏览几篇,看看哪一篇最好。
Liu Hang:	Thank you, Erick. I went to the wrong place. 谢谢您,埃里克。我进错了地方。
Erick:	It's nothing.② 不值得一提。

Dialog 4

Liu Hang: Excuse me, I am a new student of the university and not familiar with this library. Could you tell me how to use computers to check catalog?

打搅一下,我是本校的新学生,对图书馆不熟悉。您能告诉我怎么用电脑查目录吗?

Librarian: Sure. What's your topic?

当然,您要什么课题的?

Liu Hang: I'm majoring in resource recreation and tourism.

我的专业是资源消遣与旅游。

Librarian: All right. You can use any of on-campus computers. Click "find my books", then "natural resource", then enter the key words such as "resource recreation" or "tourism", and last click "research". If you know the author of the book, enter his or her name under "author".

好的,您可以用校园里的任何一台电脑,点击"找书",然后点击"自然资源",然后输入像"资源消遣"或者"旅游"这样的关键词,最后点击"查询"。如果您知道作者的名字,就在"作者"下面输入名字。

Liu Hang: That's really great. I appreciate it.

那真是很不错,谢谢。

Librarian: Anytime.[3]

不用谢。

Typical Sentences
典型句型

1) I noticed there will be a lecture about how to use the library.
我注意到有一个关于如何使用图书馆的讲座。

2) I remember it's around the reference desk or something.
我记得是在咨询台附近还是什么地方。

Online Library

3) Can I get into the library network when I go back to China during vacations or when I travel around the United States?
如果假期我回中国或者出去旅行,我能进入图书馆网络吗?

4) The professor asked us to find an article using any of qualitative methods.
教授要我们找一篇关于定性分析的文章。

5) I don't know why I couldn't find one for free.
我不知道我为什么不能找到一篇免费的。

6) Look, there comes a list of articles that include the word "qualitative".
瞧,含有单词"qualitative"的文章都列了出来。

7) Could you tell me how to use computers to check catalog?
您能告诉我怎么用电脑查目录吗?

背景知识

图书馆的书籍分类(一):在外国的图书馆里找书、借书,如果不了解书籍的基本分类和名称,就如同盲人骑瞎马,只会徒然浪费时间而已。虽然现在图书目录的管理已经实现了电脑网络化,了解一下书籍分类编号还是很有好处的。最主要的分类系统是 Dewey Decimal System(杜威十进制系统),所有的图书分为十大类(ten different classes),分别是:

第一类(000—099):Computers, information, and general reference 计算机科学、情报学与总类

第二类(100—199):Philosophy and psychology 哲学与心理学

第三类(200—299):Religion 宗教

第四类(300—399):Social sciences 社会科学

第五类(400—499):Language 语言

第六类(500—599):Science 科学与数学

第七类(600—699):Technology 技术

第八类(700—799)：Arts and recreation 艺术与休闲
第九类(800—899)：Literature 文学
第十类(900—999)：History and geography 历史与地理

除上述十大分类以外，每一大类还区分为若干小类(subdivisions)，这些小类也是依照十进制的方式来编写的。

图书馆的书籍分类(二)：除了上述"杜威十进制体系"外，还有一种常用的体系是国会图书馆制(The Library of Congress System)，简称LC分类法，主要包括一些单独的、彼此不相干的、专门的分类表。各个类别之间只有字母标记上的偶然相关，没有任何别的关联。

与"杜威"制不同，LC分类法是根据图书馆的实际，并结合现有各种分类法的优点拟订的：把图书分为20大类，外加一个综合图书类，大体上按社会科学、人文科学、自然科学、物理科学来归类。每一大类均有一个"纲要说明"，其顺序从一般到特殊，从理论到实际。

A　General Works 总类
B　Philosophy, Psychology, Religion 哲学、心理学及宗教
C　Auxiliary Sciences of History 历史科学总论
D　World History and History of Europe, Asia, Africa, Australia, New Zealand, etc. 世界历史和欧洲、亚洲、非洲、澳大利亚、新西兰等国历史
E　History of the Americas 美洲历史
F　History of the United States and British, Dutch, French, and Latin America 美国、英国历史；德国、荷兰、法国及拉丁美洲历史
G　Geography, Anthropology, Recreation 地理学、人类学、娱乐
H　Social Sciences 社会科学
J　Political Science 政治学
K　Law 法律
L　Education 教育
M　Music and Books on Music 音乐
N　Fine Arts 美术
P　Language and Literature 语言、文学
Q　Science 科学

```
R    Medicine 医学
S    Agriculture 农业
T    Technology 科技
U    Military Science 军事科学
V    Naval Science 航海科学
Z    Bibliography, Library Science, Information Resources (General) 目录学、图书馆学、主要信息资源
```

注 释

① What's up? 相当于 What's happening? 用于比较熟悉的人之间互相询问,如打电话、见到朋友、打招呼都可以说。类似的还有：

What's going on?（有什么事？）

What's happening?（发生什么事情？）

How's it going?（情况如何？）

How's everything?（一切可好？）

How's everything going with you?（你一切情况如何？）

② It's nothing. 这里是"不用谢"的另一个说法。

③ 对于别人的感谢,口头上的回应方式很多,但是用的场合并不是随意的,略举几种：

You are welcome.（对于感谢的回答,美国人用得最多,英国人也用得多起来了）

Not at all. / That's OK. / That's quite all right.（普遍用的三种）

Don't mention it.（对帮忙、送礼等感谢的答语）

It's my pleasure.（对帮忙、光临等感谢的答语）

Anytime / Any time.（对为别人做事而受到感谢的答语,同 My pleasure）

No problem. / It was nothing.（对解决麻烦而受到感谢的答语）

You bet.（美国部分地区使用）

Sure.（美国部分人使用）

Seminars and Presentations
研讨课与演示会

Topic Introduction
话题导言

研讨课(Seminar)是美国大学研究生院的课程形式,也可以是为某种职业的人提供的成人教育课程。一般地,一门研讨课开设一个学期,每周两个小时居多;也有的研讨课集中安排在一周或两周内完成。通常,如果只是参加这种研讨课而不跟着教授做研究工作或者不写什么报告,就只能得到一个学分。如果按照要求完成了相应的作业任务,就可得到两个或三个学分,这还得看教授有没有这种学分安排。参加的学生每个学期要求做一次主题发言,其余的同学和教授参与讨论。

演示会(Presentation)是其他课程过程中某个阶段或课程结束时的汇报会,主要是用语言,并结合图像和表格,以及利用现代科技如投影技术、幻灯技术、多媒体播放系统等展示自己的研究成果或者方案,然后由同学或教授提出看法和意见。

这两种形式都是培养学生的口头语言表达的很好方式。乐于为大学教授所采用,也深受学生的欢迎。

Situational Dialogs
情景对话

刘杭(Liu Hang)在研讨会上积极发言,并且赢得了一个在演示会上表现自己的机会。这对于提高她的口语大有帮助。

Seminars and Presentations 22

Dialog 1

Liu Hang: Excuse me, Professor Smith. Can I attend the seminar tomorrow?
史密斯教授,请问我可以参加明天的研讨课吗?

Prof. Smith: Sure, everyone is welcome.
当然,每个人都欢迎。

Liu Hang: What's the topic?
什么主题?

Prof. Smith: We've invited several professors from outside our department to be guest speakers. They'll report what they're doing in their research.
我们邀请了外系的几位教授来做客座发言人,他们将向我们报告他们正在做的研究工作。

Liu Hang: That's wonderful. I'd like to know them.
很好,我很想认识他们。

Prof. Smith: Yes, it's a good chance for you.
是啊,对你来说是个好机会。

Liu Hang: Do I have to speak at the seminar?
我必须在研讨课上发言吗?

Prof. Smith: No, just show up. But you may raise① your questions.
不必,只是出席而已。但你可以提出问题。

Dialog 2

Prof. Smith: You did a very good job at the seminar.
研讨课上,你讲得非常好。

Liu Hang: Thank you. I wish I had made clear the whole topic.
谢谢,我希望我把整个问题说清楚了。

Prof. Smith: It's very clear, I think.
我觉得非常清楚。

Liu Hang: I had been worrying that I couldn't make myself understood②, because of my spoken English.
因为我的口语问题,我还一直担心我不能让大家听懂。

Prof. Smith:	You are making progress in speaking English. I believe you will be better next time. 你说英语在不断进步,我相信你下次会做得更好。
Liu Hang:	I hope so. 希望如此。

Dialog 3

Prof. Smith:	Can you make a presentation this afternoon, Liu Hang? 刘杭,你能今天下午做一个演示吗?
Liu Hang:	Of course I can. How long should I take up? 当然能,我可以占用多少时间?
Prof. Smith:	How about thirty minutes or so? 大约30分钟,如何?
Liu Hang:	Okay, thirty minutes is enough, I guess. 好的,我想,30分钟足够了。
Prof. Smith:	Have you made what you will do into a Microsoft PowerPoint file③? 你把要讲的内容做成了微软演示文稿文件了吗?
Liu Hang:	Yes, I have. I use many pictures to accompany my presentation in order to make everyone understand very well. 做了,为了使每个人都听得明白一些,我用了许多图片。
Prof. Smith:	I believe you can do a very good job. 我相信你能做得非常好。

典型句型

1) What time will the seminar begin Monday afternoon?
星期一下午的研讨课几点钟开始?

2) Prof. Smith, can I attend the seminar tomorrow?
史密斯教授,请问我可以参加明天的研讨课吗?

3) What topic will you speak about at the seminar?
你在研讨课上要讲什么主题?

Seminars and Presentations 22

研讨课与演示会

4) Do I have to speak at the seminar?
   我必须在研讨课上发言吗?
5) I think their research is very novel.
   我觉得他们的研究很新颖。
6) You did a very good job at the seminar.
   研讨课上,你讲得非常好。
7) I wish I had made clear the whole topic.
   我希望我把整个问题说清楚了。
8) Could you show me how to make a hyperlink?
   你能告诉我如何做超链接吗?
9) Can you make a presentation this afternoon?
   你能今天下午做一个演示吗?
10) I use many pictures to accompany my presentation in order to make everyone understand very well.
    为了使每个人都听得明白一些,我用了许多图片。
11) Those pictures are very good. Where did you get them?
    那些图片很好,你从哪儿弄来的?

背景知识

美国高校课堂教学模式:基于不同的教学目的和教学内容,教授们往往采取不同的教学模式。

(1) 讲授课(lecture),以教师讲解为主的课堂教学模式即讲授制。美国高校开设的某些基础课程(包括演讲课)仍采取教师讲解为主的所谓"满堂灌"形式,授课的工具仍然是传统的粉笔和黑板。

(2) 实验课(lab),一般是讲授课在实验室的应用,如计算机编程、验证原理和定理、应用软件的使用等。一门实验课可以分成多次上课,学生可选择自己合适的时间去实验室。

(3) 研讨课(seminar),通常是针对研究生开设的,以讨论为主。主持人多半是在读的处于论文阶段的博士研究生或正在研究课题的教授,也邀请来自于外校或外系的本专业或相关学科的教授来交流,称作 guest speaker。主要目的是教授或其他研究人员对研究过程向同行汇报,以期望得到不同的意见而加以改进;而听课的研究生通过研讨课可就他们感兴趣的方面得到答疑解惑,并能进一步了解本学科的最新进展。

(4) 实践课(practicum),包括野外考察和现场实习,往往由一个教授带领一组研究生或高年级本科生到研究现场去调查、走访、收集资料等。教育学有关专业的研究生到学校进行教学实习,其他专业的到工厂、公司去学习实际操作等也属于这类课程。学完这样的课程,需要完成一篇报告,教授凭上交的报告给学生一个等级分数。

(5) 案例教学(case study),是美国高校管理学课程和西方财经课程教学的最大特点。案例教学法可以有助于调动学生的积极性、主动性和创新意识,有助于提高学生分析问题与解决问题的能力,也有助于提高学生的综合素质。

(6) 计算机辅助教学(computer-aided teaching),美国高校中许多课程都采用了计算机辅助教学手段,授课的工具不再是传统的粉笔和黑板,而是计算机和投影屏幕。通过计算机课件等形式的演示,使得课堂教学变得形象、生动、灵活,而且重点突出,信息量大,能给学生留下深刻的印象。由于教学内容可以回放、再现、变换等,因此增强了课堂教学的效果。

(7) 网络教学(network-based teaching),是一种新的教学手段,它在课堂中运用网络为新的教学环境,教师从讲授者转变成学生学习活动的设计者、组织者和指导者;教学媒体从过去静态单向的、书本为主的传统教学媒体转变为以书本为主,辅之以由声音、图像和影像构成的多媒体和采用超文本、超媒体链接方式、具有检索功能的网络媒体,具有动态交互的特点;教学传播也从单一的师生交流转变成教师、学生和电脑的三方交流,教学目的从使学生掌握知识为主转变为使学生学会学习为主。

实际上,很多课堂上综合了多种教学模式,如一次两个小时的课,教授先介绍观点 30 分钟,学生分组讨论 30 分钟,各组汇报讨论情况 30 分钟,教授总结和扩展 30 分钟。这中间也用到演示方法、计算机以及网络等技术。所以可以说,现在的课堂模式大都是综合性的,很难划入某一具体类别。

Seminars and Presentations

注　释

① 注意区别 raise 和 rise。两者都可以表示"升起，举起"的意思，但 raise 是及物动词，后可加名词，如：raise one's hand (举手)。rise 为不及物动词，后不能加名词，如：
The cost of living continues to rise. (生活费用继续增长。)

② make oneself understood 的本义是"让自己被听懂"，转译为"让别人听懂自己"，如：
I hope I have made myself understood. (我希望大家听懂了我说的话。)

③ make something into something 意思是"用什么东西做成什么"，如：
We used to make bamboo into water pipes. (我们以前用竹子做成水管。)

Tests and Examinations
关于考试

Topic Introduction
话题导言

考试是任何学生都躲不过的事情。美国大学的大部分课程都要进行考试,有时教授会征求学生意见,采取不同的考试形式。考试前也往往是学生们最为刻苦学习的时候,关于考试的话题也就多了起来。

重视学习到知识和真本事固然是对的,但考试和考试成绩也不能忽视,因为这些表示等级的字母关乎奖学金和以后的工作问题。关于考试有不同的词汇,如 test, examination, quiz 等;对于考试成绩的评定也有多种方法。

Situational Dialogs
情景对话

考试总是让学生紧张,李惠敏(Huimin)和韩力刚(Ligang)也一样。

Dialog 1

Huimin: I really didn't catch① what type of test Prof. Fox is going to give us next week.
我真的没有搞懂福克斯教授下周的考试是什么形式。

Tests and Examinations 23

关于考试

David: I didn't either. He never mentioned the type.
我也不知道，他从来没有提到过形式。

Huimin: I like a take-home test, whether essay writing or questions and answers.
我喜欢带回家的考试，不管是写文章还是回答问题。

David: I don't like an objective test. True-false, multiple choices, and matching always make me confused.
我不喜欢客观测试题，正误、多项选择、搭配总是让我头晕。

Huimin: Sometimes objective exams are easy to guess out the correct answers.
有时候客观考试比较容易猜出正确答案。

David: Yes, they are tricky also. I just guess sometimes.
是的，也很具有技巧性。有时我只好瞎猜了。

Huimin: Everyone does so.
每个人都是如此。

Dialog 2

Ligang: I'm worrying about the comprehensive examination.
我很担心综合考试。

Ellen: I don't care much.
我倒不是很在乎。

Ligang: The exam covers too many courses. I cannot remember so much stuff in so many courses.
这次考试涉及的课程太多，我记不住这么多课程里的这么多东西。

Ellen: It's easy to get a B, but if you expect an A, just work hard day and night[2].
得到一个B很容易，但如果要得到A，就日夜拼命学习吧。

Ligang: I need to get A's in tests, for they are too important for my scholarships.
我需要考试中得到A，对我的奖学金来说太重要了。

Ellen: I like B's. Easy to get, and no hard work is necessary.
我喜欢B，容易得到，没有不必要拼命学习。

137

Dialog 3

Ellen: I feel miserable these days.
我这些天感到很糟糕。

Ligang: Why so? Just enjoy yourself.
为什么会这样呢？过得愉快些吧。

Ellen: I got two D's in the final tests of last semester. I've got to retake these two courses or I must take another two in place of③ them.
上学期的期末考试我得了两个 D。我必须重修这两门课, 要么必须选另外两门课代替这两门。

Ligang: Heaven never seals off all the exits.④ Next time you will get two A's.
天无绝人之路。下次你就可以得到两个 A 了。

Ellen: God knows!
天知道！

Ligang: Don't be in low spirits⑤. Cheer up! Let's go to the sports center.
不要情绪那么低落。高兴起来！我们去运动中心吧。

1) I think there are too many pop quizzes, exams and tests here.
我认为这里的测验、考试太多了。

2) I really didn't catch what type of test Prof. Fox is going to give us next week.
我真的没有搞懂福克斯教授下周的考试是什么形式。

3) I like a take-home test, whether essay writing or answering questions.
我喜欢带回家的考试，不管是写文章还是回答问题。

4) I don't like an objective test.
我不喜欢客观测试题。

5) Professors here never test us with texts.
这里的教授从来不考课本。

6) True-false, multiple choices, and matching always make me confused.
正误、多项选择、搭配总是让我头晕。

7) Sometimes objective exams are easy to guess out the correct answers.
有时候客观考试比较容易猜出正确答案。

8) I'm worrying about the comprehensive examination.
我很担心综合考试。

9) I like B's. Easy to get, and no hard work is necessary.
我喜欢B,容易得到,没有不必要拼命学习。

10) I failed my mid-term. What a shame!
我期中考试没及格,真糟糕!

11) Don't wait until the night before the exam.
别等到最后一天才开始准备考试。

12) Heaven never seals off all the exits. Next time you will get two A's.
天无绝人之路。下次你就可以得到两个A了。

背景知识

美国大学的考试:考试是各级各类学校老师为了检验教学效果而采取的一种考核方式,也是学生学习成果的证明方式。

从时间上看有单元测验(Unit / Chapter Test)、临时测验(Pop Quiz)、期中考试(Mid-term Exam)和期末考试(Final Exam)。

从考试方式看,一是论文考试(essay exam),就是以文章答题或论文的形式,题目常常围绕教授所给的一个问题或题目进行。此项考试不但考察学生的知识,而且很重视学生安排材料、组织文章结构的能力。另外一种是客观考试(objective test),即考知识。教授拟定考试题目在限定的时间内完成,题型包括多项选择、简答、计算等,比论文考试相对容易些。不过,考试范围也不局限在课本所学的内容里,还有很多来自专题讲座的内容。

论文考试可以带回家完成，也有部分专业课的试卷考试可以带回家做，所以被称作 take-home exam，限定的完成时间是1至5天，不过考前要全面准备，广泛收集材料。由于考试时间短，所以拿到题后学生常在图书馆完成，以便于随时可以得到需要的资料。

由于考试用英语解答，外国留学生在事先得征求教授同意的情况下常可以破例携带词典进入考场。有时外国留学生还可以要求适当延长考试时间。这些在考试之前都有明确的说明。

考试成绩的评定：中国留学生都很熟悉百分制，按照卷面上的原始分计算成绩。一个班上，可能会出现多数人在90分以上的情况，也可能会出现很少人及格的情况。这取决于学生水平的高低和试卷的难易程度。

美国大学的成绩评定绝大多数采用等级制，有两种情况：一种是二级制，即该门课的成绩只区分合格（P=pass）和不合格（F=fail），至于多少分为合格，多少分为不合格，各科都不相同，并不是以60分为线。这种计分制度主要是针对一些讲座或技巧训练课程，这样的课程不参加GPA的计算，但照样获得学分。另一种是五级制，这是主要采用的计分方法。课程成绩分为A、B、C、D、F五个等级，其中A为优秀，B为良好，C为中等，D为及格，F为不及格。一般90分以上为A，80分以上为B，70分以上为C，60分以上为D，低于60分为F。某门课的最终成绩以期末考试(Final)为主，参考平时测验、作业、上课情况、教授的印象等进行综合评定。

实际上，不论是二级制，还是五级制，教授的主观因素起了很大的作用。但一个班上成绩的分布往往比较合理，多数人是B和C，获得优秀(A)和不及格(F)者都是少数，获得D也不是什么好事情，因为很多学科规定得D者要重修这门课。

① catch 在这里的意思是"懂得，清楚"，还有"听懂，跟上"等意思，如：Professor, would you slow down? I cannot catch what you talk about. (教授，能否慢一些？我听不懂您说的。)

Tests and Examinations 23

② day and night 是"日以继夜"的意思,也说 all day and all night,如:
They work day and night to finish the project on time. (为了准时完成这个工程,他们日以继夜地工作。)

③ in place of 的意思是"代替,而不是",和 instead of 一样,如:
You may stay here in place of me. (你可以呆在这里代替我。)

④ Heaven never seals off all the exits.这是一个谚语,本义是"上天永远不会关闭所有的出口",意思是说"总能找到一条出路。"(There is always a way out.)

⑤ in low spirits 意思是"情绪低落",in high spirits 是"情绪高涨"。如:
They are in high spirits because they have won the competition. (他们情绪高涨,因为他们赢了比赛。)

Academic Paper and Thesis Defense
论文与答辩

Topic Introduction
话题导言

国内大学本科生的功课大多没有课程论文这样一种练习,高中生更是没有这方面的训练,所以中国学生因为缺少经验到了美国上大学开始会感到很难适应。因为在美国上大学本科或读研究生,写论文是家常便饭,研究生更是天天在研究和写论文中度过。

不论是学期论文(term-paper),研究论文(research paper),调查报告(investigation paper),还是文献报告(library paper),大概步骤和体例都是一致的。写文章要注意:一是题目范围一定要具体化,不能定得太大,以免不能详尽阐述。二是文章的论题、论据、论点都要好,要会消化吸收别人的思想和观点,切忌抄袭。引用别人的观点要注明出处,直接引用别人的话,要用引号。三是语言要实在,要用学术词汇,避免说假话、大话和空话。

教授布置论文之后,并不会置之不理,而是步步紧跟着学生的写作进度,发现问题及时指出。特别是学位论文,从论文选题、写作方案、研究方法、实地调查、文献使用、统计分析、文字润色等,都会有教授一步步的指导。

学位论文答辩是毕业的必经步骤,也是几年学习的全面总结,但场面却比较随便。论文答辩通常被称为论文答辩研讨会(Thesis/Dissertation Defense Seminar),整个过程持续约为两个小时。论文是否能通过,关键在于导师组的意见和对答辩会上问题的回答。

Academic Paper and Thesis Defense

Situational Dialogs 情景对话

从论文选题到确定题目,刘杭(Liu Hang)一直都游刃有余。但是最后的论文答辩,她难免有些紧张了。

Dialog 1

James: Have you chosen your topic for your thesis?
你的论文题目选好了没有?

Liu Hang: Not yet. I submitted three topics last week, but my major professor told me that only one of them could be researchable.
还没有,我上个星期交了三个题目,但我的导师告诉我其中只有一个具有可研究性。

James: You can use that one as your topic.
你就可以用那个做题目。

Liu Hang: But the professor said it was too wide, and I have to narrow it down.
但是教授又说题目太宽,我必须把它缩窄。

James: Just choose one aspect of it.
那就选其中的一个方面。

Liu Hang: He and I will list every aspect of the topic, and then we'll have a talk about it next week.
我和他将列出这个题目的每个方面,我们下个星期再讨论。

James: That's a good idea.
那是个不错的主意。

Dialog 2

Liu Hang: How are you getting along with your research paper[①]?
你论文写得怎么样了?

James: I've already finished the literature synthesis. How about yours?
我已经完成了文献综述。你呢?

Liu Hang:	I haven't done that much. I have just finished reading some reference books and journals the professor recommended. 我没有做那么多。我刚看完教授介绍的参考书和期刊。
James:	What's your topic? 你选的是什么题目？
Liu Hang:	Mine is "College Students' Drinking Habits in Seattle Area". 我的题目是"西雅图地区大学生的饮酒习惯"。
James:	That sounds interesting. 这题目挺有意思的。
Liu Hang:	I need somebody to help me with my questionnaire investigation. 我需要有人帮助我做问卷调查。
James:	It's necessary. Every one of us, Frank, Jim, Becky and Eric, can help you then. 有必要。到时候，我们每个人都可以帮助你，有福兰克、吉姆、贝基和埃里克。

Dialog 3

John:	I hear you have finished the final draft of your thesis, haven't you? 我听说你的毕业论文已经完成定稿,是吗？
Liu Hang:	Yeah, and next Monday is the day for the defense. 是的,下个星期一就该答辩了。
John:	You're a bit nervous about it, aren't you? 你有点紧张,是吗？
Liu Hang:	You bet② I am. Do you know what I'll have to do? 当然紧张。你知道怎么答辩吗？
John:	Well, usually three of your professors form a committee and they will ask you some questions about your thesis. Those who audit may ask you questions also. 通常由三个教授组成一个委员会，他们问你一些跟你的论文有关的问题。旁听的人也可以向你提问。
Liu Hang:	How long does the thesis defense seminar last? 论文答辩会要持续多长时间？

Academic Paper and Thesis Defense 24

论文与答辩

John: Around two hours. All the professors in your department may show up there.
大概两个小时。你们系的所有教授都可能会出席。

Liu Hang: Sounds terrible.
太可怕了。

John: Don't worry, and I believe you'll make it[3]!
别担心,我相信你会通过的。

1) I'd like to get an early start on my research paper.
我希望早点儿开始写论文。

2) What do you want to work on?
你打算写什么呢?

3) What's your topic?
你选的是什么题目?

4) Is there a standard format?
有没有标准的格式?

5) Have you chosen your topic for your thesis?
你的论文题目选好了没有?

6) I have trouble choosing a suitable topic of my thesis.
选一个合适的论文题目,我有些困难。

7) How are you getting along with your research paper?
你论文写得怎么样了?

8) I've already finished the literature synthesis.
我已经完成了文献综述。

9) I need somebody to help me with my questionnaire investigation.
我需要有人帮助我做问卷调查。

10) I hear you have finished the final draft of your thesis, haven't you?
我听说你的毕业论文已经完成定稿,是吗?

11) Next Monday is the day for the defense.

下个星期一就该答辩了。

12) How long does the thesis defense seminar last?

论文答辩会要持续多长时间？

学位论文的步骤：国内大学的硕士研究生到了第二年或第三年才开始做开题报告，就是说开始写作毕业论文了。博士研究生早一些，而本科生更是最后一个学期才着手毕业论文。美国大学以研究方式获得学位的研究生论文工作要经历几个阶段：

第一阶段：选题(Topic Selection)。第一个学期的前半段就要完成选题，教授通常要求学生先选择数个感兴趣的课题，然后经过比较从中挑一个最好的最可研究的(the most researchable)的题目。中国学生往往都有奖学金，要求和教授研究相同的课题，毕业论文题目就局限在教授研究的大课题中了。

第二阶段：文献综述(Literature Synthesis)。题目确定了，就要搞清楚以前的研究者在这个课题方面做了哪些研究、到了一个什么层次、还有哪些可以创新或拓展的等等，从理论、研究方法、已经得出的结论等方面写出一篇全面的文献综述。

第三阶段：研究方法(Research Methodologies)。在进行文献综述的同时，还要确定研究方法，包括现场测量、问卷调查、访问、实验等以及分析方法、分析工具、分析软件的应用。

第四阶段：研究方案(Research Proposal)。前述三个方面的工作完成了，要进行综合并形成一个比较完整的研究方案，这个方案一定要具有可操作性，即到了现场照着就可以做了。整个方案一般规定在第一学年结束前完成，提交给导师小组讨论通过后，才可以着手研究工作。

第五阶段：研究(Research and Investigation)。导师组通过了研究方案后，就可以开始研究工作了，这个过程需要教授的指导和同学们的协助。

Academic Paper and Thesis Defense

第六阶段：初稿写作(First Draft)。研究完毕，就要把研究结果做成论文的格式。但是，从确定题目到现在可能已经过了一年或更长时间，所以需要检索文献，看有没有新的研究成果出现。根据写作的需要，也可能要补充文献。

第七阶段：定稿(Final Draft)。初稿必须得到导师小组的通过，并根据所提出来的意见，进行修改润色，确定最终上交的稿子。导师小组成员在定稿上签字后，就可以参加答辩会了。

第八阶段：答辩(Defense)，答辩的程序和国内的差别不大，首先陈述观点和研究过程，尤其要说明创新在什么方面；然后接受提问，旁听的教授和学生都可以提问，按照提问当场解答；最后决定是否通过，提问完毕后，系学术委员成员闭门讨论并投票决定是否通过答辩，当支持方和反对方势均力敌时，由学术委员会主席决定是否通过。

注　释

① **get along with** 是"与某人相处,事情进展如何"等意思,如：
How have you been getting along with your term paper?（你的学期论文进行得怎么样了？）
The newly-come teacher is getting along well with her workmates.（新来的老师与她的同事们相处很好。）

② **you bet** 在这里是"当然"的意思,与 certainly/of course/sure 的意思相同。

③ **make it** 是口头说法,指"做成功什么事情"。

Trying to Win Scholarship
争取奖学金

Topic Introduction
话题导言

海外高昂的学费和生活费相对于中国普通家庭的收入来说,简直就是天文数字。因此,很多出国留学人员把希望寄托在奖学金(Scholarship)上。

获得奖学金有多方面的条件,一是要达到该大学对你学业成绩的要求,二是要有权威人士对你进行推荐,三是你在经济上确实需要帮助。所以,一定做好这么几件事:(1)留学前就努力学习,使你申请留学时的成绩单(Academic Transcripts)令人满意;(2)托福、GRE 或 GMAT 一定要考出高成绩;(3)自荐书(Statement of Purpose)和推荐信(Reference 或 Letter of Recommendation)一定要有力度,特别是要请权威教授签字;(4)明确表示你需要经济资助;(5)考虑清楚后尽早申请也是关键;(6)了解自己所报读的学校和专业是否有足够经济实力向你提供奖学金,这才是关键之处。

很多中国学生碍于面子,不好意思向系主任或教授提出有关奖学金的问题。其实错了,你不提钱的事,他们就会以为你很有钱,根本不需要资助。所以,和系主任或教授面谈或者打个电话,让他们深入了解你的具体情况很有必要。

Trying to Win Scholarship

Situational Dialogs
情景对话

李惠敏(Huimin)和杨佳欣(Jiaxin)希望能够申请奖学金,但首先需要问清楚奖学金的一些获得条件。

Dialog 1

Huimin: I'd like to apply for a scholarship.
我想申请奖学金。

Dean: Well, certainly. But how about your GPA[①]?
这个,当然可以。但你的平均成绩怎么样?

Huimin: I don't know how to evaluate my GPA, for we use 100-point system in China.
我不知道如何评估我的平均分数,因为中国用百分制。

Dean: That will mainly depend upon your GRE score or GMAT score.
那将主要取决于你的 GRE 或 GMAT 成绩。

Huimin: Could you tell me how much the scholarship is?
您能告诉我奖学金是多少吗?

Dean: The amounts vary.
数目各不相同。

Dialog 2

Jiaxin: Could I apply for a scholarship?
我能够申请得到奖学金吗?

Dean: I am afraid we have to consider your scholarship application next year.
恐怕我们下年度才能考虑你的奖学金申请。

Jiaxin: I wonder why you won't do it now.
我不知道你们现在为何不行。

Dean: The competition for scholarships is extremely sharp, so you could try next year. I cannot give you a positive answer about your scholarship application for the time being.
奖学金竞争非常激烈,你要等到明年再试着申请。关于你的奖学金申请,我目前还不能给你一个明确的答复。

Jiaxin: What to do next?
下一步我该怎么做。

Dean: I am sending you a scholarship application form.
我会寄一份奖学金申请表格给你。

Jiaxin: How much can I get if I'm successful?
如果申请成功,可以得到多少钱?

Dean: Our scholarship does not include travel expenses, it only covers the tuition and living here.
我们的奖学金不包括来回路费,仅包含学费和生活费用。

Dialog 3

Jiaxin: Good morning, sir. Have you received my scholarship application form?
早上好,先生。请问,您收到我的奖学金申请表没有?

Dean: Yes, it reached us this morning.
是的,我们今天早上收到。

Jiaxin: Great. Do you think I could get a scholarship?
好极了。您认为我能得到奖学金吗?

Dean: Sure. But the scholarship only covers the tuition and living here.
当然可以,但这个奖学金只包括学费和生活费。

Jiaxin: That's good enough. I think I can afford travel expenses and others myself.
那也不错了,我可以自己承担交通费用和其他开支。

Dean: You can get a student loan from the bank as well.
你也可以到银行去贷款。

Jiaxin: Thank you very much.
非常谢谢您。

Trying to Win Scholarship

Typical Sentences 典型句型

1) Could I apply for a scholarship?
   我能够申请得到奖学金吗？

2) Am I qualified for this scholarship?
   我有资格获得这种奖学金吗？

3) I am afraid we have to consider your scholarship application next year.
   恐怕我们下年度才能考虑你的奖学金申请。

4) The competition for scholarships is extremely sharp, so you could try next year.
   奖学金竞争非常激烈，你要等到明年再试着申请。

5) I cannot give you a positive answer about your scholarship application for the time being.
   关于你的奖学金申请，我目前还不能给你一个明确的答复。

6) I am sending you a scholarship application form.
   我寄一份奖学金申请表格给你。

7) Our scholarship does not include travel expenses, it only covers the tuition and living here.
   我们的奖学金不包括来回路费，仅包含学费和生活费用。

8) Your RA② will cover travel, living, etc.
   你的研究助理金包括路费、生活费用等。

9) He is among the few distinguished students who are offered full scholarships.
   他是少数享有全奖的学生。

10) You can renew your TA if you do well.
    如果你学业出色，可以延续教学助理金。

11) Stanford University gives me scholarship while I do my master's degree.
    斯坦福大学为我攻读硕士学位提供奖学金。

Background
背景知识

美国大学的奖、助学金：申请读本科课程的中国学生得到校方和其他机构的经济资助的可能性非常有限，一般校方只能给本科生免除部分或全部学费(Full or Partial Tuition Waiver)。研究生奖学金主要有以下几种：

(1) 全额奖学金(Fellowship)，包括学费、杂费、生活费，全年提供的奖学金为 1～3 万美元。

(2) 研究助理金(Research Assistantship)，没有教学义务，但要参与指导教授的研究，担任其助理。

(3) 教学助理金(Teaching Assistantship)，大约每周需要协助教授 10～20 小时，教授和辅导大学低年级的实习课程以及批改作业、查找教学资料等辅助教学工作。

(4) 免学费奖学金(Tuition Waiver)，有全部或部分减免学费两种，全免学费的叫做 Full Tuition Waiver，部分免除的名称很多，如免除州外费(Out-of-State Tuition Waiver)，免除三分之一学费(1/3 Tuition Waiver)，等等。

(5) 工读奖学金(Work Study)，就是要用工作来换学费和生活费，如兼职秘书、辅助研究等。

(6) 奖学金和补助金(Scholarship 和 Grant)，是根据学生的学业成绩和经济状况颁发的一种资助。

不管哪一种，最终都取决于学校的财力。由于"9·11"及近年美国的次贷危机导致美国经济滑坡，各学校的财政拨款和所获捐赠大为减少，获得奖学金的人数和数额也大为减少。

Trying to Win Scholarship

注　释

① GPA 为 Grade Point Average（平均成绩）的缩写。所谓"平均成绩"是指学生各种成绩乘以其学分加起来的平均数。
② RA 是 Research Assistantship 的缩写；TA 是 Teaching Assistantship 的缩写。人们平时交谈也直接读缩写。

Transferring to Another University
转学

Topic Introduction 话题导言

从理论上讲,转学就是重新申请一所学校,但对于中国学生的意义则不完全是这样。中国学生"进入美国"是一件艰难的事情,特别是签证的那三五分钟就决定了你能否到美国留学。到美国后再转学是很经常的事情,比起在国内申请学校要容易得多。

问题是:转入的学校是否会全部承认你在美国获得的学分,各学校的规定不尽相同。也有学校联盟对联盟内各学校的学分转移不设任何阻碍,对外部学校则持排斥态度。转学之前一定要弄清楚对方学校接受多少学分以及奖学金的问题。

Situational Dialogs 情景对话

因为拿不到奖学金和硕士学位,李惠敏(Huimin)决定转校。

Dialog 1

Huimin: I'm thinking of transferring to another school in spring.
我想春季转到别的学校去。

26 Transferring to Another University

转学

David: Why? Isn't the school good, or don't you like this quiet city?①
怎么了？这学校不好？还是，你不喜欢这个安静的城市？

Huimin: I like this university and the city is a very good place. But the Department of Education doesn't give me any scholarship. Besides, the Department doesn't offer a Master's Degree.
我喜欢这个大学，这个城市也是一个好地方。但是教育系没有给我任何奖学金，而且这个系也不能授予硕士学位。

David: That's really a problem. Which university do you prefer?
那还真是个问题，你喜欢哪个大学？

Huimin: I'd like to go to the University of Colorado at Boulder, but I hear it's very selective.
我想转到博尔德的科罗拉多大学，但听说很难进。

David: Your grades are very excellent. They'll accept you, I believe.
你的成绩很优秀，我相信他们会接受你的。

Huimin: Yeah, mostly A's and B's.
是啊，大部分都是 A 和 B。

David: So nothing is worrying you. Why not ask your professor to write a letter of recommendation?
这样你就不用担心什么了。为什么不要你的教授为你写封推荐信呢？

Dialog 2

Huimin: I'd like to transfer to the University of Colorado at Boulder. What procedures should I go through②?
我想转到博尔德的科罗拉多大学，要履行什么手续？

Professor: Do you have an I-20 issued by that university?
你有那个大学发的 I-20 表了吗？

Huimin: Yes, I do.
有的。

Professor: There are several things you have to do. First, fill in this form and give it back to me. Second, get a copy of your transcripts from the registrar. Third, attach a financial document to your application.
有几件事你必须做，第一，把这个表填好后交给我；第二，从注册处开一份成绩单；第三，在申请上附一份资金证明。

Huimin:	Is it very complicated?
	是不是很复杂？
Professor:	Just a bit. We can help you.
	有一点儿，我们会帮你的。

1) I'm thinking of transferring to another school in spring.
   我想春季转到别的学校去。

2) Which university do you prefer?
   你喜欢哪个大学？

3) I'd like to go to the University of Colorado at Boulder, but I hear it's very selective.
   我想转到博尔德的科罗拉多大学,但听说很难进。

4) The reason is that university decided to award me a full scholarship.
   理由是那个大学决定给我全额奖学金。

5) Why not ask your professor to write a letter of recommendation?
   为什么不要你的教授为你写封推荐信呢？

6) What procedures should I go through if I transfer?
   如果转学,要履行什么手续？

7) Do you have an I-20 issued by that university?
   你有那个大学发的I-20表了吗？

8) Would you please send these documents to INS?
   把这些文件寄到移民局,好吗？

Transferring to Another University

Background 背景知识

转学(Transferring to another university)：美国的大学生若提出正当理由，又符合另一大学的入学条件，可提出转学，这就叫做转学生(transfer students)。

转学只能在开学之初进入新学校就读，学期中途是不行的。若要申请插入秋季学期(fall admission)，一般在7月1日前提交转学申请；若要申请插入春季学期(spring admission)或夏季学期(summer admission)，则须至少在开学前30天提出。申请转学者要提交成绩单(Transcripts)、申请书等材料给招生办，由招生办人员及就学专业的系主任对转学生的学习成绩评估后做出是否接纳的决定。

在美国，从一个语言学校转入其他语言学校或四年制大学，或者一般同等级的转学，均由最初学校向移民局申报。"9·11"之前，外国学生只要到第一个学校(即签证上注明的学校)报到了，就可以立即提出转到别的学校。但"9·11"之后，外国赴美留学生必须在第一个学校就读至少一个学期才能转学。

同等教育机构间的转学(same educational level transfer)，要把学生签名的I-20表交给最初入学的学校认可，签字以后由该学校将该表送至移民局，学生转入新学校后的30天内，新学校必须在I-20表上签字，认定该生已经转入新学校。

不同等级教育机构间的转学(different educational level transfer)，学生将签名的I-20表交给最初入学学校认定，并委托该校为他制定延长居留期和转学的申请书。最初入学的学校或学生本人再将入学许可表(I-20表)、延长居留并转学的表格以及学生的学生证、新学校要求的手续费、足够负担一年费用的经济证明交移民局。

对于不改变居留身份的转学生，移民局的审批往往不是什么大问题，但如果改学所谓的"敏感专业"，就要三思而后行了。

① 这样的反问句其实表达的是肯定的意义,说话人认为"这个大学很好,这个安静的城市也很好",对别人要离开感到不理解。

② go through 在这里的意思"参加某事,履行某事",如:
Certain formalities have to be gone through before one can emigrate.
(必须办妥某些手续方可移居他国。)

Changing Major
转专业

Topic Introduction
话题导言

多数美国大学对转专业非常开明，一旦你被某个专业录取，就等于你被这个大学的每个专业录取。新生换专业只需要和新旧两个专业的学业顾问(Academic Advisor)当面谈一谈，填写一张简单的表格就可以了。因为是累进学分制，即使你读到三年级时突然觉得不喜欢这个专业，还可以换专业，以前的学分大部分仍然可以算数，只需要按照新专业的规定修完课程和学分就可以了。研究生也很灵活，主要取决于新专业的系主任，如果愿意要你，即使你不符合入学规定的条件，也没有关系。例如：A专业要求GRE，B专业不要求，而你没有考GRE被B专业录取是没有问题的，但录取之后你却想读A专业，报到之后两周内和A专业的系主任面谈，提出要求并说明原因，成功的可能性是很大的。也有很多人利用这一点达到自己的目的。

Situational Dialogs
情景对话

李莎莎 (Shasha) 想从英语文学专业转到商学专业，跟同学Jack 和 Eric 讨论了，又去找系主任 Dr. Johnson。

Dialog 1

Shasha: I didn't know much about this major. Only since I got here have I found that I'm not interested in it.①
我对这个专业不太了解，我到了这里才发现我对它不感兴趣。

Jack: So what?
那怎么办？

Shasha: I'm wondering if I could change a major or not.
我在想我是否能换一个专业。

Jack: It's very easy, I think. Why not talk to the academic advisor?
我认为很简单，怎么不跟学业顾问谈一谈呢？

Shasha: I'm afraid they'll have a bad impression of me.
我恐怕他们会对我有坏印象。

Jack: No, never. Just tell them what you are thinking and feeling about the major, open-mindedly and frankly.
不会，根本不会，把你对这个专业的想法和感觉告诉他们，开诚布公地，坦率地告诉他们。

Shasha: Do you think it's good to do that?
你觉得那样做好吗？

Jack: I do. You should make them understand your trouble, and they will consider your requests.
我是这样认为的。你应该让他们了解你的困难，他们会考虑你的要求的。

Shasha: I'll have a crack at it.②
我会试试看。

Dialog 2

Shasha: I hear you transferred your major when you first came.
我听说你刚来就转了专业。

Eric: I did.
是的。

Shasha: The English literature is boring. I want to study business.
英语文学让人乏味，我想学商业。

Changing Major 27

Eric: You are talking my language!③
你和我想的一样。

Shasha: But I don't know how to transfer from English literature to business. Could you tell me how?
但我不知道如何从英语文学转到商学。你能告诉我怎么办吗？

Eric: Just talk to your academic advisor. I can go with you.
只是跟学业顾问谈谈，我可以跟你一同去。

Shasha: Sorry for getting in your hair④.
对不起给你添麻烦了。

Dialog 3

Dr. Johnson: Why the long face⑤?
怎么愁眉苦脸？

Shasha: I am wondering if the English literature is my favorite or not. So could you do me a favor?
我在想英语文学是否是我最喜欢的，您能给我帮个忙吗？

Dr. Johnson: What? You are talking over my head.⑥
什么？我听不懂你的话。

Shasha: To be frank, I'd like to transfer to the Department of Business and Accounting.
坦白地说，我想转到商业与会计系去。

Dr. Johnson: Oh, I see. You want to change your major. Please go to the Department of Business and Accounting to see if they'll accept you or not. If you persuade them, come back to me.
哦，我知道了。你想换专业，请去商业与会计系，看他们是否接受你，如果你能说服他们，再到我这里来。

Shasha: I will. Thank you so much.
我会去的，非常感谢。

Typical Sentences
典型句型

1) I didn't know much about this major.
   我对这个专业不太了解。
2) I'm wondering if I could change a major or not.
   我在想我是否能换一个专业。
3) I cannot find a job if I study mass media.
   如果我学大众传媒,我会找不到工作的。
4) Just tell them what you are thinking and feeling about the major, open-mindedly and frankly.
   把你对这个专业的想法和感觉告诉他们,开诚布公地,坦率地告诉他们。
5) I hear you transferred your major when you first came.
   我听说你刚来就转了专业。
6) The English literature is boring. I want to study business.
   英语文学让人乏味,我想学商业。
7) Is my scholarship going with me if I change my major?
   如果我换个专业,奖学金是否跟我走?
8) I'd like to transfer to the Department of Business and Accounting.
   我想转到商业与会计系去。
9) Do I have to fill any application for changing major?
   转专业要填写申请表吗?

Background
背景知识

专业名称:美国大学的有些专业名称看起来和国内大学的很相似,但其实不是一码事,要认真研究课程设置,尤其是核心课程(core courses)和专业选修课。下面列举出某大学的专业名称,以作

Changing Major 转专业

为了解。

Adult Education 成人教育	Law and Justice 法律与司法
Anthropology 人类学	Literature 文学
Applied Anthropology 应用人类学	Materials Engineering 材料科学
Applied Sociology 应用社会学	Mathematics 数学
Art History 艺术史	Mathematics Education 数学教育
Arts Management 艺术管理	News Media Studies 新闻传媒研究
Biology 生物学	Organization Development 组织发展
Broadcast 播音	Painting 美术
Chemistry 化学	Philosophy 哲学
Computer Science 计算机科学	Physics 物理学
Creative Writing 创作	Political Science 政治学
Dance 舞蹈	Print 印刷
Development Banking 银行开发	Printmaking 版画复制技术
Economics 经济学	Psychology 心理学
Education 教育学	Public Administration 公共管理
Educational Leadership 教育管理	Public Communication 公共交通
Electrical Engineering 电子工程	Public Policy 公共政策
Elementary Education 初等教育	Radio and Television 广播电视
English 英语	Russian Studies 俄罗斯研究
Environmental Science 环境科学	Sculpture 雕塑
Financial Economics 财政经济学	Secondary Education 中等教育
French Studies 法语研究	Sociology 社会学
General Psychology 普通心理学	Sociology: Justice 社会学:司法
Genetics 遗传学	Spanish 西班牙语
Health Fitness Management 健身管理	Special Education 特殊教育
History 历史学	Specialized Studies 专门研究
Information Systems 信息系统	Statistics 统计学
International Training 国际培训	TESOL 英语作为第二语言的教学
Justice 司法	Toxicology 毒物学
Latin American Studies 拉丁美洲研究	
Film and Electronic Media 电影与电子媒体	
Human Resource Management 人力资源管理	
Justice, Law and Society 司法、法律与社会	
Philosophy and Social Policy 哲学与社会政策	

Producing for Film and Video 影视制作
Resource Recreation and Tourism 资源消遣与旅游
Statistics for Policy Analysis 政策分析统计

注 释

① 这是一个倒装句,由于时间状语 since I got here 前用了 only 这个词,主句的主谓语部分倒装成了 have I ...,还如:
Only yesterday did he finish the task. (他昨天才完成那件工作。)

② I'll have a crack at it. 的意思是"我会试试看",同样的表达方法还有:
I'll have a try at it. (我试一试吧。)
I'll try. (我试一试吧。)
I'll make a try. (我试一试吧。)
I'll take a shot at it. (我试一试吧。)
I'll give it a shot. (我试一试吧。)

③ You are talking my language! 的本义是"你在说我的语言",这里指"你的想法和我一样",这样的表达在英语中很多:
We are talking the same language. (我们很谈得来。)
Now you're talking. (现在我们谈得来了。)
We are on the same wavelength. (我们想的一致。)
We're in the sync with each other. (我们很合得来。)

④ get in one's hair 的意思是"使某人困扰,纠缠某人";还可以说 get in one's face (不断纠缠某人),get on one's nerves (令某人心烦),get under one's skin (使某人生气)等。与这些短语意思相反的则可以说 get out of one's hair (不再给别人添麻烦)或 get out of one's face (不再打扰别人)。

⑤ long face 说的是"愁眉苦脸",表示情绪低落。还有:
You look down. (你看来心情不好。)
Why so blue? (为什么这么忧郁呢?)
Why so down? (怎么愁眉苦脸?)

⑥ "You are talking over my head."的意思是"我听不懂你在说什么",就等于"I don't understand."或"I can't follow you."的意思,类似的表达法还有:

You've lost me.(我不懂你的话。)

I don't know what you are talking about.(我不懂你在说什么。)

It's beyond me.(我理解不了。)

I'm not following you.(我听不明白。)

Sports Activities
体育活动

Topic Introduction
话题导言

英语有一句谚语"All work and no play makes Jack a dull boy."(只学习不玩耍,聪明的孩子也变傻。)美国人从小就培养成了一种"终生锻炼(life-long exercise)"的观念,从小学、到中学、到大学都把体育运动贯穿在整个教育过程中。

美国的大学生非常热爱体育运动,学校也具有比较好的运动条件。几乎每个大学都有一个或数个运动中心,运动设施先进齐全。只需要出示学生证就可以了,因为费用在开学交学费时就有一项是活动费(Activity Fee)。此外更有很多户外运动设施,如网球场、足球场等可以随意免费使用。中国留学生平时的学习抓得很紧,加上多数在学校打工,运动时间相对较少。

Situational Dialogs
情景对话

生命在于运动。李莎莎(Shasha)转了专业,心情也好了,也很注重锻炼了,于是她与同学 Tony 兴致勃勃地攀谈起来。

Sports Activities 28

Dialog 1

Shasha: You look strong and are always in high spirits①.
你看上去非常壮实,总是情绪很高。

Tony: A sound mind dwells in a sound body.
健康的精神来自健康的身体。

Shasha: I agree. We cannot study all the time if we want to maintain good health.
我同意。如果要保持良好的身体,我们就不能单单地学习。

Tony: I have always tried my best to keep fit for both my study and work.
为了学习和工作我一直努力健身。

Shasha: Can you give me some tips as to how to keep fit?
关于健身你能给我一些指点吗?

Tony: I think everyone has his own way of relaxing. The best way to keep fit is to go in for sports.
我认为每个人都有自己的放松方式,健身的最佳途径是去运动。

Shasha: For my age, do you think which kind of sports suits me?
对于我这个年纪,你认为哪种体育运动适合我?

Tony: I feel jogging is perhaps a good one.
我觉得慢跑可以是一个好的运动方式。

Shasha: I think so, too.
我也这样认为。

Dialog 2

Tony: Would you like to have a swimming bath?
你想游泳吗?

Shasha: Yes, but I'm only a beginner. How deep is the water?
是啊,但我不大会游。水有多深?

Tony: The depth of the swimming pool is one meter to 2.5 meters. You may swim in the shallow area.
游泳池的深度在1～2.5米之间。你可以在浅水区游。

Shasha: OK, is the water clean? Do they often change water?
好的,水干净吗? 他们经常换水吗?

Tony:	Please set your heart at rest.② They change the water of the indoor swimming pool every other day. 请你放心吧。他们每隔一天给室内游泳池换一次水。
Shasha:	What is the water temperature? 水温是多少？
Tony:	The temperature in the pool today is about 68 degrees Fahrenheit. It is a heated swimming pool. I mean you can have a swim here even in winter. 今天游泳池的水温大约是华氏68度。这是一个温水游泳池。我的意思是你甚至在冬天也能在这里游泳。
Shasha:	Thanks for your explanation. 多谢你的解释。
Tony:	There are separate locker rooms over there. If you feel tired, you can relax with soft drinks and some pastry at the poolside bar. 那里有单独的更衣室。如果你觉得累了，你可以在池边酒吧放松一下，喝点饮料，吃点糕点。
Shasha:	Okay, see you. 好的，再见。

典型句型

1) Let's go to the sports center. What would you like to play?
   我们到运动中心去吧。喜欢玩什么？
2) You can also play badminton here.
   在这里你也可以打羽毛球。
3) Doing aerobics for an hour is a lot different from lifting weights.
   做一小时有氧操与举重大不一样。
4) Lifting weights will build muscles.
   举重会增长肌肉。

Sports Activities 28

5) The bar bell is too heavy for you. Try the dumb bell.
   杠铃对你来说太重,试试哑铃吧!

6) The depth of the swimming pool is one meter to 2.5 meters.
   游泳池的深度在1~2.5米之间。

7) There are separate locker rooms over there.
   那里有单独的更衣室。

8) It is a heated swimming pool.
   这是一个温水游泳池。

9) I mean you can have a swim here even in winter.
   我的意思是你甚至在冬天也能在这里游泳。

10) We have a nine-hole golf course.
    我们有一个九洞高尔夫球场。

11) Could you tell me when it opens?
    告诉我什么时候开放吗?

背景知识

有关运动的英语单词:

football / soccer 足球	broad / long jump 跳远
volleyball 排球	skiing 滑雪
basketball 篮球	skating 滑冰
tennis 网球	figure-skating 花样滑冰
swimming 游泳	ice hockey 冰上曲棍球
diving 跳水	golf 高尔夫球
surfing 冲浪	American football / rugby 橄榄球
rowing 赛艇	baseball 棒球
shooting 射击	badminton 羽毛球
horse race 赛马	table tennis 乒乓球
hunting 打猎	dash / sprint 短跑
mountaineering 登山	cross-country running 越野跑
boxing 拳击	Olympic Games 奥运会

wrestling 摔跤　　　　　　　world cup 世界杯
high jump 跳高　　　　　　championship 冠军

注 释

① **in high spirits** 的意思是"情绪高涨"，**in low spirits** 是"情绪低落"。
② **set your heart at rest** 的字面意思是"把你的心脏放在休息状态"，意思是"别紧张，请放心"。

Festivals and Holidays
节日假期

Topic Introduction 话题导言

算起来,美国大学的假期实际上很长,如果夏季短学期(Summer Session)不上课,那么,一年上课的时间春季是从1月中旬到5月中旬,秋季是从8月下旬到圣诞节前,再扣除复活节和感恩节的两周假期,全年的上课时间加起来最多只有32周。美国很多全国性的节日也放假一天,并多被安排在星期一,这时的周末就有三天时间了。

假期是美国人朋友聚会和家人团聚的日子,而很多中国留学生会选择继续学习功课,完成像论文这样比较大的作业。因此,看到别人快快乐乐地度假去了,留学生们的心里多少感到有些异样,或孤独,或悲哀,或思念亲人,或……现在的留学生越来越年轻,又都是独生子女,节假日期间哭鼻子的大有人在。哎,毕竟,独在异乡为异客嘛。

Situational Dialogs 情景对话

假期是家人团聚,或者外出旅游的好时候。可留学生们有不同的打算,杨佳欣(Jiaxin)只能呆在学校,忙于她的论文。

Dialog 1

Shasha: The summer vacation is coming soon. Where do you plan to go for your vacation?
暑假很快就要来临,你假期准备到哪里?

Tony: I'm thinking of going to Hawaii with my wife. What about you?
我想同妻子去夏威夷。你有什么想法?

Shasha: I have a lot of things to do during the summer. Perhaps I'll stay home.
夏天我有许多事情要做,也许我就呆在家里。

Tony: It's a pity. As for me, vacation is no vacation without sea.
太可惜了。对于我来说,没有大海的假期就不算是假期了。

Shasha: I wish you a happy journey.
我祝你玩得愉快。

Dialog 2

Tony: Where are you planning to spend your Easter holidays?
复活节假期你计划到哪里去?

Jiaxin: I'm just staying on-campus.
我就呆在学校。

Tony: It's a pity. Will you join us in some activities?
真可惜,愿意参加我们的一些活动吗?

Jiaxin: I'd like to, but I'll be busy writing[①] my thesis and we Chinese students will also have a get-together.
我想参加,但我要忙于写论文,我们中国学生也有一个聚会。

Tony: Cool! Wish you a happy holiday!
好酷! 祝你假日愉快!

Jiaxin: You too.
你也一样。

Dialog 3

Ligang: Did you have a good time on your vacation?
你假期过得愉快吗?

Festivals and Holidays

Mary:	Yes, and I bet you had a wonderful time, too. 愉快,而且我敢打赌,你也一定玩得非常开心。
Ligang:	That's right. We went camping one day, which made my daughter very excited②. 对了,我们有一天去野外宿营,把我女儿激动坏了。
Mary:	That's a good experience for her. But can you guess where we've been to? 那对她来说是一个很好的经历。但是,你能猜猜我们去哪儿了吗?
Ligang:	I can't imagine. 我想不出来。
Mary:	We've been to China, your motherland. 我们去了你的祖国,中国。
Ligang:	Really? What places have you been to? 真的吗?你们去了哪些地方?
Mary:	Of course. We went to Hong Kong, Shenzhen, Guangzhou, Xi'an, Beijing and Shanghai. I remember your hometown is Xi'an, am I right? 当然,我们去了香港、深圳、广州、西安、北京和上海。我记得你的家乡就是西安,对吗?
Ligang:	Yes, Xi'an is my hometown. That's really a big trip. What is your impression? 是的,西安是我老家。你们真是玩了一大圈。印象如何?
Mary:	That's a great country with long civilizations and brilliant cultures. 那真是一个拥有古老文明和灿烂文化的伟大国度。
Ligang:	Next time I could be your guide if you like. 如果你愿意,下一次我可以给你做导游。

Typical Sentences
典型句型

1) I have to show my wife and daughter around in August.
   8月我得带我妻子和女儿到处走走。
2) Where do you plan to go for your vacation?
   你假期准备到哪里？
3) Perhaps I'll stay on-campus to polish up my thesis.
   也许我就呆在学校修改我的论文。
4) I'm dreaming about going home, but it's too far away.
   我做梦都想回家，但太远了。
5) I will make use of these nine days during Thanksgiving.
   我要好好利用感恩节期间的这9天时间。
6) I have a lot of things to take care of during summer.
   夏天我有许多事情要做。
7) I am thinking of going to Hawaii with my wife.
   我想同妻子去夏威夷。
8) We plan to climb the mountains, go fishing and swimming.
   我们计划去爬山、钓鱼和游泳。
9) As for me, vacation is no vacation without sea.
   对于我来说，没有大海的假期就不算是假期了。
10) I'd like to go around the United States by Greyhound.
    我要乘坐灰狗巴士周游美国。
11) Did you have a good time on your vacation?
    你假期过得愉快吗？
12) Did you go to the Central Park in New York?
    你去了纽约的中央公园了吗？
13) I bet you had a wonderful time.
    我敢打赌，你一定玩得非常开心。

Festivals and Holidays

背景知识

美国的节日：美国的节日名堂繁多，尤以圣诞节(Christmas Day)、复活节(Easter Day)、感恩节(Thanksgiving Day)最为隆重。

元旦(New Year's Day)，1月1日庆祝新的一年的开始。人们举办各种各样的新年晚会，到处可以听到"辞旧迎新"的钟声，为美国的联邦假日。

林肯诞辰纪念日(Abraham Lincoln's Birthday)，2月12日，庆祝林肯诞辰，为大多数州的节日。

圣瓦伦丁节(St. Valentine's Day)，2月14日，是公元3世纪殉教的瓦伦丁的逝世纪念日。情人们在这一天互赠礼物或贺卡，故又称作"情人节"。

华盛顿诞辰纪念日(George Washington's Birthday)，2月22日，庆祝华盛顿诞辰，为美国的联邦假日。

复活节(Easter Day, Easter Sunday)，一般在春分后月圆第一个星期天。该节是庆祝基督(Jesus Christ)的复活，过节时人们吃复活节彩蛋(Easter eggs)，为美国的联邦假日。

圣帕特里克节(St. Patrick's Day)，3月17日，是悼念爱尔兰的守护神圣帕特里克的节日。

愚人节(April Fool's Day)，4月1日，该节日出自于庆祝"春分点"的来临。在4月1日受到恶作剧愚弄的人称为"四月愚人(April Fools)"。

母亲节(Mother's Day)：5月份的第2个星期日，政府部门和各家门口悬挂国旗，表示对母亲的尊敬。在家里，儿女们和父亲给母亲买些礼物或做些家务。

阵亡将士纪念日(Memorial Day)，5月份的最后一个星期一，纪念为美国献身的阵亡烈士，为美国的联邦假日。

国旗日(National Flag Day)，6月14日，庆祝国旗的升起。

父亲节(Father's Day)，6月份的第3个星期天，表示对父亲的尊敬。在家里，儿女们和母亲给父亲买些礼物。

独立日(Independence Day)，7月4日，庆祝美国建国，为美国的联邦假日。

劳动节(Labor Day),9月份的第1个星期一,表示对劳工的敬意,为美国的联邦假日。

哥伦布日(Columbus Day),10月12日,纪念哥伦布在北美登陆,为美国的联邦假日。

万圣节前夜(Halloween; Eve of All Saint's Day),10月31日,孩子们多化装成鬼,打着灯笼或点燃篝火尽情地玩耍。

万灵节(All Soul's Day),11月2日,祭悼所有死者灵魂之日。

大选日 (Election Day),11月的第1个星期一后的星期二,选举美国总统。

退伍军人节(Veterans' Day),11月11日,表示对退伍军人的敬意。

感恩节(Thanksgiving Day),11月的最后一个星期四,感谢上帝所赐予的秋收,为美国的联邦假日。

清教徒登陆纪念日(Forefather's Day),12月21日,纪念清教徒在美洲登陆。

圣诞节(Christmas Day),12月25日,基督徒庆祝耶稣基督诞生的日子,是美国最隆重的节日。

注释

① be busy doing 的意思是 "忙于做什么事情", 也可以是 be busy with something, 如:
The students are busy preparing for their final tests. (学生们正忙于准备期末考试。)
也可以说:
The students are busy with their final tests. (学生们忙于期末考试。)

② 有些单词的形容词表达形式有两种,例如 excited 和 exciting 都可以表示"激动的,兴奋的",但通常情况下,-ed 形容词用来修饰人,如:
The excited children forgot to take the present to the party. (孩子们兴奋地忘了把礼物带到聚会上。)
-ing 形容词用来修饰物,如: an exciting story (一个令人激动的故事)。

Recreational Activities
娱乐活动

Topic Introduction
话题导言

  传统的清教主义思想对娱乐持冷淡甚至否定的态度,但现代西方人,尤其是消费社会的美国人,已把他们先祖的教诲置之脑后,视娱乐为生活的一部分。在他们看来,娱乐是一种放松,一种解脱,一种消遣,一种调剂。它非但不与工作相抵触,反而有助于工作效率的提高。因此,美国人有"拼命工作,尽情玩耍(work hard and play hard)"一说。事实上,在各种娱乐场合,人与人之间最易增进感情、加深关系、促进交往。在英语国家,人们在紧张的工作之余,总是争取大量的空闲时间来休闲、娱乐。

  首先,从语言表达方面来看,英语国家的人说去玩是"Let's enjoy ourselves."而不说"Let's play."其次,从方式上来说,西方人娱乐的方式很多,有消遣性的活动,也有需要消耗体力方面的活动,还有精神享受方面的活动。娱乐场所多种多样,在校园、在公司、在舞厅、在各种俱乐部、在室内大型体育场、在公园的露天草坪,都能听到风格各异、形式多样的流行音乐;在大型的娱乐中心和夜总会,人们可以看到精彩的舞蹈。对于西方人来讲,娱乐和消遣的最好方式就是舞会之类的活动了,尤其是在美国,当年轻人聚在一起时,一般都可能安排有舞会,特别是现在的年轻人,娱乐的花样翻新,并且很多都和运动结合起来。

Situational Dialogs
情景对话

平时学习生活太过紧张,杨洋(Yang Yang)他们休闲的时候会去听听音乐会或看看电影,放松一下自己。

Dialog 1

Linda: There is an open-air concert in the East City Park this evening. Will you go?
今天晚上在东城公园有一场露天音乐会,你去吗?

Yang Yang: That sounds novel[①]. What time will it begin?
听起来很新鲜,几点钟开始?

Linda: Six thirty, I guess.
我想是6点30分。

Yang Yang: Will you go, then?
那么,你去吗?

Linda: Yes, sure. Two famous local singers will perform and their band is excellent also.
去,当然去。两位当地著名的歌唱家将登台献艺,而且他们的乐队也很棒。

Yang Yang: If so[②], I will go with you.
要是这样,我将和你一起去。

Dialog 2

Yang Yang: Well, what did you think of the show?
呃,你认为今天的表演怎么样?

Linda: The show is wonderful, and I like it very much.
精彩,我非常喜欢。

Yang Yang: The actresses are very talented. This is the first time I have ever seen such a wonderful play.
演员们都很有才能,这是我第一次看到这么精彩的演出。

Recreational Activities

娱乐活动

Linda:	The orchestra is a good one as well. I'm willing to see it again. 乐队也不错,我愿意再看一遍。
Yang Yang:	The key is they have been assorting with each other very excellently. They are so beautiful and attractive. 关键是他们相互配合得很好。演员们又漂亮又有吸引力。
Linda:	I agree. 我同意你说的。

Dialog 3

Yang Yang:	Do you often come to the cinema? 你经常来这个电影院吗?
Linda:	Yes, we are here every Friday night. But sometimes they don't have very good movies. 是的,我们每周五晚上都来。但有时他们没有什么好片子看。
Yang Yang:	What kind of movie do you like best? 你最喜欢哪一类电影?
Linda:	To me, I like action films. Jackie Chan is great. 对我来说,我喜欢动作影片。成龙很了不起。
Yang Yang:	Chinese martial arts attract many people to visit China, and Jackie Chan is the most famous movie star performing martial arts. We Chinese people like him very much also. 中国功夫吸引了很多人访问中国,而成龙是表演中国功夫最著名的电影明星。我们中国人也都很喜欢他。
Linda:	Ah, the movie is beginning. The music is striking. 啊,电影就要开始了,这音乐很吸引人。
Yang Yang:	Yes. Let's watch. 是的,我们观看吧。

Typical Sentences
典型句型

1) What's up for tonight?
今晚有什么活动?

2) There is an open-air concert in the East City Park this evening.
   今天晚上在东城公园有一场露天音乐会。
3) Will you go to the concert this evening?
   你今晚去听音乐会吗?
4) Two famous local singers will perform and their band is excellent also.
   两位当地著名的歌唱家将登台献艺,而且他们的乐队也很棒。
5) Well, what did you think of the show?
   呃,你认为今天的表演则怎么样?
6) This is the first time I have ever seen such a wonderful play.
   这是我第一次看到这么精彩的演出。
7) The key is they have been assorting with each other very excellently.
   关键是他们相互配合得很好。
8) There is a dancing party Saturday night.
   星期六晚上有舞会。
9) Do you often come to the cinema?
   你经常来这个电影院吗?
10) What kind of movie do you like best?
    你最喜欢哪一类电影?
11) Jackie Chan is the most famous movie star performing martial arts.
    成龙是表演中国功夫最著名的电影明星。
12) International students often host parties when they celebrate their holidays and festivals.
    国际学生庆祝他们节日的时候经常举办晚会。

Background 背景知识

美国人的文化价值观念(一):对一个民族的价值观念,我们可以有多个方面(政治、法律、道德、教育、社会、文化等等)的概括。说到美国人的文化价值观念,最基本面包括下面几个方面:

Recreational Activities

娱乐活动

(1) 认真工作。美国人认为,工作是人们必须严肃对待的事情,不仅是人们谋生的手段,而且是人生在世必须履行的"天职"。美国人在评判一个人时,首先关注的就是一个人的工作态度和工作成就。一个人的工作成就越大,这个人的价值也就越高。

(2) 尽情娱乐。美国人对游手好闲者极其鄙视,但并不排斥娱乐本身。在他们看来,娱乐是一种放松,一种解脱,一种消遣,一种调剂。美国人有"拼命工作,尽情玩耍 (work hard and play hard)"一说。

(3) 勤奋努力。美国人具有"做点事情比闲着要强一百倍"和"勤奋努力会给人带来成功"的观念。他们遇到困难总是自己努力去克服,而不是等待他人来救助;他们认为,只要努力,就会成功,自己掌握着自己的命运。

(4) 乐观豁达。美国人对未来充满自信与憧憬,从不留恋过去,总是矢志不移地创造"明天",也从不担心未来有什么不测。

(5) 珍惜时间。美国人认为,时间是一个只朝一个方向不停地流动的东西,人们可以追忆过去,但绝不能把流逝的时间追回来。基于此,他们对时间非常珍惜,不肯轻易地浪费一分一秒,力争在有限的时间内取得最理想的成就。

(6) 金钱至上。美国的私有制经济决定了雇主与雇员之间的金钱关系。占有金钱的多少成了衡量一个人的社会地位、个人价值的主要参照系数,人们为获取更多的金钱而奋斗。

注释

① novel 在这里是形容词"新鲜的"。它还有另外的意思,作名词用是"小说"的意思。

② 这里的 so 指代的是前面 "Two famous local singers will perform and their band is excellent also." 整个句子。so 可以和从属连词 if 搭配,构成无动词的条件从句。如:
The rumor may be true; if so (=if the rumor is true), he will be indicated for treason. (谣言可能是真的,如果属实,他将要被指控为谋反。)

Chinese Spring Festival
中国春节

Topic Introduction
话题导言

春节是中华民族的传统节日,在海外留学的中国学生同样把这个节日当成最隆重的盛会。春节来临,各驻外使、领馆的教育官员纷纷到各大学去和留学生们欢度春节,带去慰问金和国内最新的影片,也带去了祖国的问候。各大学的中国学生会(Chinese Students and Scholars Association)在除夕之夜要举办一场晚会,形式多种多样,留学生们自编自演歌曲、舞蹈、猜谜、武术、小品等娱乐节目,也准备了丰富的除夕晚餐,还邀请了美国同学和老师以及各国的留学生参加这一盛会。会场悬挂着中国国旗,播放着中国音乐,气氛热烈。很多学校把这个晚会办成一个华人大团结的聚会,其他国家和地区的华人学生也欣然而至。

Situational Dialogs
情景对话

春节来临,中国留学生们将在除夕之夜举行晚会,热情的杨佳欣(Jiaxin)邀请热爱中国的外国朋友埃里克(Eric)一起来参加。

Chinese Spring Festival 31

Dialog 1

Jiaxin: Next Monday is the Chinese Spring Festival. We Chinese[①] here will have a party. Will you join us?
下个星期一是中国春节,我们中国人要办一个晚会,你愿意参加吗?

Eric: Yes, I will. Many people there?
我愿意,很多人吗?

Jiaxin: Very many. All the Chinese students, including from Taiwan and Hong Kong, professors and staff members of Chinese origin will come to the party.
非常多,所有的中国学生,包括从台湾和香港来的,华裔教授和职员都会参加这个晚会。

Eric: That's a great chance for me to know something about Chinese culture.
那对我了解中国文化是一个很好的机会。

Jiaxin: Yes, the party is full of singing, dancing, martial arts and other recreational performances.
是啊,晚会有很多唱歌、舞蹈、武术和其他娱乐节目。

Eric: Oh, I can't wait. When and where?
哦,我等不及了。什么时间,什么地方?

Jiaxin: Next Monday evening, 6:30 at the Gold and Silver Room of the Students Union Building.
下个星期一晚 6:30 在学生活动大楼的金银屋。

Eric: Okay, I will be there on time.
好的,我会准时到那儿的。

Dialog 2

Jiaxin: We've prepared some traditional Chinese food for today's party. Would you please help yourself?
我们为晚会准备了一些传统的中国食品,请随便吃吧。

Eric: I didn't know it was a potluck party[②]. I'm sorry I didn't bring food here.
我不知道是自带食品晚会,不好意思我没带东西来。

Jiaxin: You're our guest. You don't need to bring anything. Okay, let's get something to eat, shall we?
你是我们的客人,不必带食品来。那么,我们去弄点吃的东西吧,好吗?

Eric: All right. So many kinds! They must be delicious, I guess.
好的,这么多种类!我想一定很好吃。

Jiaxin: I hope you like them.
希望你喜欢。

Dialog 3

Jiaxin: You stayed in China for one year. Can you sing a Chinese song?
你在中国呆过一年,你会唱中国歌曲吗?

Eric: I used to sing some, but I forgot the words. I think I can have a try.
我以前会,但忘记歌词了。我想试一试吧。

Jiaxin: Yes. Which song would you like to sing?
好的,你要唱哪支歌呢?

Eric: Let's keep it a secret, and you'll know when I begin.
我们先保密吧,我一开始你就知道了。

…………

Jiaxin: What an outstanding singer you are!
你真是一个杰出的歌唱家!

Eric: Thank you. I think I can guess a riddle.
谢谢,我想我能猜一个谜语。

Jiaxin: You'll get a reward if you guess right.
猜对了,你将得到奖品。

Typical Sentences
典型句型

1) Spring Festival is also called the Lunar New Year's Day.
春节也叫做阴历新年。

2) I hear the Chinese New Year is the most important.
我听说中国新年是最重要的。

Chinese Spring Festival 31

中国春节

3) Next Monday is the Chinese Spring Festival.
下个星期一是中国春节。

4) We Chinese here will have a party. Will you join us?
我们中国人要办一个晚会,你愿意参加吗?

5) The party is full of singing, dancing, martial arts and other recreational performances.
晚会有很多唱歌、舞蹈、武术和其他娱乐节目。

6) We've prepared some traditional Chinese food for today's party.
我们为晚会准备了一些传统的中国食品。

7) Which song would you like to sing?
你要唱哪支歌呢?

8) You'll get a reward if you guess right.
猜对了,你将得到奖品。

9) Spring Festival also means the family reunion.
春节也意味着全家团圆。

10) On New Year's Eve we have the Family Reunion Dinner.
除夕,我们都吃团圆饭。

11) Please help yourself. Let's drink for the coming New Year!
请随便吃。让我们为新的一年干杯!

背景知识

中国春节:在这样具有传统中国特色的聚会活动中,应邀参加的美国同学或老师都是对中国文化比较感兴趣的美国人,很可能会问及春节的习俗和主要活动。可以用下面一段简短的英语进行说明:

Far and away the most important holiday in China is Spring Festival, also known as the Chinese New Year. To the Chinese people it is as important as Christmas to people in the West. The dates for this annual celebration are determined by the lunar calendar so the timing of

the holiday varies from late January to early February.

To the ordinary Chinese, the festival actually begins on the eve of the lunar New Year's Day and ends on the fifth day of the first month of the lunar calendar.

Preparations for the New Year begin from the last few days of the last month, when houses are thoroughly cleaned, hair cut and new clothes purchased. Houses are festooned with paper scrolls bearing auspicious antithetical couplet.

"Guo Nian" meaning "passing the year," is the common term among the Chinese people for celebrating the Spring Festival. It actually means greeting the new year. At midnight at the turn of the old and new year, people used to let off firecrackers, which serve to drive away the evil spirits and to greet the arrival of the new year.

On New Year's Eve, all the members of families come together to feast. Jiaozi is popular in the north, while southerners favor a sticky sweet glutinous rice pudding called Niangao.

① 这里的 Chinese 作 we 的同位语,对其做进一步的解释说明,同位语通常位于要说明的名词或代词之后,也可由 of 引出,如:the city of Beijing。

② potluck party 通常是各人自带熟食的聚会,可以在家里举办,也可以在会议室、教室举办。参加者一般要带做好的食品(如炒菜、面包、蛋糕、饮料等)。

International Friendship Association Activities
国际学生联谊会活动

Topic Introduction
话题导言

国际学生联谊会(International Friendship Association，简称IFA)是大学里各国留学生自愿形成的一种学生联谊组织，各国留学生是其当然成员，包括来自于世界五大洲不同肤色、不同宗教信仰和不同价值观念的学生。组织机构由选举产生，各国留学生自愿参加竞选。活动经费由国际学生办公室 (International Students Office) 根据具体项目拨付。尽管这一组织的名称各异，有国际学生会 (International Students Union)、外国学生联盟(Union of Foreign Students)、国际学生学者协会(The Association of International Students and Scholars)等等，但其性质都是一样的。

IFA经常组织一些户外的消遣、体育娱乐活动，如远足(hiking)、背包旅行(backpacking)、滑雪(skiing)、滑冰(skating)、摘苹果会(apple-picking)、野炊(picnicking)、观光(sightseeing)、城市购物(shopping)、国际周(International Week)等，特别是国际周举办的民族特色文艺、体育、烹调、服装展示等活动深受好评，也是美国学生了解世界的一个窗口。

Situational Dialogs
情景对话

各校的国际学生联谊会活动很多，杨洋(Yang Yang)参加了摘苹果会；杨佳欣(Jiaxin)参加了国际周活动；李惠敏(Huimin)去了科罗拉多大学后还参加了滑雪。

Dialog 1

Frank: Have you signed up for the apple-picking party?
你报名参加摘苹果会了吗？

Yang Yang: I never heard of that. When is the party? Where can I sign up for it?
我还没有听说过。摘苹果会在什么时候？到哪里报名？

Frank: You didn't receive the email from IFA, did you?
你没有收到国际学生联谊会的电子邮件，是吗？

Yang Yang: I haven't checked my email box for several days.
我好几天没有查看邮箱了。

Frank: Please go to ISO to sign up. The party is on Saturday.
请到国际学生办公室报名，摘苹果会是在星期六。

Yang Yang: That's good. Can we eat apples for free①?
很好，我们可以免费吃苹果吗？

Frank: Yes. However, if you want to take some apples away, you have to pay, but very cheap. I'm ready to buy two boxes.
可以。然而，如果你想带走苹果，就得付钱，但很便宜。我准备买两箱。

Yang Yang: Great. I'm going to sign up②.
好极了，我就去报名。

International Friendship Association Activities

Dialog 2

Jiaxin: I hear the International Week is nearing soon. We can have a cooking competition.
我听说国际周就快要到了,我们可以进行烹调比赛。

Tom: Yes. I'll cook some vegetables, such as cucumbers, eggplants, lettuce, and green beans.
是的,我要炒一些蔬菜,如黄瓜、茄子、生菜和青豆。

Jiaxin: The same vegetables can be cooked into different styles.
同样的蔬菜可以做成不同的风味。

Tom: Yes, you're an expert and Chinese people are all experts in cooking. I'd like you to cook some delicious food during the International Week.
是的,你是烹调专家,中国人都是烹调专家。国际周期间,我希望你做些美味的食品。

Jiaxin: I'm flattered, and I will.
你过奖了,我愿意参加。

Dialog 3

David: How about your weekend?
周末过得如何?

Huimin: Wonderful. The IFA and ISO arranged us to go skiing at Steamboat Springs.
好极了。国际学生联谊会和国际学生办公室组织我们到斯廷博特斯普林斯去滑雪。

David: That's fun[③].
真好玩。

Huimin: Yes, it's fun. This is the fist time I went skiing. Several times I plunged to the ground.
是很好玩。这是我第一次滑雪,我摔倒了好几次。

David: Balancing yourself is the most important. You'll learn skiing soon.
平衡自己是最重要的,你很快就学会的。

Huimin: I hope so.
希望如此。

Typical Sentences 典型句型

1) Have you signed up for the sightseeing at Spokane?
   到斯波坎观光,你报名了吗?

2) I never heard of that. When is the party? Where can I sign up for it?
   我还没有听说过。摘苹果会在什么时候?到哪里报名?

3) You didn't receive the email from IFA, did you?
   你没有收到国际学生联谊会的电子邮件,是吗?

4) I hear the International Week is just around the corner.
   我听说国际周就快要到了。

5) Will you join in the cooking competition?
   你会参加烹调比赛吗?

6) The activity for Saturday is hiking Moscow Mountain.
   本周六的活动是到莫斯科山远足。

7) The IFA and ISO arranged us to go skiing at Steamboat Springs.
   国际学生联谊会和国际学生办公室组织我们到斯廷博特斯普林斯去滑雪。

8) This is the fist time I went skiing. Several times I plunged to the ground.
   这是我第一次滑雪,我摔倒了好几次。

Background 背景知识

美国人的文化价值观念(二):国际学生办公室(ISO)和国际学生联谊会(IFA)组织的活动,目的是要外国学生尽快了解美国的文化。文化价值观念是不容忽视的内容:

International Friendship Association Activities

(7) 追求独立。个人主义强调自我实现,独立精神是其重要内容之一。孩子们从小受到的教育就是自我判断、自我决定、自我负责,切忌没有主见,人云亦云,更不可唯唯诺诺,听任摆布。

(8) 崇尚竞争。自由主义、放任哲学和民主平等观念,是人与人之间和群体与群体之间的竞争的理想条件和最根本基础。个人可以通过竞争看到自己的智慧、才能和力量;社会可以通过竞争不断充满活力,不断洋溢朝气。

(9) 希冀成功。美国人强烈的成功欲望驱使着他们在各个领域奋力拼搏,不断进取。各种各样的成功机会和范例,反过来又刺激起更大的成功欲望,开始另一个新目标的追求。

(10) 崇拜物质。在美国人看来,个人是否在社会上成功很大程度上是凭其所占有的物质财富来衡量的。高贵的服饰、豪华的轿车、漂亮的住宅和奢华的生活方式是显示社会、经济地位的最好标志,也是通向崇高政治地位的基础。

(11) 相信平等。美国人以前相信"上帝面前人人平等",后来相信"法律面前人人平等"。这种平等观念不是指人人应该平均享受社会物质财富,而是指人人获取财富的机会应该均等。机会均等(equality of opportunity)的实质是,平等竞争机会不应因其社会、政治、经济地位的低下而被剥夺;也不应该因其宗教信仰、人种肤色和语音与主流社会有差异而受歧视。

(12) 乐善好施。美国人也有互相关心、互相爱护、互相帮助、乐善好施的一面。这一面主要基于美国人对人道主义的理解:人生来应该平等,但由于一些人为的或非人为的因素,一部分人失去了平等竞争的条件。人们有义务从精神方面和物质方面帮助他们,使这部分人重新找回人的尊严和价值。

注 释

① for free 是"免费"的意思,如:
My employer will provide me with housing for free. (我的老板愿意免费提供住房。)

② sign up for 意思是"报名参加课程或俱乐部",如:sign up for a secretarial course (报名参加秘书课程),亦含有"签约之意",如:sign up for five years in the army (签约服兵役五年)。

③ fun 是不可数名词,不能说 a fun,而要说 fun 或者 a lot of fun,也容易误为形容词,而 funny 才是形容词。

Being a Guest at Professor's Home
到教授家做客

Topic Introduction 话题导言

不仅中国人好客,英美等国的西方人也比较好客。到美国等国家的大学去学习,尤其是读研究生或做访问学者,教授都可能邀请你到他家做客。指导研究生的专业导师经常在周末或节假日邀请研究生去他家聚会,形式以 potluck party 为多。接到这样的通知或邀请,不管去还是不去,都要客气礼貌地告诉教授。如果去,就明确地说"Yes, I will go."并要表示对邀请的感谢。如果不去,要先说谢谢邀请,再明确地表示"I'm sorry, I can't go to the party because …",这样就让教授心中有数,好有所准备或者另外邀请别人。

就餐的时候要对菜肴,不管是别人带去的,还是主人准备的,表示赞赏,如 This is really delicious.(这味道真好。)如果别人称赞你带去的菜肴,只要说谢谢就可以了,如 Thank you. I'm glad you like it.(谢谢,你喜欢,我很高兴。)道别的时候,也要致谢,感谢被邀请做客。

Situational Dialogs 情景对话

李惠敏(Huimin)受邀去教授家参加自带餐晚会,并因此认识了些新朋友。

Dialog 1

Jim: Let's go to a potluck dinner at Professor William's, shall we?
去威廉教授家参加自带餐晚会,如何?

Huimin: I think so. But what's a potluck party?
我想去,但自带餐晚会是什么?

Jim: Take your best food you think to Professor William's.
把你认为最好的食物带到威廉教授家去。

Huimin: Do I have to cook the food?
我要把食物做好吗?

Jim: Yes. I'll cook at five thirty this afternoon, for the party is six thirty and it'd be still hot when we get there. If you like to go with me, I can pick you up at your place.
是的。我今天下午5点30分做菜,晚会是6点30分开始,我们到那儿的时候还是热的。如果你愿意和我一块儿去,我可以到你家去接你。

Huimin: Thank you very much for your offer. Okay, come to pick me up and I'll be waiting for you in front of the bookstore, six fifteen.
非常感谢你主动提出接我。好的,来接我吧,我6点15分在书店前面等你。

Jim: Don't stand me up.① See you six fifteen there.
别失约哟,6点15分见你。

Huimin: Six fifteen, in front of the bookstore.
6点15分,书店前面。

Dialog 2

Huimin: Everything is delicious.② I like this kind of party.
每样菜都很好吃,我喜欢这种晚会。

Prof. William: We're glad you could come to my place.
你能来我家,我们很高兴。

Huimin: I wish you could like the dish I brought here.
我希望你们喜欢我带来的菜。

Being a Guest at Professor's Home 33

Prof. William:	Yours tastes great. Please help yourself to some beer or wine, or what ever you like. 你拿来的好极了。请随便喝点儿啤酒、葡萄酒,或者别的什么你喜欢的东西。
Huimin:	I will. Thank you. 我会的,谢谢。

Dialog 3

Brian:	Hello, I'm Brian. Are you a new graduate here? 你好,我叫布赖恩,你是新来的研究生吧?
Huimin:	Yes. I'm Li Huimin from China, and I came here January this year. 是的,我是中国来的李惠敏,我今年1月到这儿来的。
Brian:	Your English is very good.③ 你的英语很不错。
Huimin:	Thank you. I used to be a teacher of English at a college in China. 谢谢。我以前在中国的一所大学里当英语老师。
Brian:	You speak English like a British lady. Where did you learn your English? 你说英语像英国人似的。你在哪里学的英语?
Huimin:	I learned English in China, and I stayed in Great Britain for two years before. 我在中国学的英语,我以前也在英国呆过两年。
Brian:	No wonder. 难怪。

典型句型

1) It's my pleasure to be invited to such a dinner.
   被邀请参加这样的宴会我感到荣幸。

2) Let's go to a potluck dinner at Professor William's, shall we?
去威廉教授家参加自带餐晚会,如何?
3) But what's a potluck party?
但自带餐晚会是什么?
4) Everything is delicious. I like this kind of party.
每样菜都很好吃,我喜欢这种晚会。
5) We're glad you could come to my place.
你能来我家,我们很高兴。
6) A cup of beer is all right for me, I guess.
我想,一杯啤酒正适合我。
7) Now please be seated at the table, and help yourself to the food.
那请坐在桌上来吧,随便吃些东西。
8) All the dishes are so delicious, and I like them very much!
所有的菜都这么美味,我很喜欢它们。
9) I wish you could like the dish I brought here.
我希望你们喜欢我带来的菜。
10) This is a wonderful dinner party. I think I must be going now.
这真是一个不错的宴会,我想我该走了。

背景知识

美国人的邀请与被邀请:有正式邀请和非正式邀请两种。正式邀请多使用印好的请柬,请柬上要写明被邀者的姓名、宴席地点、时间等,常也印有"敬候回音(Respondez S'il Vous Plait 或 Please reply)"等字样,还要指明要穿全套礼服等特殊事项。主人可使用笺首印有地址的请柬,也可写明地址,不必签署姓名。答复邀请要使用回柬表示谢意。如不能去,要说明原因,请求原谅,不必签名,姓名可以打印在回柬的顶部或底部。

非正式邀请和答复与私人通信写法基本相同。开头要称"亲爱的先生",结尾则用"您忠实的某某"等。除了使用请柬外,大多数的

Being a Guest at Professor's Home

邀请是在电话里或当面提出的，通常有明确的时间和地点。至于"有空来玩"一类多是客套话，并不是真正意义上的邀请。被邀者如果愿意接受邀请，一般要问清楚时间和地点。如不认识路，则要对方把赴约路线讲清楚。如果不能出席，要打电话给主人或女主人解释原因，不能犹豫不决。

如果接受邀请，多在约定时间后的5至10分钟内到达。假如预计迟到15分钟以上，要打电话给女主人，说明不得不迟到的正当理由。如果比约定时间早到，要稍等一会儿。因为女主人一般兼任厨师，忙于烹调，直到开宴前5分钟才有时间换装。她不希望客人看到她忙乱的样子。客人到达时，可以带给女主人一些鲜花。但除在一些特殊场合之外，如庆祝生日、圣诞节、新年，不送花也可以。如果客人准备逗留过夜，或度周末，习惯上要给女主人带点小礼物——通常是1本书、1盒糖果、1瓶酒或其他类似的东西。

西方人的三餐：西方人很注重早餐的质量。早餐通常吃麦片(cereal)、烤面包片(toast)夹煎鸡蛋或火腿或咸肉片、水果，还有牛奶、果汁或咖啡等。

午餐是最马虎的一顿，有工作的人多在工作场所的餐厅或附近的快餐店中买一个汉堡包或三明治，再来一杯咖啡，就算一顿。也有人打电话到餐馆订餐，然后上门去取或由餐馆人员送到手上。

晚餐是一天中最丰盛的一顿，美国人称其为dinner，而很少用supper这个词。说是丰盛，也很难与我们的四菜一汤相比。美国人最喜欢的食品有炸牛排、炸猪排、烤鸡、炸仔鸡、糖醋鱼、烤面包、各种水果汁等，其口味特点是咸中带甜。英国人则爱吃牛肉、鸡、鸭、羊肉等，每餐都吃水果，但斋戒日的正餐却不吃肉。

以我们的标准衡量，西方人的饭量很小，似乎与他们的块头不相称。但他们的饮食结构与我们的大不相同，其中，奶制品占有很大的比例，如牛奶、奶酪(cheese)、黄油(butter)等，传统的美国食品的特点是高蛋白、高脂肪、高糖。但是，现在人们的保健意识在增强，低脂肪、低糖、低盐、高纤维的食物越来越受欢迎。

① "Don't stand me up."的字面意思是"别让我站在那里。"这里 stand up someone 引申为"失约于某人",另外一个说法是 drop cold someone (失约于某人)。例如:

Jack stood up Mary last night. (昨晚杰克失约于玛丽。)

Don't drop me cold. (别失约。)

② "Everything is delicious."用于表示对吃的东西的称赞,其他说法还有:

It tastes so great. (真好吃。)

It's out of the world. (真是棒极了。)

This meal is fit for a king. (这餐饭真是棒。)

This meal was made in heaven. (这餐饭真是人间美味。)

I couldn't ask for a better meal. (我无法找到更好的饭菜了。)

③ "Your English is very good."是称赞别人的英语说得好。其实美国人只要见到一个会说英语的外国人,都称赞别人的英语好,而再好也没有本国人说得好。还可以说:

Your English is fluent. (你的英语很流利。)

You speak English like a native. (你说英语像本地人。)

You have a genuine American accent. (你有地道的美国口音。)

You have the right intonation. (你语调正确。)

Being a Guest at Friends' Home
到朋友家做客

Topic Introduction 话题导言

美国大学的同学、朋友之间也经常聚会，美国同学也经常邀请中国留学生到家中做客。单身同学通常和别人分租公寓，已婚或有同居异性的同学则单独租房居住。到他们家去，多数情况是很多同学一起去参加周末聚会、生日晚会或节日聚餐，可以打听看别的同学是否也去，其中可能会遇到不熟悉的面孔。

不管是哪种情况，都比到教授家去要随便得多，但基本的礼节还是要讲究，如礼品、准时赴约、称赞对方、表示感谢等。同学聚餐多是烤肉和自助餐形式，要烤的肉或排骨等主要食品是由请客的主人购买，参加的同学、朋友可以带去一瓶葡萄酒、一小箱啤酒、糕点甜食、水果等；自带餐则要根据自己的手艺自己做一两种菜肴带去，分量大约比一个人吃的要略多一些。

Situational Dialogs 情景对话

杨佳欣(Jiaxin)受邀请去朋友吉姆(Jim)家参加晚会，度过了一个愉快的晚上。

Dialog 1

Jim: Hi, Jiaxin, come in, please.
嗨,佳欣,请进。

Jiaxin: Thanks for inviting me to your party.
谢谢你邀请我来参加晚会。

Jim: Just sit wherever you like. The drinks are just on the table behind you. Please help yourself.
随便坐吧,饮料在你背后的桌子上,请自便。

Jiaxin: Okay, thanks. You have so many friends. I envy you.
好的,谢谢。你有这么多朋友,我真羡慕。

Jim: Oh, yeah. I'm now introducing you to everyone here. Attention, please. This is Yang Jiaxin from China, and she is a graduate student in EP① Department.
啊,是啊。我就把你介绍给所有的人。请注意啦,这是中国来的杨佳欣,她是环保系的研究生。

Jiaxin: Very nice to meet you all. Let's be friends.
很高兴认识各位,我们做朋友吧。

Dialog 2

Jim: Your stomach is growling. Are you hungry?
你的肚子在咕咕叫了,饿了吧?

Jiaxin: Yes. Actually, I'm starving!②
是啊,其实我都快饿死了!

Jim: Why? Did you skip③ your lunch?
怎么了? 你没吃中饭?

Jiaxin: Yes, I did. I was too busy writing the research proposal. As a matter of fact④, I ate very little for today's breakfast.
没有。我忙于写研究方案。其实,我早餐就几乎没吃。

Jim: The dinner is ready, and everyone is here. I'm proposing to kick it off⑤.
饭菜已经准备好了,人也到齐了。我建议开饭吧。

Jiaxin: It's not better than that.
再好不过了。

Being a Guest at Friends' Home

Dialog 3

Jiaxin: I've very much enjoyed the meal. Well, I think I'd better be leaving now.
我这顿饭吃得很好。好了,我想我现在最好离开。

Jim: Thank you for coming to my house. I'm glad you like it. Can you stay a little while?
谢谢你到我家里来。你喜欢,我就很高兴。能多呆一会儿吗?

Jiaxin: I've got to get up early tomorrow morning. I'm going to Seattle.
我明天早上得早起去西雅图。

Jim: Do you need me to send you home?
需要我送你回家吗?

Jiaxin: No, thank you. I go with Jerry.
不用,谢谢你。我和杰瑞一起走。

Jim: Okay, see you next Monday. Take care.
好的,下周一见。保重。

Typical Sentences 典型句型

1) I feel honored to be invited for tonight's party.
   被邀请来参加今晚的聚会,我感到荣幸。

2) What should we take for the potluck?
   自带餐晚会我们应该带点儿什么去呢?

3) But if you have something special, that's better.
   但如果您有什么特别的东西,那就更好。

4) I will stir-fry something typically Chinese, I think.
   我想,我炒一些典型中国的菜。

5) This is really delicious.
   这味道真好。

6) This dish is very tasty.
   这样菜味道不错。

7) Thank you. I'm glad you like it.
   谢谢,你喜欢,我就高兴。

8) Thank you very much. That was really lovely.
   非常感谢,真是好极了。
9) I've very much enjoyed the meal, thank you.
   我这顿饭吃得很好,谢谢。
10) You're welcome. I'm glad you like it.
    不要客气,你喜欢,我就很高兴。
11) Thanks for inviting me to your party.
    谢谢你邀请我来参加晚会。
12) Well, I'd better let you have some sleep.
    好了,我得让你休息。
13) Well, I'd better let you get on with your work.
    好了,最好得让你工作了。
14) Well, I think I'd better be leaving now.
    好了,我想我现在最好离开。

背景知识

美国人的宴客:美国人喜欢在家里宴请客人,一般不去餐馆。他们认为这样更加亲切友好。常有两种方式:

一种是"家庭式",客人与主人全家大小围坐在桌子旁,食物盛在大盘中,依次传递,或由坐在餐桌两端的男主人或女主人为客人盛食物。大多数家庭通常由妻子做菜,丈夫调鸡尾酒。

另一种是"自助餐(buffet meals)",就是客人自己拿着餐盘来到摆好食品的桌边,自己动手挑选喜欢的饭菜。随后,同主人或其他人到另一间屋子内,边交谈边品尝。"自助餐"通常是非正式的,它的好处是可以让大家有更多的机会进行交谈。

美国人的餐具及使用习惯:美国人进餐所使用的餐具非常齐全。正式宴席的餐桌上每人面前所摆餐具不下二十种。

在一般家常聚餐的餐桌上也要十几种餐具,主要有餐盘、汤碗、汤匙、切肉刀、肉叉、面包碟、水果叉、咖啡和茶匙、抹黄油刀、黄油(白脱)碟、平底杯、盐瓶和胡椒瓶等。

在进餐时,美国人尽可能地只用一只手,而把另一只手搁在膝上。比如,他用右手拿起摆在左侧的叉子叉炸土豆片,他需要切肉时,就把叉换到左手,用右手拿起刀来切。切好后,又放下刀,把叉换到右手来叉切好的肉吃。想喝咖啡时,又得放下叉子用右手端着喝。美国人吃面包从来不用刀叉,而是用手掰开拿着吃。

餐桌礼节:美国人在餐馆或家庭宴会上进餐十分讲究。

(1) 每个人不能把自己使用的匙子留在汤盆或咖啡杯或其他任何菜盘上。汤匙应放在汤盆的托盘上,咖啡匙要放在茶托上。

(2) 不论是吃东西,还是喝汤,都尽量不要弄出声响。喝咖啡时要贴着杯子喝,否则,就会被认为不懂规矩。

(3) 每餐一般只上一道主菜和色拉,最后上一道甜食。如果客人没有吃饱,可向女主人夸赞她做的饭菜美味可口,并可以再要点鸡、牛排或其他菜,女主人会多加一份菜给他。

(4) 吃完饭,客人要将餐巾放在餐桌上,然后站起来。男士们要帮女士挪开椅子。人们不能在别人面前打饱嗝,不能在餐桌上抽烟。

(5) 如果主人还要留客人再吃一顿饭,餐巾可按原来的折痕折好。餐后,客人要呆上一两个小时,然后向主人道别。

(6) 如果客人被留下过夜或共同度周末,回去后的第二天要发一封便函向主人致谢,并随附一件小礼物,如一盒巧克力或一束鲜花等。

注 释

① EP 是 Environmental Protection 的缩写。很多缩写往往只有在当时的语境下才懂得其意思。美国大学的系科名称常用缩写,外人根本就摸不着头脑。如:RRT = Resource Recreation and Tourism; HRM = Human Resource Management 等。

② "I'm starving!"(我饿死了!)比 "I'm hungry."(我饿了。)程度要高。

③ skip 是"略过"的意思,可以表示略过一件事情不做、略过一顿饭不吃、略过一段文章不读,等等。

④ as a matter of fact 的意思是"其实,实际上",与 in fact 和 actually 相同。

⑤ kick off 是俚语"开始"的意思,如:
Once we're ready, we kick off the job.(一准备好,我们就开工。)

Entertaining Guests
招待客人

Topic Introduction
话题导言

俗话说"来而不往非礼也",人们重视"礼尚往来",古今中外都是如此。作为留学生经常到教授家去做客,也常常在同学家聚会,然而总不能老这样,因此请老师同学到自己家里做客也是应该的。这样可以加深了解,增进友谊,也是让老师、让其他同学了解中国文化和中国人民的一个好机会。

在美国全家人单独住在一个公寓里当然比较好招待客人,要是和别人合住,就还要和同住的人商量这个问题了。把你的意图、计划的细节摆出来,征求他或她的意见,也请对方出出主意,是合作请客还是单独请客,是否愿意参加或帮忙等等。

根据美国人喜欢猎奇的心理,招待客人可选择"中美合璧"的方式,既要尊重美国的文化传统,如礼貌原则等,也要把中国文化优秀的一面展示出来,要表现出热情好客。还要根据自己控制局面的能力确定要请客的人数,以免怠慢了某位同学或朋友,以至于获罪于人,结果适得其反。

Entertaining Guests 35 招待客人

Situational Dialogs 情景对话

受到了教授和朋友们的热情款待,作为回报,杨佳欣(Jiaxin)决定邀请他们到家里做客。

Dialog 1

Jiaxin: Prof. Smith, I'd like to invite you to have dinner with me Saturday evening. Could you come?
史密斯教授,我想邀请您星期六晚上一起吃晚饭,能来吗?

Prof. Smith: That sounds good. Anyone else?
听起来不错,还有谁?

Jiaxin: My classmates Eric, Becky and Professor Nelson.
还有我的同学埃里克、贝基和纳尔逊教授。

Prof. Smith: I think I would join you. What time?
我想我参加吧。几点钟?

Jiaxin: Six thirty. I'll cook some typically Chinese dishes for you.
6点30分,我要为你们做几个典型的中国菜。

Prof. Smith: All right. Thank you for your invitation.
好的,谢谢你的邀请。

Dialog 2

Jiaxin: Welcome. I'm very glad you could come. Come in, please.
欢迎,你们能来,我很高兴。请进来。

Prof. Smith: Thank you very much for inviting us.
非常感谢你邀请我们。

Jiaxin: Make yourself right at home.
请把这里当成你们自己家里吧。

Prof. Smith: Thank you. This is for you.
谢谢,这是给你的。

Jiaxin: That's very kind of you. The dinner is ready soon. Would you like a drink first?
您这么客气,晚饭马上就好,先喝点儿饮料,如何?

Prof. Smith: Yes, thank you.
好的,谢谢。

Jiaxin: What would you like to have? Hot tea, coffee, red wine, some beer, orange juice or apple juice?
喝点儿什么呢?热茶、咖啡、红酒、啤酒、橘汁还是苹果汁?

Prof. Smith: I'd like orange juice, please.
请给我橘汁吧。

Dialog 3

Jiaxin: The dinner is ready. Please sit at the table and help yourselves.
晚餐准备好了,请坐到桌子那里去,随便吃。

Prof. Smith: I can't wait. I have smelt the fragrance[①] from the dishes.
我等不及了,我已经闻到菜的香味了。

Jiaxin: These dishes are something typically Chinese, quite different from those in the Chinese restaurants here.
这些菜都是典型的中国菜,和这里中国餐馆的很是不同。

Prof. Smith: Yes, they are very tasty as if they were made in heaven.[②]
是啊,味道很好,像是上天的美食。

Jiaxin: Thank you. I'm glad you like them. Like to try chopsticks?
谢谢,很高兴你们喜欢。要不要试一试筷子?

Prof. Smith: Yes, please. I'd like to have a try.
好吧,我来试一试。

Jiaxin: You are using them quite well. If someone needs any more food, please let me know.
您用筷子很不错。如有人需要多一些,告诉我。

Entertaining Guests 35
招待客人

Typical Sentences
典型句型

1) Prof. Smith, I'd like to invite you to have dinner with me Saturday evening. Could you come?
   史密斯教授,我想要请您星期六晚上一起吃晚饭,能来吗?

2) Come to join us in a potluck party at my house, will you?
   到我家来参加自带餐晚会,如何?

3) I'll cook some typically Chinese dishes for you.
   我要为你们做几个典型的中国菜。

4) Welcome. I'm very glad you could come.
   欢迎,你们能来,我很高兴。

5) Make yourself right at home.
   请把这里当成你们自己家里吧。

6) That's very kind of you. The dinner is ready soon.
   您这么客气,晚饭马上就好。

7) Would you like a drink first?
   先喝点儿饮料,如何?

8) Please sit at the table and help yourselves.
   请坐到桌子那里去,随便吃。

9) I have smelt the fragrance from the dishes.
   我已经闻到菜的香味了。

10) These dishes are something typically Chinese, quite different from those in the Chinese restaurants here.
    这些菜都是典型的中国菜,和这里中国餐馆的很是不同。

11) If someone needs any more food, please let me know.
    如有人需要多一些,告诉我。

207

Background
背景知识

请客人吃什么：按照我们中国人的习俗，请客吃饭往往要准备满满一桌子的菜，而且还要说"菜不多，请包涵"或"请你来，也只是些粗茶淡饭"或"没有什么好菜，酒也不怎么样"之类的客气话。欧美人听了肯定感到莫名惊异："明明这么多，还说没有菜？"因为他们招待客人一般只准备三四个菜，往往是为了能在一起交谈、聚会而吃。西餐中很多食品是事先准备好了的，如甜食和色拉(salad)等；主菜(entrée)中的肉类菜肴则是在客人来临之前才做好。

还有，国内请客通常是女主人忙进忙出，传统些的家庭里女人和孩子不上餐桌。而欧美人宴客，主人一般不用在厨房里忙得团团转而无暇顾及招待客人，完全可以在客厅安心地同客人聊天。进餐时，只需把准备的菜肴端出来就行了。吃完饭后，主人把大家邀请到沙发上坐下，再送上咖啡什么的。通常西方人有用餐时喝啤酒、葡萄酒或牛奶的习惯。我们中国人好客，喜欢往客人碗里夹菜。但西方人却觉得这样不卫生，这点必须特别注意。即使是公勺公筷，也不太喜欢彼此夹菜，而是随一个人的意愿，吃多少自己决定。

西方人厌恶动物油，不吃鸡爪、鸡头以及动物的内脏等。所以，如果你请客，就得注意这些问题了。美国人比较喜欢中国菜，但美国中餐馆里的菜已经美国化了，你完全按照自己的烹调方式去做，口味上要适中，不能太浓、太辣、太咸、太甜。还要实行分餐制，采用美国人餐桌上吃饭的方式。用餐过程中，客人会不时对菜肴表示赞赏，要礼貌地回答说 Thank you. I'm glad you like it.(谢谢，你喜欢，我就高兴)。这一点上和我们中国人的习惯是不同的，我们爱对客人说："菜烧得不好，没有什么好吃的。"而这时就不要说了。

道别 (parting)：客人告辞时要说一些感谢主人款待的话，如 Thank you very much. That was really lovely.(非常感谢，真是好极了。)或 I've very much enjoyed the meal, thank you.(我这顿饭吃得很好，谢谢)。主人也要回答说 You're welcome. I'm glad you like it.(不要客气，你喜欢，我就很高兴)。

中国人的习惯是，全家人一拥而上去送客，而且还要送到大门口甚至更远,最后还要大声嚷道:"慢慢走;当心;走好;注意安全……"对西方人来说这种告辞方式与吵架一样,西方人一般只把客人送到门外即可,客人也无须说 Stay where you are.(不要送了。)或 Don't come any further.(不要再送了。)等话语。除非客人提出来,否则不要送得很远。如果客人对回去的路不熟悉,提出希望多送一段,主人一般也会欣然同意。当然,我们对他们也不要说 Go slowly.(慢慢走。)或 Walk slowly.(慢慢走。)或 Ride slowly.(慢慢开。)等这些汉语式的英语,否则别人会觉得莫名其妙。

注释

① fragrance 表"香气,好闻的味道",通常作单数。
② as if 引导的从句往往虚拟语气,as though 也一样。例如:
She walks as if she were drunk. (她走起路来像喝醉了一般。)(实际上没有喝醉)

Dealing with Neighbors
与邻居打交道

Topic Introduction
话题导言

中国学生到美国大学去学习,多半都是租住在公寓楼里,有的还要和美国学生合住。学校对有配偶的研究生多提供家庭式的公寓。这样的生活模式免不了要和美国学生或其他国家的留学生或当地居民打交道。

邻里关系好了,彼此也是一个照应。因此,见到邻居要主动打招呼,拉近彼此之间的距离,消除一些不必要的隔阂和偏见,但不要谈到敏感或隐私问题,如宗教信仰、政治派别、婚姻、工资收入等等,以免引起不必要的矛盾。平时有什么小问题,也可以请求帮助;可以帮助别人的时候也应该伸出友谊之手。

情景对话

左邻右舍之间难免要打交道,处理好邻里关系,对自己总是有好处的。杨佳欣(Jiaxin)和邻居 Mike 之间就总是互相帮忙。

Dialog 1

Mike: Hi, it's cold today, isn't it?
嗨,今天很冷,是吧?

Dealing with Neighbors 36

Jiaxin: Yes, but my keys have been left inside.
是很冷,但我的钥匙忘在里面了。

Mike: Oh, you mean you are locked out, right?
哦,你是说你被锁在外面了,对吧?

Jiaxin: Yeah. It's a pity. I can't go in without keys, and I don't know when my roommate will be back home.
对,真糟糕。没有钥匙我就不能进去,也不知道我的室友什么时候回家?

Mike: It's too cold outside. Please come on with me to my place. We can have a chat about something.
外面太冷,请跟我到我家去吧,我们还可以聊一聊。

Jiaxin: It's very kind of you.
真谢谢你了。

Dialog 2

Jiaxin: Hi, Mike. Could you do me favor?
嗨,迈克。能帮我一个忙吗?

Mike: Sure if I can.①
只要我帮得上。

Jiaxin: I'll be away from home for several days, but my new roommate is arriving two days later. Can you keep the key to the door for me?
我要离开家好几天,但我的新室友两天后到这儿。你能为我保管一下门的钥匙吗?

Mike: Oh, it's nothing. Do you know the exact time he'll be here?②
哦,不是问题。你知道他到的具体时间吗?

Jiaxin: Not very accurately, just around noon January 17.
不是非常准确,就在1月17日中午前后。

Mike: You'd better leave a note on the door for him, telling him where the key is. If he arrives, he may come to see me.
你最好在门上给他留一个便条,告诉他钥匙在哪里。如果他来了,他就会来找我。

Jiaxin: Good idea. I'll do as you like. Thank you very much.
好主意,就照你说的做。非常感谢。

Mike: That's all right.
别客气。

Dialog 3

Mike: What's the problem with your car?
你的车怎么了?

Jiaxin: I forgot to turn off the lights, and I'm afraid the battery is dead.
我忘记关车灯了,恐怕是电瓶没电了。

Mike: Really? Why don't we jump-start③ it? Do you have jumper cables? Just a second...
真的吗?为什么不用外接电瓶发动车子呢?你有充电电缆吗?稍等,……

Jiaxin: Yes, I do have.
我确实有电缆。
……

Mike: All right, then, no problem. Try to start your car now.
好的,没问题了,现在发动车子试试看。

Jiaxin: Wow, you did it. I owe you a big favor.④
哇,行了。非常感谢了。

Mike: It's nothing. What are neighbors for?⑤
不值一提,要邻居是干什么的呢?

典型句型

1) We can have a chat about something.
我们可以聊一聊。

2) We are neighbors. If you need some help, let me know.
我们是邻居,需要帮忙,就告诉我。

3) Could you do me a favor?
能帮我一个忙吗?

4) I'll be out for several days. Could you keep an eye on my home?
我要出门几天,能注意一下我家动静吗?

5) Can you keep the key to the door for me?
你能为我保管一下门的钥匙吗?

Dealing with Neighbors 36

与邻居打交道

6) Why don't we jump-start it? Do you have jumper cables?
   为什么不用车子上的电瓶发动车子呢？你有充电电缆吗？
7) Could you please help me jump-start my car?
   你可以用电瓶帮我发动车子吗？
8) It's nothing. What are neighbors for?
   不值一提,要邻居是干什么的呢？

背景知识

住房概况：多数美国人拥有自己的住宅,事实上,拥有私宅是进入美国中产阶级的一个重要标志。据近年的统计,70%左右的美国人拥有私人住宅。这些私宅有平房的,也有楼房的,也有些房子看上去只有一层,但有宽敞的地下室。房子前面多有一片草坪,后院则设有庭院,外加一个能停放一至两辆车的车库。

除私宅之外,还有不少美国家庭住在公寓里,这种情况主要是在大、中型城市里。公寓分各种档次,有价格昂贵的高档公寓,有条件一般、适合于中下阶层人居住的公寓,也有政府出资建造、供低收入者安居的福利性公寓。此外,有近5%的美国人住在"活动房子(mobile homes)"里,即那些装有轮子、可用拖车拖走的房子。这类房子比较便宜,颇受收入低下的青年夫妇和退休老年夫妇的青睐。还有部分退休老人一年四季开着一辆房车（recreational vehicle,简称RV）,周游北美各地。

不管哪一类房子大多都是工厂化生产的, 主要的建筑材料是木材,有些看上去是砖结构,实际上只是外表贴了一层红砖以作装饰。

美国人的拜访礼节：预约虽然是美国人见面的主要形式,但对于临时拜访也不是完全不欢迎。特别是邻里之间, 觉着可以去看看,就可以敲门而入,但要关系比较熟悉才好。

美国人拜访时,进屋前都要先敲门,征求对方的同意后,方可入内。进屋后,首先要脱帽,并询问是否方便,当对方回答说"无妨"时,方可说明来访者的意图。如果来访者看到门外写有"请勿打扰"

的小纸牌,一般要改个时间再来。一般来说,早上8点之前或晚10点之后,除非有急事或要事,否则一般不去拜访别人。在朋友家做客想去厕所时,美国人一般不问主人,尽量自己去找。如果被主人引入卧室,客人一般不坐在床上,这在美国人看来是忌讳的。未经主人同意,客人不能随便翻动屋内东西,特别是钢琴。如果拜访女士,除非女主人主动让你脱去外衣,客人通常不能随便脱掉,因为来访者不知道女主人是否喜欢让其久留。

中国人进屋还有脱鞋的习惯,但在美国没有这个必要,因为地毯就是铺在地上供人踩的,不管多漂亮多干净,都不用脱鞋,而当众脱鞋也被认为是不礼貌的行为。

注释

① **Sure if I can.** 是一个省略句,可以补全为:
I sure help you if I can help you. (如果我能帮你的,我一定帮你。)

② 一套房有数间卧室供各人使用,因此男女合租的现象比较普遍,只是共用客厅、厨房和卫生间。

③ **jump-start** 是用外接电瓶发动汽车,往往是由于停车时忘了熄灯,电瓶(battery)里的电已经消耗完了,只好请求别人用电缆连接到他的车上,以发动汽车。

④ **I owe you a big favor.** 是表示感谢的另外一个说法。使用 owe 表示感谢的还有:
I owe you. (我感谢你。)
I owe you one. (我感谢你。)
I owe you a lot. (我非常感谢你。)

⑤ **What are neighbors for?** 的字面意思是"邻居是用来做什么的?",这里的含义是:作为邻居,我就应该帮你这个忙。

Renting a Bicycle
租用自行车

Topic Introduction
话题导言

美国大学的校园都比较大,而且大部分学生都租房住在校外(off-campus housing),特别是小城市的大学区,公共交通很不发达。学生的汽车只能停放在校园边缘的停车场,而且大多数校园都规划为步行区(campus walkway system),只有行人和自行车被允许自由通行。

以自行车代步就成了比较理想的交通手段,一则可以到超市或自行车商店买一辆新车;二则可以在庭院售卖(yard-sale)或旧货商店(如Goodwill等)碰机会买到一辆旧自行车;三则可以到国际学生联谊会(IFA)设立的自行车租赁处去借一辆车。

Situational Dialogs
情景对话

自行车不仅停放方便,而且无污染。杨洋(Yang Yang)为了交通方便去国际学生联谊会租借自行车。刘杭(Liu Hang)毕业了就去还车。

Dialog 1

Susan: Hi, good morning. May I help you?
嗨,早晨好,可以帮你吗?

Yang Yang: I'd like to borrow a bike.
我想借辆自行车。

Susan: All these bikes are over here. You may choose whatever you like.
所有的车子都在这里,你可以挑一辆你喜欢的。

Yang Yang: What formalities should we go through[①]?
我们要履行什么手续?

Susan: That's easy. Please sign this "Bike Renting Contract" and pay 25 dollars as a deposit.
那很容易,请在"自行车租用合同"上签字,交 25 美元的押金。

Yang Yang: How long can I keep the bike?
我可以用这辆车多长时间?

Susan: As long as you stay here or you need the bike. If you find something wrong, please send it back, and we'll have it repaired.
只要你呆在这里或者需要这辆车,都可以用。如果发现车坏了,请送回来,由我们维修。

Yang Yang: Is all the service free or do I have to pay?
所有的服务是免费的还是我要付钱?

Susan: Everything is free of charge, including labor and parts.
一切都是免费的,包括人工费和零部件。

Yang Yang: Thank you very much.
非常感谢。

Susan: Any time.
愿意效劳。

Dialog 2

Susan: What's the problem with your bike?
你的自行车出了什么问题?

Renting a Bicycle 37

Yang Yang:	The hind tire is broken, I guess. 我想是后胎破了。
Susan:	Let me check it. Would you give me a hand? 我来检查一下，帮我一把，好吗？
Yang Yang:	Yeah. I pumped up the tire Saturday evening, but it got flat Sunday morning. Before then I never pumped it up. 好的，我星期六晚上打的气，星期天早上就瘪了。在此之前我从没有打过气。
Susan:	Yes, it's too worn out. How long have you used this bike? 是啊，太旧了。这辆车你用了多久了？
Yang Yang:	Around one year, eh, I mean eleven months. 大约1年，呃，我是说11个月。
Susan:	I'll change a new one for you. Will you come to get it next week or wait about ten minutes? 我为你换一个新的。你是下周来取，还是等10分钟？
Yang Yang:	Thank you. I may wait here, and just take it easy. 谢谢你，我可以等一下，你也别急。

Dialog 3

Brian:	Return your bike? 还车吗？
Liu Hang:	Yeah. I'm going back home next week. 是啊，我下周就回家了。
Brian:	Going home? Have you finished school here? 回家？你毕业了吗？
Liu Hang:	Yap. I've got my degree here, and found a job in Los Angeles. I will go back to China to stay with my parents for some time and then come back to Los Angeles to take up[2] the job. 是的，我得到这里的学位了，并在洛杉矶找到了工作。我将回中国和父母呆一段时间，然后回到洛杉矶开始工作。
Brian:	Congratulations on your degree and your new job! 恭喜你得到学位和找到新工作！
Liu Hang:	Thank you very much. I'd like to donate the deposit to bike repairs. 非常感谢。我想把这押金捐给你们维修自行车。

Brian:	Thank you so much. Would you sign here?
	非常感谢,请在这儿签字,好吗?
Liu Hang:	Yes. Anything else?
	好的,还有别的事情吗?
Brian:	No more, and have a nice trip!
	没有了,祝你旅途愉快!

典型句型

1) I'd like to borrow a bike.
   我想借辆自行车。
2) Would you please check this bike for me?
   帮我检查一下这辆车,好吗?
3) I prefer the light bike.
   我喜欢这辆轻便车。
4) How long can I keep the bike?
   我可以用这辆车多长时间?
5) If you find something wrong, please send it back, and we'll have it repaired.
   如果发现车坏了,请送回来,由我们维修。
6) What's the problem with your bike?
   你的自行车出了什么问题?
7) The tires become flat very easily.
   车胎很容易漏气。
8) The hind tire is broken, I guess.
   我想是后胎破了。
9) I'd like to return this bike.
   我要把这辆车还给你。
10) How long have you used this bike?
    这辆车你用了多久了?
11) I'd like to donate the deposit to bike repairs.
    非常感谢。我想把这押金捐给你们维修自行车。

Renting a Bicycle

Background 背景知识

租借自行车： 国际学生联谊会(IFA)设立的自行车租赁处一般只对外国学生服务。

(1) 自行车的来源：自行车都是当地社区的居民捐赠的，大部分是七八成新的旧车，也有少数新车。

(2) 工作人员：不管是国际学生办公室(ISO)还是国际学生联谊会(IFA)都没有正式的工作人员安排在这个岗位上。这里的工作人员不领一分钱的工资或报酬，是完全的义务工作者(volunteers)，不管是管理人员，还是修车"师傅"，有当地居民，有学校职员，更有大学教授和学生。

(3) 手续与维修：租车时要凭学生证或其他有效证件，但其实工作人员一听口音就知道是不是外国留学生。租车时要签署一个简单的租用合同，交纳押金25美元，自己在存放的车辆中挑一辆就行了。租借时或使用的过程中，如果车子出现了什么问题，可以随时在开门时间送回维修，既不收人工费(labor)，也不收零部件费用(parts)。

(4) 换车与还车：觉得自己租借的自行车不好用，可以随时去换一辆自己喜欢的。如果学成毕业或离开学校或觉得自己不再需要，可以将车退回给自行车租赁处，并可以全额拿回自己的押金。实际上，很多人并不要求拿回押金，而是捐给他们作维修资金。

(5) 损坏与丢失：如果严重损坏了自行车，但仍然送还了主体部分，就要从押金里扣一部分作为赔偿。如果丢失了自行车，就要扣掉全部押金。

注 释

① go through 的意思是"经过,通过(手续、步骤等)",如:
You have to go through many formalities before you leave our school.
(你要办理很多手续才能离开我们学校。)

② take up 的意思是"开始从事某事(尤指职业)",如:
She has taken up a job as a teacher. (她当上老师了。)

University Cafeteria
学校食堂

Topic Introduction
话题导言

大学食堂是为方便学生和部分教师就餐而设立的,一般供应点菜和快餐。点菜的价格相对比较贵,点菜其实就是事先做好了数十种菜肴和主食,每种分别订价。快餐,也叫自助餐(buffet),就是划卡入门后,随意挑选自己喜欢吃的种类,数量也不限制,但不能带出食堂,一般供应汤、三明治、肉类、甜食、热狗、比萨饼、各式蔬菜沙拉、水果、冰淇淋和饮料等,周末的品种比平时少。

实际上,大学食堂并不是由大学本身自己来经营的,而是由某个大型的饮食或服务公司(如Sodexho)经营的。一个大学食堂只是该公司一个很小的经营实体,所以,食堂和学校的关系只是服务合作关系。食堂的工作人员一部分为该公司的雇员,一部分则为临时工作(part-time job)的本校学生,特别是亚洲学生比较多,也有当地高中生。

Situational Dialogs
情景对话

杨洋(Yang Yang)开始到美国时是在食堂用餐。

Dialog 1

Clerk: Hello, this is the University Dining Service. May I help you?
你好，这里是大学饮食服务公司，能帮你吗？

Yang Yang: This call is from a new student. I'd like to know something of your meal plans.
我是一名新来的学生。我想了解一下你们的就餐计划。

Clerk: Do you stay in any of the university residence halls?
你是住在学生宿舍吗？

Yang Yang: No, I don't. Any difference?
不是。有什么不同吗？

Clerk: So, you should pay US$4.95 for lunch or dinner and US$1.95 for breakfast. But if you stay in residence halls, nineteen meals per week have been included in your residence plan.
这样的话，你中餐或晚餐要付4.95美元，早餐要付1.95美元。但是，如果你住在宿舍，那你的住宿方案中就已经包含了每周19餐饭。

Yang Yang: US$4.95 for lunch or dinner and US$1.95 for breakfast. Oh, I see. Thank you very much.
中餐或晚餐要付4.95美元，早餐要付1.95美元。哦，我明白了。非常感谢。

Clerk: You are welcome.
别客气。

Dialog 2

Clerk: Hi, how are you today?
嗨，今天好吗？

Yang Yang: Pretty good. Thank you. And you?
很好，谢谢。你呢？

Clerk: I'm fine. What kind of bread do you like today?
我很好，你今天要什么面包？

Yang Yang: Whole wheat, please.
请给我全麦面包。

Clerk: Vegetables?
什么蔬菜？

University Cafeteria 38
学校食堂

Yang Yang:	Lettuce, onions, and tomatoes, please. 请给我生菜、洋葱和西红柿。
Clerk:	How about meat? 肉呢？
Yang Yang:	Turkey, I guess. 我想要火鸡。
Clerk:	Do you like cheese? 你要奶酪吗？
Yang Yang:	No, thank you. And please don't cut. May I have two sandwiches? 不要，谢谢。请不要切。我可以要两份三明治吗？
Clerk:	I'm sorry. You can't get two at the same time. If you really need two, please line up behind once more. 对不起，你不能同时要两份。如果你确实需要两份，请到后面重新排队。
Yang Yang:	Okay, it's all right. 好的，没有关系。

Dialog 3

Yang Yang:	Excuse me. May I see your manager? 请问，我能见你们经理吗？
Clerk:	For what? 为什么呢？
Yang Yang:	I've got complaints. It's no picnic.① 我要投诉，这不是小问题。
Clerk:	But the manager isn't at work now. You may write down here and then put it into the box. You'll get a response soon. 但是经理现在不当班。你可以写下来，然后放进那个箱子里。很快就会得到答复的。
Yang Yang:	That's the only thing I can do.② 只好如此了。

Typical Sentences
典型句型

1) I'd like to know something of your meal plans.
   我想了解一下你们的就餐计划。
2) I eat at the cafeteria, for I don't like cooking.
   我在食堂吃饭,因为我不喜欢做饭。
3) What kind of bread do you like today?
   我很好,你今天要什么面包?
4) Please don't cut.
   请不要切。
5) May I have two sandwiches?
   我可以要两份三明治吗?
6) You can't get two at the same time.
   你不能同时要两份。
7) If you really need two, please line up behind again.
   如果你确实需要两份,请到后面重新排队。
8) Excuse me. May I see your manager?
   请问,我能见你们经理吗?
9) I've got complaints. It's no picnic.
   我要投诉,这不是小问题。

Background
背景知识

食堂主食及甜食名称:到食堂吃饭,不了解食品的口味,不知道食品名称,会带来很多不方便。对于中国学生来说,这些名称的很多词汇也确实难读难记:

cracker 饼干　　　　　　　　　macaroni 通心面
assorted cracker 什锦饼干　　　muffin 松饼,小松糕
bread 面包　　　　　　　　　　oatmeal 燕麦片

University Cafeteria 38
学校食堂

brown bread 黑面包	pie 馅饼,派
French bread 法式面包	pumpkin pie 南瓜饼
rye-bread 黑麦面包	pizza 比萨
whole wheat bread 全麦面包	popcorn 玉米花
bun 小圆面包	potato chips 炸土豆片
hamburger 汉堡包	pudding 布丁
cake 蛋糕	sandwich 三明治
cream cake 奶油蛋糕	soufflé 蛋奶酥
cereal 玉米片,谷类食物	toast 烤面包
cheese 奶酪	wafer 威化饼
cookie 甜饼干	yogurt 酸奶
dessert 甜食	tart 小烘饼
doughnut 炸面饼圈	trifle 甜糕
French fries 炸土豆条	waffle 华夫饼干
hotdog 热狗	spaghetti 意式细条实心面
ice-cream 冰淇淋	jelly 果冻

注 释

① It's no picnic. 的意思是"这不是轻松的事"。"轻松、容易的事情"或"易如反掌的事情"用英语说还有 a piece of cake/a snap/a cinch/a breeze 等。

② That's the only thing I can do. 的本义是"那是我能做的唯一的事情",指的是没有别的办法了。

University Residence Hall
学校宿舍

Topic Introduction 话题导言

大学宿舍的房产属于大学所有,但由某个公司(如 Sodexho)经营,所以学校并不给学生分配宿舍。要想住在宿舍里,就得和经营公司签订租房合同。学校向新生邮寄入学通知的时候,往往也包括住房情况的有关资料、入住手续、合同样本、费用情况等。所以,要想住在学校宿舍,就得提前预订,临时到了才想入住往往不能保证有空位。

学校宿舍住宿有严格的规定,集体宿舍不能做饭,不能随便增加人员,只能在食堂就餐,算起来价格很贵。实际住在宿舍的中国留学生非常少,主要是经济上难以承受。学生们称宿舍为 hall,也叫做 dormitory,日常交谈中常称为 dorm。

Situational Dialogs 情景对话

学生宿舍的费用对于杨洋(Yang Yang)来说太高了,他决定在找到别的住所前先暂住一个月。

University Residence Hall

Dialog 1

Yang Yang: I'm a new student, and I like to stay in any of the residence halls.
我是新来的学生，我想住学校宿舍。

Clerk: You are very lucky. A boy just moved out yesterday.
你很走运，一个男生昨天刚刚搬出去。

Yang Yang: So, you mean there is a vacant place for me?
这样，你是说有一个空位给我吗？

Clerk: Correct. You may move in first, and come to sign a contract with us.
正确，你可以先搬进去，再来和我们签一个合同。

Yang Yang: How soon should I do all this?
我应该多长时间做完这些事情？

Clerk: Within one week. You don't need to pay for the first week if you are not satisfied with① the dorm. But once you sign the contract, you have to pay at least two weeks' rent.
一个星期之内。如果你觉得宿舍不满意，第一个星期可以不付钱。但是，你一旦签了合同，你最少要付两个星期的房租。

Yang Yang: I just want to stay here for one month. How much?
我只想住一个月，多少钱？

Clerk: Do you eat in the cafeteria?
你要在食堂吃饭吗？

Yang Yang: Yes, I prefer eating here.
要，我想在这里吃。

Clerk: You should pay $495.00 one month.
你一个月要付 495 美元。

Yang Yang: Oh, it's too expensive. Let me see.
哦，太贵了，我要想想。

Dialog 2

Jones: Hello, my name is Jones. I'm your new roommate.
你好，我叫琼斯，我是你的新室友。

Yang Yang: I'm Yang Yang from China. Can I help you with your luggage?
我是从中国来的杨洋，要我帮你拿行李吗？

Jones:	Thanks. It's very nice of you.
	谢谢,你真好。
Yang Yang:	What's a roommate for?② Where are you from?
	室友是用来干什么的呢？你是从哪里来的？
Jones:	I'm from Anchorage, Alaska. Do you like it here?
	我是来自于阿拉斯加的安克雷奇,你喜欢这里吗？
Yang Yang:	Yes, but it's much colder than my hometown.
	喜欢,但这儿比我家乡冷多了。
Jones:	Cold? You call this cold? Alaska is still colder than here.
	冷？你说这里冷？阿拉斯加比这里还要冷？
Yang Yang:	I can't stand③ that.
	我受不了。

Dialog 3

April:	Are you staying in the school dormitory?
	你住在学校宿舍吗？
Yang Yang:	Yes. But I think I will move into my fraternity's house next quarter.
	是的,但我想下一季度会搬到我的校友住宅去住。
April:	I applied for student housing but there's a long waiting list.
	我申请了学生宿舍,但排了很长的队伍。
Yang Yang:	The housing problem in the university district is becoming very serious these days.
	这些日子,大学区域内的住房问题日益严重。
April:	You may rent a small apartment nearby; it's not expensive at all.
	你可以在附近租一个小套间,一点也不贵。
Yang Yang:	I'm considering that.
	我正在这样想呢。

University Residence Hall
学校宿舍

Typical Sentences
典型句型

1) Are you staying in the school dormitory?
   你住在学校宿舍吗?
2) Is this a co-ed dorm?
   这是男女混住的宿舍吗?
3) Are there any rules in this dorm?
   宿舍有哪些规定?
4) I'm glad to be your roommate.
   我很高兴成为你的室友。
5) Is there a reception room in this dorm?
   这里有会客室吗?
6) Do I have to pay any deposit for this furniture?
   我要支付家具押金吗?
7) I think I will move into my fraternity's house next quarter.
   我想下一季度会搬到我的校友住宅去住。
8) Can I apply for a family apartment?
   我可以申请家庭公寓吗?
9) I'm a new student, and I like to stay in any of the residence halls.
   我是新来的学生,我想住学校宿舍。
10) So, you mean there is a vacant place for me?
    这样,你是说有一个空位给我吗?

Background
背景知识

学生宿舍的类型:大学为了满足各种不同层次的学生需要,提供了各种不同类型的宿舍供学生选择:

(1) 集体宿舍(Residence Hall),学生使用公共卫生设施或者与室友共用卫生设施,一般备有床、椅子、书桌、书架、壁柜和衣橱,学生需要自己购买床单、枕头、毛巾和其他个人物品。实际上,这些东西在美国比较便宜,不必要从中国带到美国去。烹调用具可以使用的有微波炉(microwave oven)、炒锅(hotpot)、烤面包机(toaster oven)、爆米花机(popcorn popper)、咖啡壶(coffee machine)等,但这些必须是有自动开关(automatic shutoffs)的才准许使用。微波炉和冰箱可以在住房管理办公室租用。

(2) 环球村(Global Village),这种宿舍鼓励美国学生和国际学生之间的互相交流,住在这里的学生既有国际学生,也有一小部分美国学生。学生们经常举行舞会(dance club)、化妆晚会(costume parties)以及国际论坛(forum on global issues)。

(3) 研究生宿舍(Graduate Student Residence),是一种单间的宿舍(studio),全部都是研究生住在这里,房间都是一个人住的单间并有个人卫生间,并配有联网电脑和方便的洗衣设施。

(4) 已婚学生宿舍(Married Student Housing),这种房子是公寓式(apartment)的,一般为两间卧室和一间客厅、一个厨房,室内还有卫生间和洗衣设备,租金根据套间的大小来决定。

除已婚学生宿舍外的其余三种,有男女混住(co-ed dorm)的,每个房间还是同性合住;也有不混住(single gender)的,即整栋楼都是男生或女生,不过也有异性朋友留宿的情况。当然还可以挑选自己喜欢的室友,如是否抽烟、是否喝酒、是否很多社会交往、是否喜欢安静等等。

注 释

① be satisfied with 的意思是"对……满意",也有以说 be pleased with 或 be delighted about 等,如:
The professor is satisfied with what you did yesterday. (教授对你昨天做的事情很满意。)

② What's a roommate for? 和前文所用的 What's a neighbor for? 是一个意思,意思是说:作为室友,帮忙是应该的事情。

③ stand 的意思是"忍受",如:
You have to stand the sufferings. (你必须忍受苦难。)
还有几个词语也可以表示这个意思,如 bear, tolerate, put up with 等,例:
I really can't bear the noise any more. (我再也受不了这噪音了。)
Can you tolerate his attitude? (你受得了他的态度吗?)
I can't put up with her. (我受不了她。)

Off-Campus Housing
校外租房

Topic Introduction
话题导言

新到一个国家去读书,衣食住行样样都不能少。在目前各大学纷纷扩大办学规模的情况下,校内宿舍只能供部分学生居住,而且校内宿舍的租金特别贵。中国学生一般住在校外的出租屋,找房子、租房子、与邻居相处等等都是必须处理的问题,势必要和房东(男房东叫 landlord,女房东叫 landlady)、房地产公司(realty 或 properties)或者租房经纪人(house agent)打交道。

租房如同买东西一样,一定要把什么都问得清清楚楚、明明白白,虽然美国人都不愿意讲价钱,但作为学生,经济能力有限,提出价格问题是可行的,特别是在房源比较多的区域:如 I'm here as a student. I'm afraid I can't afford so much.(我是个学生,我恐怕付不起这么多钱。),The rent is too high. Can you lower a bit? (租金太高,能低一些吗?);尤其与那些也是学生在找室友(roommate)的转租者更要讨价还价。千万不能感到不好意思,怕讨价还价得罪了当地人,其实相反,他们可能会因为你讨价还价觉得你很精明呢。

Off-Campus Housing 40
校外租房

Situational Dialogs
情景对话

校内宿舍对于杨洋(Yang Yang)来说实在太贵,出外找房子是一个不错的选择。但是还是要先向房东问清楚水电杂费如何缴纳,是否允许合租为好。

Dialog 1

Landlady: Hello, may I help you?
您好,可以帮您吗?

Yang Yang: Yes, do have any vacancies①?
是的,您有空房出租吗?

Landlady: Yes, what kind of apartment would you like?
有,你们要什么样的公寓?

Yang Yang: We'd like to have an apartment with three bedrooms and two bathrooms. Do you have such one?
我们要有三个卧室,两个卫生间的公寓。您有吗?

Landlady: What a coincidence!② We do have such an apartment. The previous tenants just moved out.
那是巧了!我们就有这样的公寓。前面的住客刚刚搬走。

Yang Yang: So we are lucky. Can we have a look?
那么我们很走运了。我们能看看吗?

Landlady: Sure. This way, please.
当然,这边请。

Dialog 2

Yang Yang: Good morning. Do you still have a one-bedroom apartment for rent?
早晨好,您还有一个卧室的套房出租吗?

Landlady: Yes, we do. How many people are there in your party?
那么一起有几个人呢?

Yang Yang:	I plan to live with a roommate. We are students. 我打算两个人合住，我们是学生。
Landlady:	Great! Students are most welcome. Our terms are very simple. The rent is $200 per month and is due on the first day of the month. 好极！我们尤其欢迎学生，我们的条件很简单，每月房租200美元，每月第一天付。
Yang Yang:	Is the cleaning fee included? 清洁费包括在内吗？
Landlady:	Of course, but you have to pay for utilities in addition. 当然，但您要另外付公共设施费。
Yang Yang:	No problem. Is it quiet at night? 没问题，晚上安静吗？
Landlady:	Yes, please set your heart at rest. 安静，请您放心。

Dialog 3

Landlady:	Good morning. Can I help you? 早晨好，能为您效劳吗？
Yang Yang:	Yes, I'd like to rent an apartment to live in. 是的，我想租个套房住。
Landlady:	What's your request then? 那么，您有什么要求？
Yang Yang:	I am a student and just want a place to eat and sleep. 我是个学生，只想找个地方可以吃住就行了。
Landlady:	That's simple indeed. 那是够简单的。
Yang Yang:	How much is the rent for the small furnished apartment? 这套备有家具的小公寓住宅租金得多少？
Landlady:	It is $350 a month, but that includes gas, water and electricity③ 一个月350美金，包括煤气和水电费。
Yang Yang:	It's a bit expensive for me. Can I ask a roommate to share with it? 对我来说有点儿贵，我能邀一个室友来合住吗？

Off-Campus Housing 40

校外租房

Landlady: Yes, that's your business.
可以,那是您的权利。

Yang Yang: Well then, I'll take it.
那好,我租下了。

典型句型

1) I am calling about the apartment in today's paper.
   按照今天的报纸,我正在打电话问询那间公寓的事情。

2) I am a student and just want a place to eat and sleep.
   我是个学生,只想找个地方可以吃住就行了。

3) Could you tell me if you have an apartment with furniture?
   请问,您是否有带家具的公寓?

4) How much is the rent if I just want an unfurnished bedroom?
   如果我只要一间不带家具的卧室,多少钱?

5) How much is the rent for the small furnished apartment?
   这套备有家具的小公寓住宅租金得多少?

6) How about the deposit and the utilities?
   押金和水电费怎么出?

7) I was wondering if I could have a look at the apartment.
   我想来看看那套房子。

8) I'd like to have a visit. What time is available for you?
   我想看一看,您什么时候有空?

9) Please go over your lease and sign your name where necessary.
   请过目你的租约,然后签名。

10) Now you have to pay $350 advance rent.
    你要预付350美金租金。

11) Can I pay in cash?
    我可以付现金吗?

12) This is your copy of the lease.
    这是你的租赁合同。

Background
背景知识

校外租房: 美国大学宿舍有限,要申请住宿舍不太容易,因此大部分留学生要在外面自租房子,称为"off-campus housing"。租房有几种方式:一般是看当地的报纸广告中的租房信息。如果看中,可直接去逛逛,看到哪一幢有牌子(如 For Rent,For Lease 等),就直接找房东或管理公寓的人。最好先到 "校外租房办公室(Off-Campus Housing Office)"打听消息,这是学校中提供房屋出租消息的办公室,它除了拥有各类房屋出租资料外,并有专人解答有关问题。"校外住房"(Off-Campus Housing)并不是指离学校很远的房子,有的可能比较远,有的就在校园内,但不属学校所有。一般分3 种:公寓、互助宿舍(co-op)和家庭客房(rooms in a house)。

出租公寓: 一般都归一些房地产公司所有。其类型包括 studio(一室无厨房,只有小火炉及小冰箱或者一室一厨)和单元套房(有 one-bedroom, two-bedroom 或 three-bedroom apartments 等)。有包括家具的及不包括家具的两种。若一人居住,可选择 single 或 bachelor;两人以上可考虑去租 one bedroom 等。

寄宿家庭: 就是 rooms in a house 的形式,这种安排通常有两种情形:一是在一家中租一个房间,按月交租,可共用厨房,有的早餐和晚餐由房东提供;二是半工半住(live-in),不交房租或只交少许租金,但要帮房主做一点事情,如带孩子或整理庭院、照顾老人之类的工作。如果运气好,可以找到很便宜的房子,并且可以和房东交上朋友。这种形式在英国比较多,称作 home-stay,在美国不多见。

签订租约: 无论是以哪一种方式租住校外,最重要的是在搬入之前,把一切条件都弄清楚,譬如租金是否包括电话费、水电费、煤气费,租约、租期以及停车地方、退房条件和其他规定(有时,不同的房主规定相差很大),还要亲自去看房子。社会治安在大城市是个值得关注的问题,要特别注意。太差的区域,房租虽较便宜,但不安全。这一切必须在签契约之前确保弄清楚明白,否则契约一旦签订后,你和房东就都必须遵守它。因为契约受法律保护,反悔要受罚。如果是寄宿家庭式的,就更要弄清楚工作性质、工作时间。如果

Off-Campus Housing

不是约定该做的事,到时就要拒绝。如果你自愿帮忙,要让房主知道这是在帮他的忙,而不是你份内工作。有些学生因为人地生疏,不懂得当地习惯,又不好意思拒绝别人,以至于后来工作愈来愈多,几乎成为佣人,这就不值得了。

注 释

① vacancy 这个词可以表示"空着的,未被占用的职位、座位、住房、床位等",如求职时可以问 Do you have any vacancies?(你们有空余职位吗?)

② 这是一个感叹句,表示巧合的情况可以使用,如:
What a coincidence! I am just ready to phone you. (真是巧了,我正要给您打电话。)

③ 在美国,通常煤气、水和电是计算在一起的,称作 utilities(公共设施费),而往往租房的时候房东会表示支付水的费用,也就是说水费包含在租金里面。

Utilities Sharing 费用分摊

Topic Introduction 话题导言

要生活,就要消耗能源和使用通讯设施,就要负担自己该付的费用。学生日常消费的费用主要包括供水、供电、污水排放、垃圾处理、煤气、电话、网络使用、有线电视等等,几乎项项都要钱,煤气只是在少数地方开通了家用。

项目有这么多,但费用的计算却没有这么复杂。一般地,这些费用分成三个部分:(1)杂费(utilities),包括供水、供电、污水排放、垃圾处理、煤气等;(2)电话费(phone bill),包括电话、网络使用等;(3)有线电视(cable TV),主要是收看有线电视节目费用。不管什么费用,租房要和房东谈清楚,合住要和室友谈清楚,以免惹出什么不必要的麻烦。

Situational Dialogs 情景对话

租房总是要涉及到水费、电费等房租之外的费用。杨佳欣(Jiaxin)要与合租者共摊费用,对有问题的收费要投诉。

Utilities Sharing 41

费用分摊

Dialog 1

Jiaxin: Can we talk about the utilities?
我们可以讨论一下费用问题吗?

Becky: Sure. Besides the rent, we have to pay utilities, phone and cable TV.
可以。除了房租以外,我们还要付杂费、电话和有线电视。

Jiaxin: What do the utilities include?
杂费包括那几项?

Becky: Power and water supply, sewage, and trashcan dumping. The utilities are collected by one department called Department of Public Affairs of the City Hall.
包括水、电、废水处理和垃圾清理,是由市政厅的公共事务局收取的。

Jiaxin: How much for one month?
一个月多少钱?

Becky: Around $40, but it varies from① month to month.
大约40美元,但月月不同。

Jiaxin: How about the other two items, I mean phone and cable TV?
另外两项呢? 我是说电话和有线电视。

Becky: These two items are fixed, $22.80 for phone and $18.90 for cable TV. But they keep rising.
这两项是固定费用,电话是22.80美元,有线电视是18.90美元,但总在上涨。

Jiaxin: We three stay in this apartment. So, in my opinion②, each of us pays one-third per month for the whole amount of all these items.
我们是三个人住一套公寓,所以我的意见是,每个人每个月负担总额的三分之一。

Becky: I have no objection.③
我不反对。

Dialog 2

Becky: All the bills of last month have come. $68.89 for the utilities, $22.10 for the phone, and $19.80 for cable TV.
上个月的所有账单都来了,杂费是 68.89 美元,电话是 22.10 美元,有线电视是 19.80 美元。

Jiaxin: How much all together?
总共多少?

Becky: $110.79, right?
总共 110.79 美元,对吗?

Jiaxin: Quite right. Let's get it divided by 3, how much?
很对,我们分成三份,多少?

Becky: $36.93. I'll pay to collectors together by writing a check, I think.
是 36.93 美元,我想我用支票一起付给收费单位。

Jiaxin: Then we'll pay our shares to you?
然后,我们再把我们的那份付给你?

Becky: Sure.
对。

Jiaxin: OK. This is $36.93 I should pay.
好的,这是我该付的 36.93 美元。

Becky: Cool! Thank you a lot.
好酷!多谢了。

Dialog 3

Jiaxin: I don't know why we should pay so much this month?
不知道为什么我们这个月要付这么多钱。

Becky: We've made the rooms too hot.
我们把房间搞得太暖和了。

Jiaxin: Any change in the amount of phone and cable TV?
电话和有线电视的费用有什么变化吗?

Becky: No. Only the utilities cost us $98.10.
没有。光杂费就是 98.10 美元。

Jiaxin: That's too much. Can anything be wrong?
太多了,可能有问题吧?

Utilities Sharing 41

费用分摊

Becky: I hope not. However, we can complain about that, and they will check the wires and meter for us.
希望没有。不管怎样我们可以进行投诉,他们就会来检查电线和电表。

Jiaxin: Then we can make it clear.
那么,我们就可以搞清楚了。

Typical Sentences 典型句型

1) Can we talk about the utilities?
我们可以讨论一下费用问题吗?

2) The landlord pays water, and we'll pay electricity.
房东付水费,我们付电费。

3) Besides the rent, we have to pay utilities, phone and cable TV.
除了房租以外,我们要付杂费、电话和有线电视。

4) What do the utilities include?
杂费包括那几项?

5) In my opinion, each of us pays one-third per month for the whole amount of all these items.
我的意见是,每个人每个月负担总额的三分之一。

6) I'll pay to collectors together by writing a check, I think.
我想我用支票一起付给收费单位。

7) The phone is free, for we use the campus line.
电话免费,因为我们用的是校园电话线。

8) Then we'll pay our shares to you?
然后,我们再把我们的那份付给你?

9) I don't know why we should pay so much this month?
不知道为什么我们这个月要付这么多钱。

10) Any change in the amount of phone and cable TV?
电话和有线电视的费用有什么变化吗?

11) That's too much. Can anything be wrong?
太多了,可能有问题吧?

背景知识

各种收费：在美国租用公寓，房租付给房东，其他费用按照约定和规定支付。作为租户，一定要搞清楚这些问题。

(1) 供水 (water supply)，每户都有单独的水表 (water meter)，但其实大部分情况下，水费是由房东负担的。

(2) 供电 (power supply)，电费是杂费中最主要的一项，你不能看到电表，因为电力管理实行了电脑化，只有在公共服务部门的电脑系统里才能通过账户看到用电数量。

(3) 污水排放 (sewage disposal)，污水排放不单独计费，而是和使用自来水一同计算的，即使用了多少吨自来水，就收多少吨污水处理费的钱。

(4) 垃圾处理 (trashcan dumping)，清洁公司每天都要定时到各家各户去清理垃圾箱，收取一定费用，有的地方将这个费用加在污水处理费中一起征收。

(5) 煤气 (gas supply)，美国的煤气使用没有中国城市那么广泛，只在餐馆、酒店等商业机构才开通了煤气管道，大部分地方的住宅没有开通，因为美国人都习惯于用电力做饭、取暖等。

(6) 电话 (phone bill)，电话是一项单独的费用，由电话公司收取。

(7) 网络使用 (networking)，如果使用了电话线进行网络连接如 ADSL，这项费用就由电话公司收取。

(8) 有线电视 (cable TV)，有线电视公司提供多种服务，你可以选择不同的方案，价格比较固定。价格越高的方案，可以收看的频道就越多；你也可以按小时购买节目，来收看一些特殊的收费电影节目 (主要是我们所谓的"性爱片")。

以上这些费用，都是发生之后收取，只有个别项目需要交纳押金或预先支付。所以每个月的第一个星期都要付这些钱，开支会猛然多了起来。交费时可以交支票，也可以到窗口交现金，还可以用信用卡进行网上支付。

① vary from 意思是"因……而变化",如:
Price varies from seasons.(价格因季节而变化。)
② in my opinion 的意思是"按照我的意见,在我看来"。
③ I have no objection.的意思是"我没有反对意见",表示支持或赞同别人的意见,还可以表达为:
I quite agree with you.(我完全同意你的意见。)
That's my opinion, too.(这也是我的意见。)
I couldn't agree with you more.(我完全同意。)
How right you are!(你对极了!)
There's no doubt about it.(毫无疑问。)
I'm afraid it's true.(恐怕是对的。)

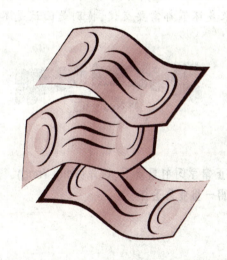

Finding an On-Campus Job
校内找工作

Topic Introduction
话题导言

作为一个中国学生,如果你去国外留学,在以学业为重的前提下,一般总希望找到一份业余工作,以便尽可能地挣些钱,这对于自费留学生尤其重要。其实,很多美国学生从高中阶段起就开始在业余时间打工挣钱,以减轻父母的经济负担,特别是孩子多的家庭。

工作期间用到的英语,是活生生的语言。找工作时要了解是否招工(help wanted 或 recruiting),需要什么条件,递交申请材料,面试,试工等。这中间很多环节都需要交谈,特别是面试是不可忽视的一关。

Situational Dialogs
情景对话

在保持正常学习的情况下,杨洋(Yang Yang)、杨佳欣(Jiaxin)希望在校内寻得一份业余工作。

Dialog 1

Clerk 1: University Dining Service, can I help you?
大学饮食服务公司,能帮您什么忙?

Finding an On-Campus Job 42

Jiaxin:	Yes, I read your ad in yesterday's newspaper, and I'm calling for the job. 是的，我读到了昨天报纸上你们的广告，我是为那个工作打电话的。
Clerk 1:	Are you a full-time international student? 您是全日制的国际学生吗？
Jiaxin:	Yes, I'm a graduate student at this university. 是的，我是本校的研究生。
Clerk 1:	And have you had any experience as a server[①] before? 您以前有做服务员的经验吗？
Jiaxin:	Yes, I worked as a waiter for two and a half years before I came here. 有，我来这儿之前做过两年半服务员。
Clerk 1:	That's fine. And do you want to work part-time or full-time? 那很好，您是做全职还是兼职？
Jiaxin:	If possible, I'd like to work part-time. But can I work full-time during summer vacations? 如果可能的话，我想做兼职工作。但是，暑假我可以做全职吗？
Clerk 1:	Yes, you can. Please come and fill some forms. 可以，请过来填一些表格。
Jiaxin:	Yes, I'll be there this afternoon. 好的，我今天下午就来。

Dialog 2

Jiaxin:	Hello, Mr. Smith. I'm Yang Jiaxin and I'm coming for an interview. 您好，史密斯先生。我叫杨佳欣，来面试的。
Smith:	Yes. You have an appointment with me. Please sit down here. Are you interested in the job? 好的，您和我有个约会，请坐这里，您对这个工作感兴趣吗？
Jiaxin:	Yes, I like the job. On the other hand, I need do some physical job after class. 是的，我喜欢这工作。另一个方面，上完课后，我需要干些体

力活。

Smith: Could you tell me what your outstanding feature is during work?
您能告诉我您工作时的最大特点是什么吗？

Jiaxin: I think it is that I can do everything on time.
我想是我做什么事情都很准时。

Smith: Do you have any references?
您有推荐信吗？

Jiaxin: They are available on request.
如果需要我可以随时拿来。

…………

Smith: Thank you for your time, Jiaxin.
佳欣，谢谢抽时间来。

Jiaxin: Thank you, Mr. Smith. When can I know the result?
谢谢您，史密斯先生。我什么时候能知道结果？

Smith: You may stop by[2] and check next Monday morning.
您下个星期一上午可以顺便来看看。

Jiaxin: Thank you.
谢谢。

Dialog 3

Yang Yang: Excuse me, can I talk to the manager?
打扰一下，我能同经理谈谈吗？

Clerk 2: Do you have an appointment with him?
您同他预约了吗？

Yang Yang: No, madam. I learnt from the classified ads in yesterday's newspaper that you are looking for an accountant.
没有，小姐。我从昨天的报纸上得知，你们正在招聘一名会计。

Clerk 2: We need an accountant badly.
我们确实需要一名会计。

Yang Yang: I am confident I'd be able to learn to do this job.
我相信，我能够做好这项工作。

Clerk 2: Do you have previous experience?
你以前做过这个工作吗？

Finding an On-Campus Job 42

Yang Yang: Yes, I used to be an accountant for eight years. When shall I request an interview?
做过,我以前做过8年会计。我什么时候可以进行面试?

Clerk 2: Would you please fill in this application form?
请填这张申请表,好吗?

Yang Yang: Certainly I will.
好的,我会填的。

Clerk 2: Our manager is out on business. Could you please come again Friday morning③ at 9 o'clock for an interview?
我们经理因公外出。请你在周五早9点钟再来面试,好吗?

Yang Yang: All right. By the way, I can only work part-time because I have to attend classes at the university.
好的。顺便说一下,我只能兼职,因为我还在大学上课。

Clerk 2: I don't think that's a question.
我认为那不是问题。

1) I read your ad in yesterday's newspaper, and I'm calling for the job.
我读到了昨天报纸上你们的广告,我是为那个工作打电话的。

2) I'm a graduate student at this university.
我是本校的研究生。

3) I'm Larry and I'm coming for an interview.
我叫拉瑞,来面试的。

4) Could you tell me what your outstanding feature is during work?
您能告诉我您工作时的最大特点是什么吗?

5) I think it is that I can do everything on time.
我想是我做什么事情都很准时。

6) The references are available on request.
如果需要推荐信,我可以随时拿来。

7) I am confident I'd be able to learn to do this job.
   我相信,我能够做好这项工作。

8) Would you please fill in this application form?
   请填这张申请表,好吗?

9) And have you had any experience as a server before?
   您以前有做服务员的经验吗?

10) I worked as a waiter for two and a half years before I came here.
    我来这儿之前做过两年半服务员。

11) That's fine. And do you want to work part-time or full-time?
    很好,您是做全职还是兼职?

12) If possible, I'd like to work part-time. But can I work full-time during summer vacations?
    如果可能的话,我想做兼职工作。但是,暑假我可以做全职吗?

背景知识

美国移民局关于打工的规定:外国学生(F-1 签证持有人)一般不能在校外工作,平时只能在校内工作(称作 on-campus employment,如为图书馆整理图书、食堂餐饮服务、教学办公楼清洁等),每周最多可以工作 20 小时,按规定得到报酬。寒假和暑假也只能在校内工作,但每周可以工作 40 个小时,当然由学校根据专业学习安排的实习(practicum)可以不在校内。在美国学习满一年后,由于意料不到的情况而发生经济上的困难,经过移民局批准,可以在一定范围内参与校外工作。F-1 的配偶和子女(F-2)在任何情况下都不能工作。J-1 签证持有人经过请求可以从事与专业相关的工作,J-1 的配偶和子女(J-2)若其本身需要可以工作,由移民局批准。

Finding an On-Campus Job 42

注 释

① 单词 server 在这里的意思是"服务员",与 waiter 和 waitress 同义。英语用词的趋势是弱化性别差异,如称呼 fireman 为 firefighter、称呼 stewardess 为 flight attendant 等等,都是因为性别不同而产生多个词汇的例子,人们在交往中尽量选用中性的无性别差异的词汇来表达。再如:actress → actor, poetess → poet, woman doctor → doctor, saleswoman → salesperson, policeman/policewoman → police officer, chairman/chairwoman → chairperson, spokesman/spokeswoman → spokesperson 等等。

② 短语 stop by 的意思是"顺便看看",而非刻意拜访。其他如 drop by, drop in, pass by, look up 等词语也可以表达这个意思。开学的时候,系里要把全系研究生的照片和简历办个专栏,秘书就说:
Please stop by and take a picture when you feel free. (有空的时候顺便经过照个相。)

③ 美国英语中省略介词的时候很多,这里就是一例。这里把 on Friday morning 中的 on 略掉了。

Working On-Campus
校内打工

Topic Introduction
话题导言

外国留学生第一年只能在校内工作（on-campus employment），对于没有获得奖学金或只有很少资助的学生来说，打工是必要的，一来可以增加收入，二来可以调节紧张的学习节奏。校内工作就要和美国人打交道，如工作安排、班次排定(shift)、计算工时、刷卡出错、领取工资等等。在学生打工比较多的地方，如食堂、图书馆等，往往有一、两名学生经理负责管理学生打工。

对于中国学生来说，要注意安排好工作和学习的关系，不要把工作看作一个负担；还要摆脱"惧上媚上"的心态，有什么问题直接大方地向经理提出来；工作过程中，也可能会遇到种族歧视或民族偏见之类的麻烦，要挺起腰杆，据理反驳。实际上，任何具有种族歧视倾向的人都惧怕正义和法律。

Situational Dialogs
情景对话

杨佳欣(Jiaxin)顺利找到了兼职工作，但是工作中也会碰见些意想不到的事情，例如打卡机出错、调班、代班等。

Working On-Campus 43

校内打工

Dialog 1

Kasson: Hi, Jiaxin. Can you do me a favor?
嗨,佳欣。能帮我一个忙吗?

Jiaxin: Why?
什么事情?

Kasson: Can you work tomorrow morning? Some students asked for leave① because they have to celebrate their festival, and I hope you can substitute one of them.
你明天上午能工作吗?一些学生因为要庆祝节日而请假了,我希望你能顶替他们中的某一个。

Jiaxin: You mean those Indian students?
你指的是那些印度学生?

Kasson: Yeah.
是的。

Jiaxin: From what time to what time, and what should I do?
从几点到几点,我该做什么?

Kasson: From 9:30 AM to 2:30 PM, in the dish room.
从上午 9:30 到下午 2:30,在洗碗间工作。

Jiaxin: All right. I can do it.
好的,我可以干。

Kasson: Thank you very much. Please check in at 9:25.
非常感谢,请你 9:25 签到。

Jiaxin: Okay, see you tomorrow.
好的,明天见。

Dialog 2

Jiaxin: Excuse me, Kasson?
凯森,打搅一下?

Kasson: Yes?
什么事情?

Jiaxin: I scanned my card this morning, but the time clock② displayed "WRONG CARD". What should I do?
我今天早上刷卡的时候,但计时钟显示"错卡",我该怎么办?

Kasson: Oh, I see. Please fill in a correction form and I'll sign for you.
哦,我明白了。请填写这张更正表,我为你签字。

Jiaxin: So they will add this morning to my working hours?
这样,他们就把今天早上加到我的工作时间里了吗?

Kasson: Yes, I assure you.
是的,我保证。

Dialog 3

Kasson: Hi, Jiaxin. I'd like to change your job.
嗨,佳欣。我想把你的工作换一下。

Jiaxin: No problem. What will I do next month?
没问题,我下个月做什么呢?

Kasson: We need a person to work on the deli③ bar. Are you willing to work there from next Monday?
我们需要一个人在"现点现做食品"柜台,你愿意从下个星期一起到那儿干吗?

Jiaxin: But I never work there. I know nothing about deli.
但我从来没有在那儿干过,我对"现点现做食品"一无所知。

Kasson: It's easy. Just making sandwiches.
很容易,就是做三明治。

Jiaxin: Sandwiches?
三明治?

Kasson: Yes. Someone will train you next Monday. Are you with me?④
是的,星期一有人培训你的。明白了吗?

Jiaxin: Yes, I understand, and I will begin working there from next Monday.
好的,我懂了。我从下周一开始在那儿干。

Kasson: Thank you very much. You can do a good job.
非常感谢,你一定能做好的。

Typical Sentences
典型句型

1) Can you work tomorrow morning?
   你明天上午能工作吗?
2) Can you substitute me next Sunday on the salad bar?
   你能下个星期天在沙拉吧代替我吗?
3) From what time to what time, and what should I do?
   从几点到几点,我该做什么?
4) Please clock in at 9:25.
   请你 9:25 打卡签到。
5) I scanned my card this morning, but the timer displayed "WRONG CARD".
   我今天早上刷卡,计时钟显示"错卡"。
6) So they will add this morning to my working hours?
   这样,他们就把今天早上加到我的工作时间里了吗?
7) I doubt there's something wrong with my paycheck.
   我怀疑我的工资支票有些问题。
8) I'd like to change your job.
   我想把你的工作换一下。
9) Are you willing to work there from next Monday?
   你愿意从下个星期一起到那儿干吗?
10) Someone will train you next Monday. Are you with me?
    星期一有人培训你的。明白了吗?
11) I understand, and I will begin working there from next Monday.
    我懂了。我从下周一开始在那儿干。
12) I think I'll call in sick today.
    我今天想请病假。

Background
背景知识

美国人的工作观：据笔者观察，美国人对待他们的工作有他们自己的观念和态度，概括如下：

(1) 工作无贵贱。一个人的工作，无论怎样低下，都应受到尊重。工作既是正常生活的一部分，又是给人以自豪的一种手段。所以，哪怕是一个做清洁工的美国人，谈起他们的工作也是津津乐道。

(2) 工作要认真。工作是人们必须严肃认真对待的事情，它不仅是人们谋生的手段，而且还是人们活在世上必须履行的"天职"。根据《圣经》的教旨，"既然人总得以某种方式从事某种事业，所以，工作本身就是一件好事。"

(3) 个人价值看工作。美国人在评判一个人时，首先关注的就是一个人的工作态度和工作成就。一个人的工作成就越大，这个人的价值也就越高。

(4) 珍惜时间。时间对于美国人来说，就是工作、生命和金钱，所以很多时候的工资报酬都是以时间来计算，特别是律师更把时间看作一种商品，出售给委托人。工作时如果闲聊或上班迟到、早退被发现，要受到严厉批评，甚至遭到解雇。

(5) 考虑公司盈利。美国人认为，没有这家公司，自己就没有工作的地方，公司是否盈利跟自己的利益密切相关，所以，就连普通员工也很关心公司的整体利益。

(6) 严格遵守制度。美国是一个法治国家，公司的制度就是公司的法律，所有员工都认真遵守，而且还会提醒他人也遵守制度。

① ask for leave 的意思是"请假"。"请病假"是 call in sick，"休产假"是 on maternity leave。关于因病、因事等而请假、休假的表达还有几个：
He is on vacation. (他正在休假。)
He is out sick today. (他因病没有上班。)
He is off today. (他今天休假。)
I took seven days off for Christmas. (圣诞节我休假七天。)
She's three days off now. (她正休假三天。)

② time clock (也称作 timer) 是公司、工厂对工人上、下班时间进行记录的一种装置。原来使用纸质卡片把时间打印在上面，现在则是电脑化的计时钟，纸质卡片也被智能 IC 卡所取代。该计时钟和人事部的电脑连接在一起，什么时候上班、什么时候下班一目了然。

③ deli 是 delicatessen 的缩写，指现成食品或熟食品。这里是食堂里现点现做的食品，但原料都是现成的熟食，如三明治等。

④ Are you with me? 的意思是"你明白我的意思吗？"用于确认对方对所听到的话的理解。还有些类似的表达方法：
You have me, don't you? (你明白了，是吗？)
Is it OK so far? (懂了吗？)
Did you get the picture? (你明白了吗？)
Know what I'm getting at? (明白了我的意思了吗？)
Do you follow me? (你明白了吗？)
Can you see the point? (你能明白吗？)
Did I make everything clear? (我都说清楚了吗？)
Have you got it? (清楚了吗？)
Do you understand the point? (懂得了吗？)
Does that make sense? (说清楚了吗？)

TA and RA
助教和助研职位

Topic Introduction 话题导言

助教(Teaching Assistantship，简称 TA)和助研(Research Assistantship，简称 RA)是校内工作的另一种形式，只不过不使用体力而是用脑力挣钱，相对于食堂、图书馆、楼房清洁等来说，可能更靠近自己的专业知识，有的职位甚至就是自己的专业教学和研究辅助工作。这样的工作是所有研究生梦寐以求的。

申请助教职位一般向系主任提出，也可以向自己的专业导师提出，由他与系主任和其他教授商议。助研职位多半就是自己的专业导师提供的，也有其他教授或研究机构面向研究生公开招聘的。美国各州对研究生做助教和助研的工资待遇有明确规定，如某州规定，硕士研究生不能低于每小时 10.16 美元，博士研究生不能低于每小时 13.86 美元。也有的地方按年度支付工资。

Situational Dialogs 情景对话

相对于其他的业余工作，助教或者助研总是要轻松很多。李惠敏(Huimin)的英语口语不错，因而决定申请助教职位。

Dialog 1

Huimin: Professor Smith, do you have any positions open?
史密斯教授,您有空余职位招人吗?

Prof. Smith: Some TA and RA are open for next semester. If you feel interested, you may apply.
下学期有几个助教和助研职位,如果你感兴趣,可以申请。

Huimin: I'd like to apply for a TA. Do I have to fill in any form?
我想申请一个助教职位,要填表吗?

Prof. Smith: Yes. You may download the applications from our department website. When you finish it, please turn it in to Mrs. Scott, department administrative assistant.
要填。你可以从我们系的网站上下载申请表,填好以后,请交给斯科特夫人,就是系行政助理。

Huimin: By the way, do I need to attach a copy of TSE[①] score report?
顺便问一下,我要附上一份英语口语考试成绩报告吗?

Prof. Smith: Yes, you do.
要。

Dialog 2

Huimin: Will you apply for the RA position provided by Ford Foundation?
你要申请由福特基金会提供的助研职位吗?

Edwin: Yes, I will. How about you?
我要申请,你呢?

Huimin: I haven't got a clear picture about it[②].
我对这个还是不太明白。

Edwin: You have to do the research programs if you are selected. But I think there's too much work to do. It's hard to finish six research proposals in one year.
如果你被选中,你就得做这些研究项目。但我觉得工作太重,一年之内很难完成六个研究方案。

Huimin: Yes, that's too much. But the money is attractive indeed.
是的,太重了。但工钱也确实诱人。

Edwin: Sure, it is. The Ford Foundation provides 27,000 dollars.
确实，福特基金会提供 27,000 美元。

Huimin: I couldn't finish six proposals even if they would provide much more money③, and I have a TA at hand.
他们给再多的钱，我也完成不了六个研究方案，而且我已有一个助教职位在手上。

典型句型

1) Prof. Smith, do you have any positions open?
   史密斯教授，您有空余职位招人吗？

2) Some TA and RA are open for next semester. If you feel interested, you may apply.
   下学期有几个助教和助研职位，如果你感兴趣，可以申请。

3) By the way, do I need to attach a copy of TSE score report?
   顺便问一下，我要附上一份英语口语考试成绩报告吗？

4) What would my job entail?
   我的工作将包括哪些？

5) What should a teaching assistant do for the professor?
   助教要为教授做些什么？

6) What salary would you expect to get?
   你希望拿多少钱？

7) You have to do the research programs if you are selected.
   如果你被选中，你就得做这些研究项目。

8) It's hard to finish six research proposals in one year.
   一年之内很难完成六个研究方案。

9) The Ford Foundation provides 27,000 dollars.
   福特基金会提供 27,000 美元。

Background 背景知识

助教的主要内容：顾名思义，Teaching Assistantship 就是教学助手，主要任务包括批改本科生的作业或平时的测验试卷(scoring)，辅导本科生的作业练习课(tutoring)，查找教授所需要的教学参考资料(references)，在实验室上实验课(labs)，以及制作上课需要用的教具或示范用具等。但是，并不是每门课都有这么多事情要做，很多课就只需要批改一下作业，工作量是固定的，如批改 ACCT204(会计学概论)的作业每周计算为 10 个小时工作量，就按照 10 个小时计发工资。

助研的主要内容：同样，Research Assistantship 也是为教授或有关研究机构在研究上提供协助，主要包括查找以往的相关研究成果(previous research achievements)以了解研究的起点或动向，撰写研究方案和研究计划(research proposal)，如设计问卷，参与实地调查，分析研究过程中所取得的相关数据资料，整理研究资料，写研究报告等等。当然，这些工作都是在教授的指导下完成的。有时候所研究的课题就是自己的专业，所以，很多研究生就以此完成自己的学位论文，真可谓一举数得。

Notes 注释

① TSE 是 Test of Spoken English (英语口语考试)的缩写。
② haven't got a clear picture about something 的意思是 "对……不是太明白"。
③ 这是一个虚拟语气的句子，表示一种假设。还如：
If I were you, I would live in the countryside. (如果我是你，我就住在乡下。)

On-Campus Recruitment Fair
校内招聘会

Topic Introduction
话题导言

虽然美国的大学没有中国大学的所谓"毕业生分配办公室",但也有一个机构关心毕业生的就业问题,就是职业服务处(Career Service),其主要职责就是求职技巧培训、简历整理、咨询服务、举办招聘会等。

因此,每年的春秋两季有学生毕业的学期,这个服务处都邀请部分公司和机构到学校来举办多次招聘会,毕业生可以利用这个机会和招聘单位接触,以促进相互了解。实际上,招聘会主要是进行面试(interview),具体落实还要等待招聘单位以后确定。

Situational Dialogs
情景对话

"养兵千日,用兵一时",李莎莎(Shasha)转入商业与会计系以后,顺利地获得了会计学的硕士学位,现在要求职了。

Dialog 1

Eric: I hear there's a career fair this Saturday. Will you have a try?
我听说本周星期六有个招聘会,你要试一试吗?

On-Campus Recruitment Fair

Shasha: Yes, I've just got my résumé ready①.
是的,我刚把简历准备好。

Eric: I really don't know what kind of men they need. Today, good jobs are hard to find.
我真不知道他们需要什么样的人,现在,好工作很难找。

Shasha: Yes, you're right. But we'll try our best.
是的,你说得对。但我们还是要尽力。

Eric: You're the most excellent. God bless you.
你是最优秀的,上帝保佑你。

Dialog 2

Interviewer: Good morning, Ms. Li. Take a seat, please.
李女士,早上好,请坐。

Shasha: Thank you.
谢谢。

Interviewer: We've known something about you from your résumé. Could you tell us about your previous experience as an accountant in China?
我们从你的简历中对你有了一些了解。你能和我们谈谈你以前在中国做会计的经历吗?

Shasha: Yes. I graduated from Shanghai College of Finance and was sent to Qingdao Customs as an accountant. My job there was managing import accounting files.②
好的,我毕业于上海财经学院,并被分配到青岛海关当会计,我在那里的工作就是管理进口会计账目。

Interviewer: How long did you work there?
你在那里干了多久?

Shasha: I worked there for almost ten years.
我在那里几乎干了十年。

Interviewer: During these ten years, were you in the same position?
在这十年中,你一直在同一个职位上吗?

Shasha:	No, I was promoted to be the Vice Director of Financial Department in 1998, and then Director of Financial Department in 2002. 不是，我1998年被提拔为财务处副处长，然后2002年晋升为财务处处长。
Interviewer:	Great. Have you ever worked in America? 很好，你之前在美国工作过吗？
Shasha:	Not yet, but I'm very familiar with American accounting systems and operations through the two years' study here. 还没有，但是我通过这里两年的学习，对美国的会计制度和运作非常熟悉。
Interviewer:	We'll inform you of our decision later. Thank you for your interest in our corporation. Thank you for your time. 晚些时候我们把决定通知你。谢谢你对我们的公司感兴趣，谢谢你抽时间来面试。
Shasha:	I hope to be working with you. Thank you so much. 我希望和你们一起工作，非常感谢。

Dialog 3

Interviewer:	There's one point we have to make clear. 有一点我们必须搞清楚。
Shasha:	Yes? 什么事情？
Interviewer:	You're an international student now. If we employ you, we'll file③ for immigration for you and your family. 你现在是国际学生，如果我们雇用了你，我们就要为你和你的家人申请移民。
Shasha:	I hope so. 希望如此。
Interviewer:	But the problem is, are you willing to pay any fees for immigration? 但问题是，你愿意支付移民费用吗？

On-Campus Recruitment Fair

校内招聘会

Shasha: In my opinion, I can do that, and the company just provides all the certifications and files needed for immigration.
在我看来,我可以支付,公司只要提供申请移民所需要的证明和文件就可以了。

Interviewer: Okay, the matter is settled.
好的,这个事情解决了。

Typical Sentences 典型句型

1) I've just got my résumé ready.
   我刚把简历准备好。

2) Today, good jobs are hard to find.
   现在,好工作很难找。

3) I hear there's a career fair this Saturday. Will you have a try?
   我听说本周星期六有个招聘会,你要试一试吗?

4) We've known something about you from your résumé.
   我们从你的简历中对你有了一些了解。

5) Could you tell us about your previous experience as an accountant in China?
   你能和我们谈谈你以前在中国做会计的经历吗?

6) During these ten years, were you in the same position?
   在这十年中,你一直在同一个职位上吗?

7) Young as your company is, you had an impressive growth record last year.
   你们公司虽然年轻,可去年的增长速度很令人瞩目。

8) I believe that I'll have a great deal to learn from and to contribute to your company.
   我相信我能从你们公司学到很多东西,也能为你们做很多贡献。

9) I would expect the appropriate rate of pay for a person with my experience and educational background.
   我希望能得到一个有我这样的经历和学历的人在你们公司应该能得到的待遇。

10) I'm very familiar with American accounting systems and operations through the two years' study here.
是我通过这里两年的学习，对美国的会计制度和运作非常熟悉。

背景知识

个人简历(résumé)：在美国找工作，首先要求邮寄个人资料给招聘单位，包括自荐信、个人简历、推荐信以及相关证书复印件，也可以通过电子邮件发送到招聘单位的电子信箱。最重要的就是个人简历，注重个人简历的格式和写法：

(1) Personal Information(个人资料)：包括 Given Name(名)、Family Name(姓)、Address(通讯地址)、Zip Code(邮政编码)、Phone Number(电话号码)、Birth Date(出生日期)、Birthplace(出生地点)、Sex(性别)、Height(身高)、Weight(体重)、Health(健康状况)、Date of Availability(可到职日期)、Driver's License or ID Number(驾驶执照或身份证号码)、Marital Status(婚姻状况)。

(2) Job/Career Objective(应聘职位)：Name of Position(职位名称)。

(3) Education Background(学历)：排列顺序为学位名称、获得学位的时间、专业名称、毕业学校名称、其他内容(如奖励、荣誉等)。

(4) Working Experience(工作经历)：排列顺序为职位名称、担任该职位的时间、所在部门、所在公司以及其他内容(如奖励、晋升)。

(5) Qualifications(资历)：包括荣誉称号、职业或特殊技能证书、业绩证书等。

(6) Hobbies / Interests(兴趣爱好)：包括体育特长、文艺修养、特别爱好等等。

① get something ready 的意思是"把某事情准备好",如:
Have you got ready everything we need at the party? (你把晚会上需要的所有东西都准备好了吗?)

② My job there was managing import accounting files. 这是一个系表结构,不是进行时态,was 是系动词。又如:
My job is teaching English at this college. (我的工作就是在这个学院教英语。)

③ file 在这里用作动词,意思是"提交申请文件",如:
Have you filed for graduation this semester? (你这学期申请毕业了吗?)

Practicum in Summer
暑期实习

Topic Introduction 话题导言

美国大学的暑期从5月中旬开始一直到8下旬结束,说是假期,但很多学校都在暑期安排一些实践性很强的课程。对研究生而言,主要包括实地研究和实习,所以也被称为夏季学期(Summer Session)。暑期实习不仅可以增加收入,也可以积累在美国的工作经验,还可以提高英语口语交际能力。

实习(practicum)机会既可以是专业导师或某教授一门课程的一部分,也可以自己根据专业学习联系实习单位。不管哪一种,只要经过导师同意,实习完毕后上交一篇实习报告,就可以获得学分。有时候,暑期实习做得好,还会为以后求职埋下伏笔呢。所以,暑期实习是一举数得的好事情。

Situational Dialogs 情景对话

暑期到了,杨佳欣(Jiaxin)想申请暑期实习,既可增加收入,也能积累工作经验,还有学分可得。

Practicum in Summer 46

暑期实习

Dialog 1

Jiaxin: Professor Simpson, I'd like to take the practicum during this summer. How do I apply for it?
辛普森教授,我想参加暑期实习,如何申请?

Prof. Simpson: Fill in the application and give it back to me.
填这个申请表,交回给我。

Jiaxin: I notice the practicum is at a tourist attraction. How long will it be?
我注意到实习是在一个旅游点,要干多久?

Prof. Simpson: Twelve weeks, eight hours per day. Can you accept shift work[①], including Saturday and Sunday?
12个星期,每天8个小时。你能接受轮班工作吗?周六和周日也要干活。

Jiaxin: Sure, I can. How will they pay us?
我当然能。工资怎么付?

Prof. Simpson: Around 15 dollars per hour.
每小时约15美元。

Jiaxin: Cool! I like it. I'll finish the form as soon as possible.
好酷!我很喜欢,我会尽快把这个表填好。

Dialog 2

Clerk 1: Hello, this is the State Wilderness Management Center. May I help you?
你好,这里是州莽原区管理中心,能帮您吗?

Jiaxin: Yes. I've learned you have some positions open for graduate students in summer. I'm very interested in working at hunting inspection station[②].
是的,我得知你们有些职位在暑期提供给研究生。我对在狩猎检查站工作很感兴趣。

Clerk 1: You may fill in the form on our website first.
你可以先在我们的网上填表。

Jiaxin: Yes, I will. But I have one question. Is only one person staying at the station at night?
我会的,但我有一个问题。夜间只有一个人呆在检查站那儿吗?

Clerk1:	No, we've prepared mobile homes for you and at least three persons stay there at night. 不是,我们准备了活动房屋,夜晚至少有三个人。
Jiaxin:	OK. I'll apply for it online. Thank you. 好的,我会在线申请的。谢谢。

Dialog 3

Clerk 2:	Hi, Jiaxin. How are you getting along here? 嗨,佳欣。你在这里过得怎么样?
Jiaxin:	Pretty well. I've been used to working③ here. I have learned a lot of new things. 很好,我已经习惯在这儿工作了。我学到了很多新东西。
Clerk 2:	I'm confident in④ your success. 我相信你会取得成绩。
Jiaxin:	I have to write a practicum report to my professor. Possibly you are a great help when I need some data⑤ and information. 我要写一个实习报告给教授。我需要资料的时候,也许你能帮我一大把。
Clerk 2:	Let me know when I am needed any time. 任何时候只要需要我,就告诉我。
Jiaxin:	It's very kind of you to say so. I can't thank you enough.⑥ 你这样说真是太好了。我不知如何感谢你才好。
Clerk 2:	It's nothing. 不值一提。

Typical Sentences
典型句型

1) It must be nice to work outdoor.
   在户外工作肯定不错。

2) Prof. Simpson, I'd like to take the practicum during this summer.
   辛普森教授,我想参加暑期实习。

Practicum in Summer   46
暑期实习

3) I'd like to apply for a part-time job in summer.
   我想申请一个暑期兼职。
4) I notice the practicum is at a tourist attraction.
   我注意到实习是在一个旅游点。
5) I've learned you have some positions open for graduate students in summer.
   我得知你们有些职位在暑期提供给研究生。
6) I'm very interested in working at hunting inspection station.
   我对在狩猎检查站工作很感兴趣。
7) Do you have any special skills?
   你有什么专长吗?
8) I'll apply for it online.
   我会在线申请的。
9) I have learned a lot of new things.
   我学到了很多新东西。
10) I have to write a practicum report to my professor.
    我要写一个实习报告给教授。
12) I think I'd enjoy doing that sort of work.
    我想我会喜欢这种工作的。
13) Practicum is a very good chance for me to know more about this country.
    实习对我来说是一个更多了解这个国家的很好机会。

背景知识

与实习有关的两个问题:其一,美国人认为,既然你是在为一个公司或一个机构工作(work)而取得收入,就应该交税,所以,要了解一下个人所得税问题。其二,作为研究生的实习,多半和研究工作有关,用电脑的几率很高,因此,要了解一下电脑词汇。

(1) 美国的个人所得税:美国的个人所得税属于综合所得税类型,也就是个人在一年之内,从各种渠道所取得的收入,不管是劳动所得还是资本利得,均汇总为当年的收入总额。根据年收入总额划分不同的档次,分别规定相应的税率,按超额累进税率方式进行征收。美国个人所得税的应税所得,要经过成本费用扣除、个人免税扣除和家庭生计扣除。其中,家庭生计扣除就是从净所得中减去规定的数额,这种扣除往往对配偶与子女规定不同的标准,有时对子女还要按照他们的年龄规定不同的标准。美国对每个纳税人抚养的家属给予个人宽免额。从1985年起,美国联邦个人所得税的税率表、各种扣除和抵免额等,每年均按物价指数调整,这被认为是对税法的重要创新,相当于大幅提高了起征点,降低了个税的有效税率,这对占美国家庭总数90%以上的中低收入家庭非常有利。

(2) 电脑常用词汇:

computer terminal 电脑终端　　hardware 硬件
cpu 中央处理器　　　　　　　　input 输入
dialog box 对话框　　　　　　　interface 界面
drive 驱动器　　　　　　　　　keyboard 键盘
enter 进入,回车　　　　　　　 memory 内存
exit 退出　　　　　　　　　　　mouse 鼠标
extended memory 扩展内存　　　multimedia 多媒体
file name 文件名　　　　　　　 operation system 操作系统
floppy disk 软盘　　　　　　　 path 路径
format 格式化　　　　　　　　　screen protect 屏幕保护
hard disk 硬盘　　　　　　　　 software 软件
hard drive 硬盘驱动器　　　　　video card 视频卡

注释

① shift work 指的是某些工作场合需要轮流上班的情况,分为早班(morning shift)、中班(afternoon shift)和晚班(nigh shift),需要轮班的有工厂、食堂、旅游点、酒店等。

② 在美国,打猎需要狩猎证(hunting permit)才能进入狩猎区打猎,对开放时间、猎取的动物种类和数量都有明确规定,在进出口往往设有检查站。

③ 这是一种容易出错的情况,其实,use,used 和 used to 是三个不同的词或词组,容易让人混淆:
use 是动词,"使用"的意思,如:
We use wood to make paper.(我们用木头造纸。)
Wood can be used to make paper.(木头可以用来造纸。)
used 是形容词,"习惯的"意思,如:
Natalie has been used to living in China. / Natalie has been used to the life in China.(纳塔莉已经习惯了中国的生活。)
used to 相当于情态动词,是"过去常常"的意思,如:
Alice used to come late to class.(爱丽斯以前上课常常迟到。)

④ be confident in 的意思是"对……感到自信",如:
She's confident in passing the test.(她自信能通过考试。)

⑤ data 的意思是"资料,材料",是 datum 的复数。但 datum 罕用,一般即以 data 作为集合词,在口语中往往用单数动词,如指一份资料,则说作 this data。

⑥ I can't thank you enough. 也是一句表示感谢的话,有强调感谢之意。类似的表达法还有:
How can I ever repay you?(我怎么报答你呢?)
How can I ever thank you?(我怎么感谢你呢?)
I don't know how to thank you.(我不知道怎么感谢你。)
Thank you very very much.(非常非常感谢你。)
Thanks a million.(太感谢你了。)

Students Health Service
学生健康服务

Topic Introduction
话题导言

几乎所有的大学都设立了学生健康服务中心（Students Health Center）这样的机构为学生服务。这个机构与校外医院或诊所不同的是，一是看病就在校园内，二是费用低廉，三是有接待国际学生的经验，如果刚到美国不久的中国学生听不太懂英语，他们还会请人翻译，以便更好地掌握病情。遇到比较严重的问题，医生们就介绍你到好一些的机构或医生去看。

美国移民局规定，国际学生必须购买学生健康保险（Student Health Insurance Program，简称 SHIP），否则不能注册上课。当然，也可以购买包含 SHIP 内容的其他公司的保险，但要经过国际学生办公室（International Students Office）同意。有了这样的保险，每次看病只要交很少的费用，药费也是象征性地交一点儿。

与到其他医疗机构一样，到学生健康服务中心看病也要预约，但临时去看也会接待，特别是上午医生们一般不怎么忙。据笔者所知，中国学生去看病的极少，因为大部分人从中国带去了不少药，遇到头疼脑热之类的小毛病，就自己吃点药算了，舍不得花那几十块美元给医生。

Students Health Service

学生健康服务

Situational Dialogs
情景对话

人难免会生病,杨洋(Yang Yang)也不例外,她因为感冒需要看医生,幸好学生健康服务中心的收费都不高。

Dialog 1

Nurse: Students Health Center, may I help you?
学生健康服务中心,能帮你什么吗?

Yang Yang: I'd like to make an appointment to see the doctor.
我想预约来看医生。

Nurse: Can you come now? The doctors are not busy this morning.
您能现在来吗? 医生们今天上午不忙。

Yang Yang: Yes, I can.
能,我能来。

Nurse: By the way, do you have the SHIP?
顺便问一下,您买了学生健康保险吗?

Yang Yang: Yes, I do. But I haven't got the insurance card yet.
买了,但我还没有得到保险卡。

Nurse: We don't use the card any longer. We check your insurance status on the campus web.
我们不再用保险卡了,我们可以在校园网上查到您的保险情况。

Yang Yang: That's fine. I'll be there.
好的,我就到。

Dialog 2

Yang Yang: Doctor, I have a bad cough① and I feel a burning pain in my throat whenever I cough.
医生,我咳嗽得厉害,咳嗽的时候也感到喉咙烧痛。

Doctor:	The nurse just took your temperature. You have a fever. How long have you suffered from this? 护士刚才查过您的体温了,您发烧了。您这样多久了?
Yang Yang:	Two days. From Monday morning, I believe. 两天,我想是从星期一早上。
Doctor:	Let me listen to your chest. Now, breathe in ... hold it ... breathe out. Once more. Okay. Do you feel any pain in your chest? 我来听一下您的胸部,注意,吸气……憋住……呼气,再来一次。好的。您感到胸部疼痛吗?
Yang Yang:	Yes, a little when I cough. Is it serious, doctor? 是的,咳嗽的时候有一点儿疼痛。严重吗,医生?
Doctor:	Perhaps it's the flu. Take the medicine before every meal and drink more water. 可能是流感。每餐饭前服药,多喝些水。
Yang Yang:	Yes, doctor. 是的,医生。
Doctor:	Keep yourself warm and do some sports. You will get better soon. 注意保暖,做些运动。您很快就好了。
Yang Yang:	Thank you very much. 非常感谢。
Doctor:	You are welcome. 不用谢。

Dialog 3

Yang Yang:	I've finished here. I'd like to check out. 我看医生看完了,我要走了。
Nurse:	I need to give back your student ID card. The first letter of your last name, please? 我要把您的学生证退还给您,请问您姓氏的第一个字母?
Yang Yang:	Y. Y。
Nurse:	Here is your card. Would you pay now or later?[2] 这是您的证件。您是现在付账还是以后再付?

Students Health Service

学生健康服务

Yang Yang: I will pay later together with other expenses, I think.
我想我以后和其他费用一起付吧。

Nurse: That's OK. See you later.
好的,再见了。

Yang Yang: See you.
再见。

Typical Sentences
典型句型

1) By the way, do you have the SHIP?
   顺便问一下,您买了学生健康保险吗?

2) I haven't got the insurance card yet.
   我还没有得到保险卡。

3) I have a bad cough and I feel a burning pain in my throat whenever I cough.
   我咳嗽得厉害,咳嗽的时候也感到喉咙烧痛。

4) I will pay later together with other expenses, I think.
   我想我以后和其他费用一起付吧。

5) My back went out.
   我扭到腰了。

6) I pulled my muscle.
   我肌肉拉伤了。

7) I have a cramp in my foot.
   我的脚抽筋了。

8) I've had many dreams in my sleep recently.
   我近来睡觉总是做很多梦。

9) Are you allergic to certain foods like shrimps?
   您对某些食物,比如虾,有过敏反应吗?

Background
背景知识

关于疾病的词汇：

dry cough 干咳
easily excited 容易兴奋
fatigue 疲劳
general aching 遍身疼痛
general malaise 全身不适
loose to bowels 拉肚子
nausea 恶心
neurasthenia 神经衰弱
poor appetite 胃口不佳
ringing in the ear 耳鸣
routine check-up 常规体检
run a fever/temperature 发烧
rundown 疲乏无力
running nose 流鼻涕
shortness of breath 气促
sick leave 病假
sneeze 打喷嚏
sore throat 咽痛
stuffed nose 鼻子不通
thorough check-up 全面体检
mandatory health insurance
必须投的健康保险

insomnia 失眠
inflammation 发炎
carcinogen 致癌物
benign tumor 良性肿瘤
malignant tumor 恶性肿瘤
lung cancer 肺癌
lymphoma 淋巴瘤
bone tumor 骨肿瘤
liver cancer 肝癌
breast cancer 乳腺癌
sarcoma 肉瘤
metastatic carcinoma 转移性癌
cancer spread 癌扩散
suspected cancer 可疑癌
leukemia 血癌
insured amount 保险额
insurance premium 保险费
social security 社会保障
minimum coverage 最低保险额
policy 保险单

注释

① I have ... 和 I have got ...是比较有用的句型,说明得了什么疾病或什么症状都可以表达:

I have a tight muscle around my neck. (我落枕了。)
I have a cramp in my foot. (我的脚抽筋了。)
I have pins and needles in my leg. (我腿脚麻了。)
I have calluses on my palm. (我手上长茧了。)
I have chapped lips. (我嘴唇裂了。)
I have got a fever. (我发烧了。)
I've got a headache. (我头痛。)

② 有了 SHIP 这样的健康保险,看病的时候只要付很少的费用(相当于国内的挂号费和很小比例的药费)。若生了重病,则只需付保险条款规定的上限,其余的费用由保险公司支付。

Family to U. S.
申请家属赴美

Topic Introduction
话题导言

从理论上讲，已婚的外国学生可以申请配偶和孩子到美国团聚。大学需要的手续非常简单，一是告诉国际学生顾问你的配偶和孩子的姓名、出生年月日、国籍，一是提供足够的资金证明，国际学生顾问就会签发家属赴美的 I-20 表。

得到这样的 I-20 表，就要把你在美国情况的有关证明材料一同寄回中国，包括学生证复印件、注册证明（从网上打印）、驾驶执照复印件、社会安全卡复印件、教授或系主任的说明信、国际学生顾问的说明信、成绩单(transcript)等。家属得到这些资料后，就可以到美国驻中国的使馆或领馆申请学生家属签证(F-2)了。"9·11"之后，学生家属签证变得难起来了，被拒签的关键原因就是签证官认为有"移民倾向"(tendency of immigration)。

Situational Dialogs
情景对话

离开家太久了，杨佳欣(Jiaxin)很希望能够全家团聚，所以她想申请家属赴美。

Family to U.S.

申请家属赴美

Dialog 1

Tammy: How can I help you?
我能帮到你什么？

Jiaxin: I need my husband and daughter to be here with me, Tammy. Could you issue an I-20 for them?①
塔米，我想要我的丈夫和女儿到这里来和我团聚，您能给他们签发一个 I-20 表吗？

Tammy: Sure. Please write down their names, date of birth and nationality. Be careful, you should write first name first and last name last.
当然可以。请写下他们的名字、出生日期和国籍。注意，你要先写名，后写姓。

Jiaxin: Yes, that's it. Do I need to provide any financial certification?
好的，这就是了。我需要提供资金证明吗？

Tammy: Yes, better give me one of your bank statements. The total amount for them is US$12,000.
要，最好把你的银行对账单给我一份，总额是 12,000 美元。

Jiaxin: I'll get it for you later. Anything else?
我晚一些时候拿来，还要别的吗？

Tammy: Nothing more.
没有别的了。

Dialog 2

Jiaxin: Could you please make a bank statement for me?
请给我开一张银行对账单，好吗？

Teller: Sure. Your account number, please.
当然可以。请告诉我你的账号。

Jiaxin: It's 000 1234 8888.
账号是 000 1234 8888。

Teller: It's a savings account. I'll make one for you. Please wait a minute.
是储蓄存款账户。我给你开一张。请等一会儿。
…………

Teller:	I've got the bank statement ready. 我已经开好了银行对账单。
Jiaxin:	Thank you very much. 非常感谢。
Teller:	You are welcome. 别客气。

Dialog 3

Jiaxin:	This is one of my monthly bank statements. Is it okay? 这是我的一份月对账单,行吗?
Tammy:	Yes, it works. I'll write a letter for you, and your husband may take it to the local American consulate general. 好的,可以。我将给你写封信,你丈夫可以拿它去当地美国总领事馆。
Jiaxin:	Thank you. Can I also ask my department head to write a letter? 谢谢。我可以要系主任也写封信吗?
Tammy:	I think it'll be better. You'd go to the registrar's website and print an enrollment verification. 我认为更好。你上注册处的网,打印一份注册确认书。
Jiaxin:	Yes, I will. I'm not sure about② their visas. 好的。我对他们得到签证没有把握。
Tammy:	Your husband and daughter will be lucky enough. 你的丈夫和女儿会很走运的。

Typical Sentences
典型句型

1) What should I do if I want to ask my family here?
我要是想让我的家人到这儿来,该怎么做?

2) I need my wife and daughter to be here with me.
我想要我的妻子和女儿到这里来和我团聚。

3) Is my original I-20 available for them to get visas?
我原来的I-20表可以用于他们得到签证吗?

4) Could you issue an I-20 for them?
   您能给他们签发一个 I-20 表吗？

5) Can they get B-1/2 visa if they just come for a visit?
   如果他们只是来看看，能得到 B-1/2 签证吗？

6) Do I need to provide any financial certification?
   我需要提供资金证明吗？

7) Could you please make a bank statement for me?
   请给我开一张银行对账单好吗？

8) I've got the bank statement ready.
   我已经开好了银行对账单。

9) This is one of my monthly bank statements. Is it okay?
   这是我的一份月对账单，行吗？

10) Your wife may take the letter to the American Embassy.
    你妻子可以拿这封信去美国大使馆。

11) You'd go to the registrar's website and print an enrollment verification.
    你上注册处的网，打印一份注册确认书。

12) I've found a spelling mistake of my daughter's name.
    我发现我女儿的名字有个拼写错误。

背景知识

签证拒签(Visa Denials)：当申请美国签证被拒签时，签证官会告诉你说："你的签证申请被拒绝了，你不符合美国《移民与国籍法案(Immigration and Nationality Act)》第214(b)条的规定"。

美国《移民与国籍法案》第214(b)条的规定是：任何一个外国人都被认为是有移民倾向，直到他申请的时候能满意地说服签证官应该给予他非移民身份。

按照美国国务院的提示，要想成功获得签证，必须说服签证官你在美国以外的地方有紧密的联系，包括工作、房子、银行账户、家庭关系、社会联系、其他财产等等，并且这些联系是不会被放弃的。

其实,这些所谓的紧密联系对于各个国家、地方和个人是被不同看待的,签证官考虑问题时也会注意到这种差异性。

有鉴于此,对于学生家属申请签证,移民官的移民倾向怀疑是肯定的,如何说服他或她就是一个难题了。有人选择先到其他西方国家去旅行,创造出国记录;有人选择一个人先申请,另外一个后申请的办法;如此等等。

注 释

① I-20表上有多个选项,如学生初次入境、学生返回美国、家属入境、语言学校等。家属和学生的I-20表完全一样,只是选项不同而已。

② be sure about/of 的意思是"对什么有把握",如:
I am sure about your success. (我肯定你能成功。)

Acknowledgements（致谢）

　　本系列能够以目前这种状态面世，得感谢很多人：德高望重的我国著名英语教育家、英语语法学界权威张道真教授，多年以来对笔者的教导和关心；广州乃至全国许多高校的前辈和同行，从他们身上笔者学到了很多东西，尤其值得一提的有恩师胡光忠教授、周力教授；美国爱达荷大学（the University of Idaho）的 Edwin Krumpe 博士、Steven Hollenhorst 博士和我的美国同学 Andrew Stratton、Natalie Meyer 以及路易斯安那州萨夫市 W. W. Lewis 中学校长 Oci McGuire 夫妇等都曾从不同方面给我以帮助；北京大学出版社外语编辑室的编辑们为本系列的选题、编校付出了辛勤的劳动；特别值得一提的是，本系列的部分前身是在广东语言音像出版社的有关领导及编辑的帮助下出版的，他们的约稿促使我编写了那个系列；还要提到的有广东涉外经济职业技术学院的刘乐老师，通读了全书初稿并提出了很多很好的意见和建议，还对人物的设计提出了独到的见解；更有其他许多朋友、领导和同事，对书稿的编写工作和出版从不同的侧面给我以支持和鼓励，如张婷婷女士、黄雨鸿先生、赵宁宁小姐、杜传贵先生、胡德奖先生、葛彬女士、何传春女士、王正飞先生等等，恕不一一枚举。

邱立志
2008 年 5 月 5 日